Revolution, Defeat and Theoretical
Underdevelopment

Historical Materialism Book Series

The Historical Materialism Book Series is a major publishing initiative of the radical left. The capitalist crisis of the twenty-first century has been met by a resurgence of interest in critical Marxist theory. At the same time, the publishing institutions committed to Marxism have contracted markedly since the high point of the 1970s. The Historical Materialism Book Series is dedicated to addressing this situation by making available important works of Marxist theory. The aim of the series is to publish important theoretical contributions as the basis for vigorous intellectual debate and exchange on the left.

The peer-reviewed series publishes original monographs, translated texts, and reprints of classics across the bounds of academic disciplinary agendas and across the divisions of the left. The series is particularly concerned to encourage the internationalization of Marxist debate and aims to translate significant studies from beyond the English-speaking world.

For a full list of titles in the Historical Materialism Book Series
available in paperback from Haymarket Books, visit:
https://www.haymarketbooks.org/series_collections/1-historical-materialism

Revolution, Defeat and Theoretical Underdevelopment

Russia, Turkey, Spain, Bolivia

Loren Goldner

Haymarket Books
Chicago, IL

First published in 2016 by Brill Academic Publishers, The Netherlands
© 2016 Koninklijke Brill NV, Leiden, The Netherlands

Published in paperback in 2017 by
Haymarket Books
P.O. Box 180165
Chicago, IL 60618
773-583-7884
www.haymarketbooks.org

ISBN: 978-1-60846-818-8

Trade distribution:
In the US, Consortium Book Sales, www.cbsd.com
In Canada, Publishers Group Canada, www.pgcbooks.ca
In the UK, Turnaround Publisher Services, www.turnaround-uk.com
All other countries, Ingram Publisher Services International, ips_intlsales@
ingramcontent.com

Cover design by Jamie Kerry of Belle Étoile Studios and Ragina Johnson.

This book was published with the generous support of Lannan Foundation
and the Wallace Action Fund.

Printed in Canada by union labor.

10 9 8 7 6 5 4 3 2 1

Library of Congress Cataloging-in-Publication data is available.

Contents

Introduction

The essays in this volume, written over the past four years (2010–14) and collected here, deal with the legacy bequeathed to the contemporary revolutionary left by four key historical experiences: the Russian Revolution, the Communist International's first experiment in 'anti-imperialism' in the early years of the Turkish Communist Party (1917–25), the failings of anarchism in the Spanish Revolution and Civil War (1936–9) and the failure of the Trotskyist Fourth International in the run-up to the Bolivian Revolution (1952) and beyond. In short, they probe the theoretical and practical legacies bequeathed to us as Leninism, anti-imperialism, anarchism and official Trotskyism, as it evolved after Trotsky's assassination in 1940.

At first glance, such a selection may appear arbitrary and open to the charge of 'ancient history' to new generations of self-styled revolutionaries emerging from the nearly four decades of quiescence, defeat and dispersion that followed the ebb of the world upsurge of 1968–77. Those familiar with the cutting edge of a certain Marxist 'renaissance' in recent years, after the long post-1970s glaciation, may wonder: why I do not instead attempt a reckoning with the work of Backhaus and the 'new Capital reading', Postone, communization, Italian workerism and autonomism, Dauvé, Camatte, or (stretching the envelope) the insurrectionists, the last, 'aleatory' Althusser, Badiou or Zizek, and beyond them, perhaps even Deleuze and Guattari?

The answer is fairly simple, if undoubtedly unsatisfactory to some: the theories of such figures, of highly uneven interest (to me, at least), have not been tested, to date, in practical revolutionary processes comparable to what occurred in Russia, Turkey, Spain and Bolivia in the first half of the twentieth century. The historical period has not, to date, been kind to us contemporaries. All this theoretical heavy lifting, in the old E.P. Thompson quote I like, has yet to produce a single practical mouse.

Evidenced in dozens, perhaps hundreds of *Capital* and *Grundrisse* study groups around the u.s. and Europe, or in widely attended conferences on Marx (which would have been unthinkable as late as the mid-1990s), one finds the healthy impulse: *back to Marx*, freed from the faded (but still with us) twentieth-century legacies of Lenin and Trotsky, not to mention Mao and lesser figures (Baran and Sweezy) who still dominated debate, pro and con, into the 1970s. While I had to emit a belly laugh perusing the preface to Ingo Elbe's book on the 'new *Capital* reading'[1] in which he wrote, 'We can now read Marx for

---

1 Ingo Elbe 2008.

the first time without discussing politics', not so many today accord the canon-
ical status granted a few decades ago to the work of the revolutionaries of the
Second and Third Internationals, even the best of them, such as Luxemburg,
Pannekoek, Gorter, and Bordiga, or those who, breaking with Trotsky and Trotskyism, produced some of the most original theories of the shop-floor revolt
of the immediate post-World War Two period, such as James or Castoriadis, or
finally those who broke with them in turn, such as Debord. Not so many people
today seek orientation in Lenin's *What Is to Be Done?* or – God forbid – *Materialism and Empirio-Criticism*, or even in his (improved) *Philosophical Notebooks*,
or finally in Trotsky's *The Revolution Betrayed*, not to mention in Mao's 'On the
Resolution of Contradictions among the People'.

Most movement comrades I knew in the late 60s and early 70s had not read
the three volumes of *Capital*, let alone drawn specific political conclusions
from them about what capitalism and communism are. Nor had I. This new
focus on Marx's critique of political economy cuts through the assumptions of
forty years ago that its lessons were 'assumed' in the writings of Lenin, Trotsky,
Luxemburg, Pannekoek and lesser lights. The best currents then said there
would be the international power of the workers' councils and soviets, and that
would be that. The hard knocks of subsequent history have also distanced us
from that seemingly optimistic view. The question today is no longer global
worker management of *this* production and reproduction, but of a profound
recasting of all such spheres, in which as many jobs would be eliminated as
placed under 'workers' control',[2] and work itself would be superseded in that
'all-sided activity' articulated in Marx's *Grundrisse*.

I nonetheless part ways with a swath of currently fashionable theories: I still
see the wage-labour proletariat – the working class on a world scale – as the key
force for a revolution against capital. Since the 2008 world financial meltdown,
the world has seen unprecedented 'social movement', 'citizens', 'multitudes'
uprisings, confrontations and riots: the Arab spring, Greece from 2008 to 2012,
the Iranian 'green revolution' in 2009, America's Occupy, the Spanish indigna-
dos, the Ukrainian maidan (not ignoring its fascist component), the London
riots of 2011, the successful Brazilian 'anti-fare hike' movement of summer 2013,
the relentless Chilean student strikes of 2011–12, the 2014 Hong Kong democracy movement, or the ongoing (January 2015) movement against racist police
killings of black and brown youth in the u.s.

What has been unfortunately missing from most of these movements was
none other than the wage-labour proletariat, workers participating in them *as*

---

2   See my 2010 article 'The Historical Moment that Produced Us' (Golder 2010).

workers, or more up to date, as proletarians seeking the self-dissolution of the proletariat into a realised humanity (which was, it should not be forgotten and *pace* the contemporary communizers et al., always the conception of the best elements of the older movement).[3]

True, the Egyptian working class staged some impressive strikes before and after the fall of Mubarak, and at this writing remains unbowed; true, the Brazilian anti-fare hike movement included many workers on the peripheries of the big cities. But we can see the predominantly middle-class character – the downsized and frayed middle class produced by decades of global crisis – of most of these movements when we counterpose to them the unending wave of strikes, large and small, many underreported or unreported, in China; several recent general strikes in Vietnam; strikes of textile workers in Cambodia and Bangladesh; the new workers' movement in India in such places as Faridabad and Gurgaon; the strike wave lasting for years in the South Africa mining industry; the ongoing, multiyear IKEA strike in Italy; or the burgeoning $15-an-hour, fast food movement in the U.S. Or, finally, in 2011–12, the near-convergence of the beleaguered longshore (ILWU) local in Longview (Washington state), with elements of the west coast Occupy 'precariat', which almost led to a head-on confrontation with the U.S. Coast Guard and, behind it, the Obama government.

To take only the United States, of the 130 million people who go to work every day, how many are, by any standard, blue, white or pink collar proletarians? How many millions of them labour in transportation, whether in the ports (longshoremen and above all truckers), on railroads and in the mass transit systems of 100 cities? In oil, gas or the newer fracking? How many millions do the scut work in health care, or work as precarious teachers' aides or secretaries in education at all levels? How many work in supermarkets and the massive distribution centers, not to mention the hyper-computerised time-and-motion hell of the warehouses of Walmart or Amazon? How many are fast food workers, or workers in the meatpacking and food processing plants of the Midwest? How many at the post office, at FedEx or UPS? How many both in construction and in building maintenance, as repair people and janitors? How many airline employees, and the skilled workers maintaining the planes? How many in the back rooms of Wall Street or Silicon Valley? As public employees at the Federal,

---

3   Already in 1920 Amadeo Bordiga criticised Gramsci's conception of factory councils as confining workers to their place in the division of labour (i.e. the factory) bequeathed by capitalism, to which he counterposed the soviet, a regional body including all proletarians, employed or unemployed, and freed from workplace-bound roles. See John Chiaradia, 'Amadeo Bordiga and the Myth of Antonio Gramsci' (Chiaradia 2013).

state and local levels? And last but hardly least, how many in the factories that remain in the U.S., starting with twenty (mainly foreign) auto plants scattered in 'green field' plants throughout the South, that still produce as many cars in the U.S. as the 'Big Three' did 40 years ago?

Despite the appearances of 'post-industrial' capitalism in the West, and the clouds of ideology that have 'disappeared' the working class, there are more wage-labour proletarians in the world today than ever before. All the new, complicated forms of profit, interest and rent go back to surplus-value produced by them.

To return, then, to Russia, Turkey, Spain and Bolivia. Having hopefully countered, somewhat, the deep sense of 'farewell to the proletariat' that underpins many currently fashionable (and untested) theories (which, not accidentally, proliferate most in world cities where the 'creative classes' help set the tone) we can now ask how these upheavals of the first half of the twentieth century can speak to revolutionaries today.

We might begin by reminding ourselves, much as we did with the newly-formed working classes of Asia, that political spinoffs of the Russian Revolution are still in evidence. Shall we first recall the mass Maoist parties of Nepal and India, each having tens of thousands of members and still parading with silkscreens of Stalin? Or the rural Maoist insurgency of the Indian Naxalites, reborn from post-1970s oblivion in recent years? Shall we remind ourselves of the reach of Latin American Trotskyism, from Mexico to Argentina, in which latter country Trotskyist militants have been key in impressive subway strikes in Buenos Aires? Of the not negligible Trotskyist presence in and around the Brazilian Workers Party?

A sceptic might quickly point out that these mini-mass phenomena exist in countries of the underdeveloped or semi-developed 'periphery', and that their counterparts in the 'centres' of Europe, the U.S. and Japan are at best small sects. Shall we then consider the emergence of new mass left-wing parties such as Syriza in Greece, Podemos in Spain, or the (not so new) Linke Partei in Germany? How will revolutionaries relate to them if and when they enter the state, whether as brokers or partners in some new left-wing coalition? Granted that none of these are classical Social Democratic or Communist parties, are the lessons of such parties in power from the 1920s to the 1970s, and how revolutionaries attempted to relate, or not relate to them, of no use to us today? Not so long ago a not negligible wave of *chavismo* was palpable in some broad left circles in the U.S. and Europe, wishing to see in Venezuela, its close ally Stalinist Cuba, and other left-wing governments or parties in Ecuador, Bolivia or Brazil a new 'anti-imperialist' bloc. Some of that sentiment even extended to decidedly non-Marxist forces such as Hezbollah or Hamas in the Middle East.

If one central theme has emerged in the resurgence of interest in Marx in the past two decades, and of some of the theorists mentioned above, it is the eclipse of the 1960s/1970s focus on workers' control of production by the deeper understanding of communism, for which Marx's work is the indispensable starting point, as inseparably the destruction of value, wage labour, and hence as the *self*-dissolution of the proletariat as the class 'whose dissolution is the dissolution of all classes'.[4] But such an understanding goes hand in hand with a recognition that on a world scale such a transformation is, as before, 'the task of the working class itself', and not some shapeless mass of 'multitudes' as some contemporary theory would have it. An 'individuality as all-sided in its production as in its consumption'[5] was and remains the goal, once individuals are freed from the shadowy husks of 'identity' allotted them in commodity relationships.

Hence the articles presented here draw on the new, deeper retrieval of Marx. I begin with the agrarian question in the Russian Revolution, in which I show how the Russian peasant commune, which fascinated Marx in the last decade of his life, was suppressed by a century of the 'developmentalist' Marxism begun partially by Engels, which latter then became a world-conquering ideology at the hands of Kautsky, Lenin and their lesser acolytes. I argue that all the leading Bolsheviks were blinded to the reality of the peasant commune, which in 1917 laid claim to 98 percent of all land in Russia, and which survived until Stalin's collectivisations after 1928, and that, further, this 'blind spot' became as fatal as any relationship between 'party and class' in the industrial-urban centres, which was the dominant focus of all the 1960s and 1970s debates on the origins of Stalinism. This analysis does not mean that the Bolsheviks 'had the wrong ideas', but rather that their ideas, and the practice those ideas expressed, were part of a transition in world capitalism they only partly understood, and ultimately abetted.

The second article, on the very early years of Turkish communism, questions the widespread view that Soviet interests as a nation-state, within the international capitalist balance of power, only became dominant with Stalin's 'socialism in one country' in 1924. I show on the contrary that the massacre of the central committee of the Turkish CP in January 1921, in all likelihood by Kemalist (nationalist) forces, did not prevent the Soviet government from concluding a trade agreement with that same Kemalist regime mere months later (March 1921), from saying nothing about the massacre for further months,

---

4   Marx 1975b [1844], p. 186.
5   Marx 1973 [1857], p. 325.

and did not prevent the attendant subordination of the Turkish CP to support for one of the first 'national liberation' struggles, a subordination which would have, to put it mildly, a long legacy around the world. I take off from Trotsky's little-known secret memo to the top Bolshevik leaders in June 1920:

> All information on the situation in Khiva, in Persia, in Bukhara and in Afghanistan confirm the fact that a Soviet revolution in these countries is going to cause us major difficulties at the present time ... Until the situation in the West is stabilized and until our industries and transport systems have improved, a Soviet expansion in the east could prove to be no less dangerous than a war in the West ... *a potential Soviet revolution in the east is today to our advantage principally as an important element in diplomatic relations with England.* From this I conclude that: 1) in the east we should devote ourselves to political and educational work ... and at the same time advise all possible caution in actions calculated to require our military support, or which might require it; 2) we have to continue by all possible channels at our disposal to arrive at an understanding with England about the east [my emphasis – LG].

and show its consequences over the next five years, and ultimately into the 1970s.

The third article is addressed to the contemporary revival of anarchism in looking at the 'grandeur and poverty' of the biggest mass anarchist or anarcho-syndicalist movement in history, that of Spain, culminating in the revolutionary period 1936–7, but not fully defeated for two additional years. I take seriously the comment of the anarcho-syndicalist Diego Abad de Santillán in 1940, one year after the final defeat, to the effect that 'Even in our revolutionary ranks we worked much more intensely and with more inclination preparing the insurrection than in really preparing for what we would build afterwards'. This critique, to my knowledge, applies all the more to the different shades of anarchism and anarcho-syndicalism abroad in the world today. No revolutionary process to date, which even Leon Trotsky acknowledged was at its outset a deeper social revolution than that which occurred in Russia, better illustrates how the absence of Marx's project of the abolition of value and wage labour, and a programme based on it, cripples the most powerful revolutionary surge. Again, as in the cases of Russia and Turkey, this absence of theory ultimately expressed the backwardness of conditions.

The fourth and final article deals with the lesser-known Bolivian Revolution of 1952, led by the ex-fascist turned left-corporatist MNR (*Movimiento Nacional Revolucionario*). As with the article on Turkey, I begin with the deep influence of German populist (Fichtean) romanticism, in this case in the career of Franz Tamayo, one of the founders of Bolivian (and Andean) *indigenismo*, a nationalism which shaped a faction of the Bolivian officer corps deeply alienated by the debacle of the Chaco War (1932–5). The interest for this collection is, however, more the attempt to situate the emergence of one major Latin American corporatism in the overall shift from the formal to the real domination of capital on a world scale, along with the corporatisms of the Brazil of Vargas, the Argentina of Peron and the Mexico of Cardenas. In the Bolivian case, the philofascist origins of the movement were quietly effaced for the emerging post-1945 period dominated not by fascist Italy and Nazi Germany but by the United States. What is decisive here, finally, is the way in which the Trotskyist POR (*Partido Obrero Revolucionario*) tailed this corporatism in the name, once again, of 'anti-imperialism' to the point where a majority of its members simply liquidated themselves into the MNR. True, a small minority, including the Trotskyist leader Guillermo Lora, stopped short of that final step, but the die was cast for the Paris-based Fourth International, which went on to a long career of supporting decades of dubious 'anti-imperialist' movements from the Algerian FLN to the Iranian mullahs, via the Nicaraguan Sandinistas and the Vietnamese NLF.

Hence, in conclusion, what is modestly attempted here is a critical undermining in turn of Leninism, anti-imperialism, anarchism, and Trotskyism as a contribution to clearing away the 'poetry of the past' for the creation of a world communist movement fully at the level of the founding work of Marx, and beyond that, of the uncompleted project which is ours to deepen and extend.

The Agrarian Question in the Russian Revolution: From Material Community to Productivism, and Back[1]

> If Russia follows the path that it took after 1861, it will miss the greatest chance to leap over all the fatal alternatives of the capitalist regime that history has ever offered to a people. Like all other countries, it will have to submit to the inexorable laws of that system.
>
> MARX, Letter to Vera Zasulich, 1881

• • •

> Socialism has demonstrated its right to victory, not on the pages of *Das Kapital* ... not in the language of dialectics, but in the language of steel, cement and electricity.
>
> TROTSKY, *The Revolution Betrayed*, 1937

•
• •

Buried under almost a century of ideology, the 'Russian question', the historical meaning of the defeat of the Russian revolution, is the question that will not go away. World capitalism since the 1970s has been in a crisis without end, yet the reigning ideology, despite all the headwinds of the years since the 2007–8 meltdown, still proclaims: 'get used to it; there is no alternative to capitalism'. And yet, for anyone who does think about an alternative to the disintegrating world visible all around, even in the unfathomable historical amnesia of the present, the question of 'what went wrong in Russia?' is never too far from the surface.

The following article is not a rehash of the debates of the 1960s and 1970s on the 'class nature of the Soviet Union', important as those debates may

---

1 I am indebted to John Marot, Henri Simon, James D. White and Hillel Ticktin, in addition to friends who read various drafts, for help with this article.

have been and in some way still are. In the subsequent four decades, a whole broadly-shared framework for discussing that question has been largely lost, in the contemporary world of post-history, post-modernism, identity politics, the World Social Forum and NGOs. That framework was obviously lost because it no longer seemed a viable guide to the contemporary world, especially after 1989–91.

This chapter had its origin in a series of talks I gave in summer 2013 on the Russian, German, Chinese and Spanish revolutions.[2] The background (re)reading for those talks got me thinking about how the political void of the past 40 years influences our ability to relate those revolutions to present developments. Even more, it got me thinking about all the alternative currents – anarchism, anarcho-syndicalism, revolutionary syndicalism, the IWW, council communism – which were effectively steamrollered by Bolshevism and by the reach of the Third International for a whole epoch, an epoch which began to end c. 1968. In fact, the article was conceived as Part One of a three-part series which would be: 1) the revolutionary epoch 1917–23, and the ultimately disastrous international influence of the Russian Revolution, illustrated in the cases of the very early French, German, Italian and U.S. Communist Parties; 2) the failed return of the 'vanguard party' (Trotskyism, Maoism) in the period from 1968 to 1977; and 3) the ongoing recomposition of the world working class, and forms of worker organisation and self-organisation, today and tomorrow.

Thinking about the historical semi-oblivion of non-Bolshevik 'projects for a different society' brought me up against the (hardly original) question of why revolutionary Marxism (at least in the ideologised variant of the Second International) had (seemingly) been embraced by hundreds of thousands, perhaps millions of working people in mass movements in the West from the 1880s to the 1920s, and had then, after the mid-1920s, increasingly become the outlook of 'generals without an army', small sects of whatever stripe existing on the fringes of the mass movements of the 1930s and 1960s, but in no way hegemonic in the way revolutionary Marxism had seemed to be just before and after World War I. Rosa Luxemburg in that earlier period had spoken all over Germany to large crowds; Angelica Balabanova similarly recounts[3] regularly speaking to crowds of 5000 in a series of small towns in Italy in the same period.

A large part (at least) of the answer to that conundrum was tied up with the 'Russian question'. Not merely (to reiterate) in the finely-tuned debates of 40

---

2   The talks on Russia and Germany are on the Break Their Haughty Power web site: http://home .earthlink.net/~lrgoldner; the China and Spain talks drew from the content of recent articles on Maoism and Spain on the same site.

3   In her memoirs, *My Life as a Rebel* (Balabanoff 1968 [1938]).

years ago about whether the Soviet Union was state capitalist or bureaucratic collectivist or a degenerated workers' state; the problem lay deeper. Virtually all the protagonists in those debates seemed to rather casually assume that Russia in 1917 was something close to a fully European capitalist society, very backward to be sure, but ultimately on a continuum with the rest.[4] Didn't Trotsky – whose framework shaped, consciously or otherwise, those debates more than anyone, pro or con (at least among most anti-Stalinist would-be revolutionary currents) – talk about Tsarist Russia having the largest and most modern factories in the world, alongside a vast population of petty producer peasants?[5] Hadn't the two dozen best-known Bolsheviks of 1917 (when Stalin was totally unknown, though already fundamental in the underground apparat)[6] spent decades in European exile?

The timing seemed too perfect: Marxism, even in ideological form, receded as a mass phenomenon in most 'advanced capitalist' countries in the decade after 1917, following 1) the Russian Revolution; 2) the emergence of mass movements of workers and still more of peasants in the semi-colonial and colonial world from China and Vietnam to Africa by way of India; and, last but hardly least, 3) in the transition from the formal to the real domination of capital, which overlaps with what some people call the decadence of the capitalist mode of production. Max Eastman wrote in his memoirs of the mindset of Greenwich Village radicalism before 1914: 'We were living in times innocent of world war, of fascism, of nazism, sovietism, the Führerprinzip, the totalitarian state. Nothing we were talking about had ever been tried. We thought of political democracy with its basic rights and freedoms as good things permanently secured. Planting ourselves on that firm basis, we proposed to climb

---

4   Lost to view by most Western Marxists was the fact that Marx, Plekhanov, Lenin, Trotsky, Luxemburg and later Riazanov all at different times discussed the 'Asiatic' or 'semi-Asiatic' character of the Tsarist state. See Marx's 1856 pamphlet 'History of the Secret Diplomacy of the 18th Century'.

5   Old myths die hard. British investors visiting those factories before 1914 did in fact find them to be huge, with thousands of workers, but were also shocked at the shoddy goods and by the absence of techniques, such as the Bessemer process in steel making, which had been in use in Britain since the 1860s.

6   Stalin did not make even a cameo appearance in either John Reed's 1918 classic *Ten Days That Shook the World* or in Max Eastman's documentary film *From Tsar to Lenin*, made in the early 1920s but released only in 1937, when it was boycotted worldwide by throngs of idolisers of Stalin (DVD available through http://wsws.org). But already in November 1917, he was one of only two people – the other being Trotsky – authorised to walk into Lenin's office without an appointment.

higher to industrial or "real" democracy'.[7] To this we can add, where Western Marxism was (with few exceptions) concerned, times innocent of a successful mass insurrection of three million Russian workers greatly abetted by 100 million peasants who were in fact not – *pace* the entirety of Russian Marxists, starting with Lenin – capitalist petty producers but living overwhelmingly in household economies only tangentially related to any market; similar movements with even smaller working classes and larger peasantries in China or Vietnam or India; or, in our own time, mass movements in the Moslem world ostensibly (at least) fighting for an Islamic republic or even the restoration of the caliphate.

In short, pre-1920s Marxism broke up, as a mass movement in the West, on the shoals of the 'Russian question', and beyond that, the realities of the world's huge peasant populations, in countries where capitalism had an even more tenuous hold than in Russia, and where, after 1914, little real development, and a lot of outright retrogression, took place.

Looking back, it seems clear that the transformation of the work of Karl Marx into a modernisation ideology for developing or backward countries, at the hands of his ostensible followers, the very people who prompted him to exclaim 'I am not a Marxist', bears an important responsibility for that crack-up. (I should make clear that I am not saying that the mainstream Marxists of the Second International 'had the wrong ideas'. Their 'ideas' were integral to their role in propelling capital from its phase of formal to real domination, of which more below.)

We know today, more clearly than was possible in the 1960s and 1970s, that Marx himself was already deeply interested in the non-Western world,[8] and specifically said that the theses of *Capital* and *Theories of Surplus Value* were valid only for western Europe and the U.S., and that other parts of the world might well follow 'different roads'. The collapse of Stalinism, the post-1978 emergence of a dynamic capitalism in China, and the ebb of 'Marxism-Leninism', Maoism and Third Worldist development ideologies in much of Asia, the Middle East, Africa and Latin America has revealed the great diversity, and adaptability, of social formations in those parts of the world that were hidden behind the apparent march toward 'modernisation' under the likes of the Shah of Iran, Nasser, Nehru, or Sékou Touré.

---

7   See my article on Eastman at http://home.earthlink.net/~lrgoldner/eastman.html.

8   See Kevin Anderson's *Marx at the Margins* (Anderson 2010), and, before him, the work of Lawrence Krader on the Asiatic mode of production (Krader 1975), as well as his edition of Marx's *Ethnological Notebooks* (Marx 1972).

Only in 2010 did the world's rural population drop below 50 percent of the total. The great majority of those remaining in the countryside are petty-producer peasants, artisans and rural proletarian labourers. Considering only India and China, with close to 40 percent of the world's population between them, it is clear that the 'agrarian question', on a world scale, remains central to any possible creation of a renewed communism. This is all the more urgent in light of the one million people a *day* who arrive from the countryside in the world's cities, as capitalism increasingly makes their way of life unviable and draws them into a dubious future in the world's shantytowns,[9] or China's 270 million migrant workers.

To reconnect with the political and social realities of the world's rural population, both historically and for today, in a project to create a viable, non-developmentalist Marxism for the world after Stalinism, Maoism and Third Worldism, also takes us back to another largely forgotten dimension of Marx: the critique of the separation of city and countryside as a fundamental alienation; the separation of the producers from their means of production in the sixteenth and seventeenth centuries as '*the*' original alienation to be overcome in a future 'activity as all-sided in its production as in its consumption' (*Grundrisse*);[10] Marx's call for the 'more even distribution of the population around the earth's surface' (*Communist Manifesto*) when cities, owing their existence to the centralisation of capital, can be superseded; and finally, and hardly last, the ever more pressing question of the environment.

All these dimensions are opened up by an inquiry into the agrarian question in the Russian Revolution.

1   Karl Marx, Friedrich Engels and the Russian Peasant Commune: Origins of an Ideology

In the 1870s, Karl Marx first took a serious interest in the Russian revolutionary movement, partly through the (initially) surprising impact of his own work[11] in a country he had previously viewed as the colossal 'gendarme of Europe', and even more so by contact with the Russian Populists, both through their impressive actions[12] and through their correspondence with him, requesting advice on strategy and tactics.

---

9   See Davis 2006.

10   Marx 1973, p. 325.

11   The first translation of vol. 1 of *Capital* in any foreign language appeared in Russian in 1872.

12   From 1878 to 1881, one faction of the group Zemla I Volya (Land and Freedom) waged a

In short order, Marx set aside work on volumes II and III of *Capital*, taught himself Russian, and spent much of the last decade of his life studying Russian agriculture. He concealed this turn in his work from his lifelong collaborator, Engels. Aside from important correspondence with Russian revolutionaries, he never wrote a text of any length based on his new interest, but at his death left two cubic metres of notes on Russia.

What ensued was a fundamental step in the transformation of Marx's work into an ideology, one whose influence reached into the 1970s. When Engels discovered these materials after Marx's death, and realised they were the reason that Marx had not finished *Capital*, he was furious, and apparently wanted to burn them.[13]

Marx, in his research on Russia (as well as on other non-Western countries and regions),[14] had discarded his earlier claims of a single path of world capitalist development, one in which 'England held up to the world the mirror of its own future', and had also recognised that the validity of his work up to that point was confined to the conditions of western Europe.

At the centre of Marx's 'Russian road'[15] was the peasant commune, or mir (also called the obschina). The mir had been studied in depth in the early 1840s by the German Baron Haxthausen, whose three-volume work of 1843 led to a controversy in Russia about the mir's significance, involving every Russian intellectual faction from the backward-looking Slavophiles to the exile Alexander Herzen to the Westernisers.[16] The commune then became central

---

campaign of terror that virtually paralysed the Tsarist government, culminating in the assassination of Tsar Alexander II in 1881. Marx supported them for waging what seemed to be the sole form of struggle available in conditions of extreme repression, and also kept at arm's length Russian self-styled Marxists who wrote learned treatises in the safety of Swiss exile. Marx, unlike his followers, was never troubled by the problem of being an orthodox Marxist.

13   See White 1994, p. 281.

14   Again, see Anderson 2010.

15   See Shanin 1983, and White 1994, Ch. 5.

16   The anti-Enlightenment Slavophiles idealised the commune as an eternal expression of a Slavic soul; Herzen was aware that such communes had once existed in much of Europe, but thought they could be part of a Russian revolution; the westernisers tended to deride its importance as a 'judicial imposition' and looked forward to its speedy disappearance with the advance of capitalism. Cherneschevski, who had written pioneering sociological works on Russian society, did not idealise the commune, which he knew from childhood experience growing up in a provincial town, but did anticipate Marx's later view that it could, in a revolutionary upheaval, 'provide the basis for a non-capitalist economic development'. See Kingston-Mann 1983, pp. 23–4.

to the Populists' claim that Russia could, or should, skip the capitalist 'stage' of development, a sentiment reinforced by Marx's preface to the 1882 Russian translation of the *Communist Manifesto*,[17] not to mention the portrayal of real conditions in England which they found in *Capital*.

In his discovery of the still-viable Russian commune, Marx was reconnecting with his 1840s writings about 'community' (*Gemeinwesen* in German).[18] He was reasserting that for him, communism was first of all about the 'material human community', and not about forced-march industrialisation and productivist five-year plans.[19]

This debate between the self-styled Marxists of different kinds and the 'romantic' 'subjectivist' Populists about the viability of the mir lasted into the early 1900s, greatly skewed by Engels's suppression of Marx's Russian studies.[20] Even some of the Populists who had received Marx's letters about Russia's unique possibilities resulting from the mir, who had then become Marxists themselves, all but participated in the suppression.[21] Later, the Social Revolutionaries (SRs), the rivals to the Bolsheviks, many of whose members considered themselves Marxists, claimed to be the true heirs of Marx based on his suppressed letters on the mir.[22]

One should not romanticise the mir; Chernyshevsky, who had known it close up near the provincial town of his boyhood, had distinctly mixed feelings about it as a prototype for socialism, yet he was one of the first, in the 1850s, to argue that the mir, combined with Western technology after a successful revolution in Europe, could be the basis for a 'communist development', as Marx and Engels later put it in 1882.

---

17   'If the Russian Revolution becomes the signal for a proletarian revolution in the West, so that both complement one another, the present Russian common ownership of land may serve as the starting point for a communist development'.

18   He was also reconnecting with personal memories of a similar Germanic commune near Trier, his birthplace, which had disappeared only one generation before his birth, as well as his 'determinate negation' of elements of German romanticism. See White 1996, pp. 205–6, for Marx's letter to Engels of March 1854, in which he writes of the resilience of the communal form in Germany and elsewhere, preceding his discovery of the Russian commune by almost two decades.

19   White 1996; Bordiga 1975.

20   Plekhanov refused to confront the issues of Marx's correspondence with Daniel'son, Mikhailovski, and Zasulich. 'In early writings he had referred to Marx's favorable comments on the commune, but in *Our Differences* (1885) no longer did'. See Kingston-Mann 1983, p. 33.

21   This included Vera Zasulich, who later worked with Gyorgi Plekhanov in Switzerland.

22   See Jacques Baynac 1979.

What exactly was the mir as a lived experience for Russian peasants? Franco Venturi, author of the classic study of the Russian Populist movement of the nineteenth century, wrote about how the mir figured in the modernising plans of the Tsarist state prior to the serf emancipation of 1861, which was intended to put Russia on the path of capitalist development, and sketched themes that would remain present right up to Stalin's destruction of the mir in his 1929–32 collectivisations:

> The enquiry of 1836 had shown how much this spirit of equality, latent in the very forms of serfdom and peasant tradition, had in fact been undermined by the rise of a group of richer farmers who began to have considerable influence on the entire life of the obshchina [or mir – LG]. These farmers, for instance, tipped the scales of periodic redistribution in their own favor and ... subjected the community of poorer peasants to their control. But the enquiry had also shown how deeply these traditional forms were rooted. The assiduous inspectors were often shocked by the disorder, the vulgarity and the violence which prevailed in the meetings of the mir, and also by its many obvious injustices. Nevertheless it was in the obshchina and the mir that the peasants expressed those ideas on land ownership which had so impressed and irritated Kiselev and Périer.[23] It was through these organizations, the only ones at its disposal, that peasant society defended itself. The communities naturally differed from district to district, reflecting the entire range of peasant life ... Yet, despite all this variety, there was one common factor; the obshchina represented the tradition and ideal of the peasant masses. How then could it be broken?[24]

That latter question would continue to vex Tsarist planners right up to 1917, and, in a different way, would be the barrier on which different Bolshevik plans for industrialisation as well would break up in the 1920s.

From Engels to Plekhanov, 'the father of Russian Marxism', to Kautsky and Lenin, the linear, evolutionist, 'matter-motion' view of 'dialectical materialism' spread worldwide as the orthodoxy of the Second International. With the consolidation of Stalinism, it became identified with 'real existing socialism' itself. 'Dialectical materialism' was in fact the vulgar recapitulation of the bourgeois materialism of the eighteenth century, and not accidentally promoted

23   Key figures of the Tsar's investigating commission.
24   Venturi 1960, p. 70.

by movements and regimes which were, like the eighteenth-century template, completing the bourgeois revolution, in the eradication of pre-capitalist agriculture, whatever their ideology and stated goals. Elements of this ideology persist today in various types of productivism that confuse the tasks of the bourgeois and socialist revolutions.[25]

But a still larger context was shaping this post-Marx ideological development: the global transition from the formal to the real domination of capital. In the formal phase, capital takes over pre-capitalist production (e.g., guilds, cooperation, manufacture) without modifying them materially; in the latter, real phase, capital reduces all aspects of production, reproduction and of life generally to its adequate capitalist form. In industry, the German and American 'rationalisation movements' (i.e., capital-intensive innovation) of the 1920s were the cutting edge of this 'materialization of a social relationship';[26] in agriculture, this meant, ultimately, California-style agribusiness, and comparable developments in other major grain exporters such as Canada and Australia,[27] as well as the professional, agronomy-trained farmer who has replaced western Europe's classical peasants since World War Two. In the arc from the u.s. to Russia, by way of the smaller agricultures of France, Italy and Germany, one finds a near-perfect congruence of lingering pre-capitalist agriculture, i.e., the agriculture of formal domination (exemplified in the individual land-owning peasant who emerged from the French Revolution) and, later, Communist Parties: the stronger pre-capitalist agriculture, the stronger the Third International parties after 1917.[28] Pre-1914 Social Democracy and post-1917 Communism were the

---

25   'The Bolshevik revolution had shattered the old Marxist assumption that industrialization was the exclusive task of capitalism' (in Cohen 1973, p. 170). Or, as Amadeo Bordiga put it more succinctly and accurately in the 1950s, responding to Stalinist propaganda: 'It is exactly right that the "foundations of socialism are being laid in the Soviet Union"', which was exactly why he considered it as a capitalist society.

26   See Brady 1933; and Sternberg 1932. In both Germany and the u.s. in the 1920s, chronic unemployment remained at eight percent or higher in the brief boom years before 1929, an unprecedented level compared to pre-1914 standards. For some material on the similar link between rationalisation and structural unemployment in the u.s., see Irving Bernstein 1960.

27   The Argentine Raúl Prebisch, founder of the 1950s and 1960s 'import substitution' strategy of development and hardly a Marxist, studied the differences between Argentina, a major exporter of grain and beef by the 1880s, and similar exporters such as Australia and Canada, concluding that Argentina, unlike the British Commonwealth countries, was hobbled by the pre-capitalist legacy of Spanish colonialism in the persistence of the latifundia, into the twentieth century. See Dosman 2008, p. 49.

28   See my articles 'The Non-Formation of a Working Class Party in the u.s., 1900– 1945'

adequate form of working-class organisation to propel this transition, and were notably marginal in countries like the U.S. or Great Britain, where these tasks were complete. We can thus agree with Lars Lih when he argues[29] that Lenin was an 'Erfurtian Social Democrat' in the extreme conditions of Tsarist autocracy, as long as we recognise that Erfurtian Social Democracy in Germany,[30] like the Russian Social Democratic Labor Party (RSDLP) of the Bolsheviks and Mensheviks, were the organisational expression for this transition. One might sketch the two phases like this:

Formal domination (extensive accumulation)	Real domination (intensive accumulation)
1. trade unions combated promoted	1. trade unions tolerated
2. parliamentarism	2. state bureaucracy
3. non-militarist	3. Militarist
4. colonialism	4. Imperialism
5. liberal professions	5. technical professions
6. peasants into workers	6. expansion of tertiary sector
7. state as minimal consumer	7. state as major consumer
8. laissez-faire capitalism	8. concentration, regulation
9. secondary role of finance capital	9. hegemony of finance capital
10. low financial-interrelations ratio[31]	10. high FIRO
11. gold standard (Ricardo)	11. fiat money (Keynes, Schacht)
12. working class as pariah class	12. 'community of labour'[32]
13. urbanisation	13. suburbanisation

(Goldner 1983) and 'Communism is the Material Human Community: Amadeo Bordiga Today' (Goldner 1991).

29   Lih 2006. 'Erfurtian Social Democrat' is Lih's term for a disciple of Karl Kautsky and pre-1914 German Social Democracy (the SPD), which Lenin surely was. Curious that Lih makes little or nothing of Engels's critique of the Erfurt Progam, which resulted from the SPD's 1891 congress in that city.

30   See the classic on the integration of the SPD into German capitalism: Groh 1973; and the earlier book of Carl Schorske: Schorske 1955.

31   The 'financial interrelations ratio' measures the total capital assets in manufacture to total assets in finance and real estate.

32   Absolute surplus value, for Marx, is obtained by the lengthening of the working day above and beyond the reproduction time for labour employed; relative surplus value is obtained by technical intensification of the production process, i.e. by increasing the productivity of labor.

(cont.)

Formal domination (extensive accumulation)	Real domination (intensive accumulation)
14. absolute surplus value[33]	14. relative surplus value
15. primitive accumulation of petty producers	15. primitive accumulation by internal wage gouging
16. labour retains craft aspects	16. rationalisation, Taylorism
17. labour struggles to shorten the working day	17. technical intensification of the labour process

The roots of 'Erfurtian Social Democracy' as a project for state power, then, were ultimately in the absolutist state of the sixteenth to eighteenth centuries, which in its Tudor phase in England (1485–1603) had began the process of clearing the countryside,[34] a process which then spread to the continent, in the French Bourbon state and its taxation of the peasantry, and the Prussian state, with the Stein-Hardenburg top-down reforms during and after the Napoleonic wars.[35] Thus the linear evolutionist 'matter-motion' worldview developed by Engels, Plekhanov, Kautsky and inherited by Lenin, as opposed to Marx's discovery of 'another road' for Russia in the combination of the mir with a western European revolution, amounted to a latter-day 'modernisation' ideology for countries still dealing with pre-capitalist agriculture, a 'substitute bourgeois revolution' with a key role played by the working class, a continuation of the bourgeois revolu-

---

33   The glorification of labour, common to fascist, Stalinist and Popular Front/New Deal ideology in the 1930s, was the common ideological thread that mobilised the working class for the new phase of accumulation in the interwar period. This little-studied phenomenon, expressed in the Italian dopolavoro, the Nazi 'Kraft durch Freude' campaigns and in the social realist art of the Stalinist school, or in that generated by the American New Deal, was the *condensed* form of mass consumption which, after 1945, achieved its *diffuse* form in the mass-consumer ideology of the 'affluent society' (Debord).

34   See Marx's chapter on 'Primitive Accumulation' in Volume 1 of *Capital* and the draconian methods used by the Tudors to herd peasants off the land and into the wage-labour work force, destitution and the work house.

35   See P. Anderson 1974. Other important absolutisms in countries that later developed important Communist parties were in Bourbon Spain, the Portugal of Pombal, and regional absolutisms (Piedmont, Naples) in what became Italy. All of them were, in different ways, involved in the capitalisation of agriculture. See, again, my article on the non-formation of a working-class party in America (Goldner 1983).

tion with red flags. This was, for obvious reasons, hardly recognised or articulated at the time, and required an historical unfolding over decades of the
American, German or Russian variants to become visible. Nor were these out-
comes a 'telos' of the earlier (Lassallean, Social Democratic, or Bolshevik) formulations on organisation; the road was hardly straight and narrow and major
working-class defeats were required to bring the later form to maturity. Nonetheless, looked at in comparative perspective, the road is there, as it emerged
in the pre-1914 world when capitalism was converting peasants and farmers
into production workers in the advanced sector,[36] whereas after World War
One and especially World War Two it was increasingly using high productivity to support the rapidly growing population of unproductive consumers in
the 'service sector', with production workers as a declining percentage of the
total work force.

It is hardly surprising to find agriculture and the vast Russian peasantry (85–
90 percent of the population in 1917) as the decisive factor in the fate of the
revolution, once the anticipated world revolution that would materially aid
backward Russia failed to materialise. The Reds won the civil war ultimately
because they had at least the grudging support of a significant part of the peasantry against the Whites who, with their ties to the old regime, could not bring
themselves to accept land reform. Stalin triumphed in the debates of the 1920s,
which centred on the agrarian question.[37] Stalin's collectivisation of 1929–32

---

36   The industrial working class in both Britain and Germany peaked in the pre-1914 period
     at roughly 40 percent of the total work force.

37   See Erlich 1960; see also Marot 2012. As is generally known, three factions confronted each
     other in these debates: the advocates of rapid industrialisation in the Trotskyist left, the
     'socialism at a snail's pace' Bukharinist right, and the most dangerous faction of all, the
     'vacillating' Stalinist 'centre'. The victory of the Stalinist 'centre' ruined communism inter-
     nationally for an epoch, whereas Bukharin had rightly said, in the course of the debate,
     that the implementation of the left's programme would require a huge bureaucracy and
     that the social costs of regulation would be much greater than the potential downside of
     market-driven stratification of the peasantry (see below). The entire left except for Trotsky,
     seeing Bukharin as the threat of 'capitalist restoration', capitulated to Stalin, on a product-
     ivist basis. See the analysis of the Italian Communist Left on the fiftieth anniversary of the
     Bolshevik Revolution, 'Bilan d'une revolution' (Italian Communist Left 1960) for a bal-
     anced rectification of Bukharin as a 'right communist' against the far more dangerous
     Stalin. See also Marot 2012, Ch. 2, for a devastating account of how the Trotskyist 'left'
     embraced Stalin's collectivisations. The Trotskyists to this day retain the blind spot of
     seeing Stalin as a 'centre' and Bukharin as the 'right', and as the cat's paw of a 'capital-
     ist restoration', as if that, had it taken place, would have been worse for world socialism
     than what actually happened.

irreversibly ruined Russian agriculture, costing the regime the previous, reluctant acceptance by the peasantry, with ten million dead and the destruction of 40 percent of all livestock (horses, cows and pigs) by the peasants themselves. For the remaining six decades of the Soviet Union, Russian agriculture, prior to 1914 a major grain exporter to the world, never fully recovered, making impossible the decisive cheapening of food as a portion of working-class consumption that had opened the way for mass consumer durables in the West, and Russia was itself compelled to import grain by the mid-1950's.

Most Marxist attempts outside the Soviet Union to analyse the mode of production there, with the important exception of the Italian Communist Left (which had other problems), had the same urban-industrial bias as the Second International, focused on the relations between the party, the state and the working class, to the neglect of the peasantry, and in their own way embraced elements of the linear-evolutionist assumptions of the Engels-Plekhanov-Kautsky worldview that emerged from the suppression of Marx's Russian studies.

2   The Agrarian Question in the Second International and in Russia

Karl Kautsky's 1899 book *The Agrarian Question*[38] set down the 'official Marxist' position on that subject for the world socialist movement prior to World War One. It is symptomatic of a whole, industry-centred sensibility that the book was largely forgotten within a decade, despite Marx's earlier extensive comments on the agrarian world in volumes I and III of *Capital*[39] and in *Theories of Surplus Value*, especially on the question of ground rent, and his insistence (against common coin on the left to this day) that there were *three* classes in society: capitalists (who live from profits), proletarians (who live from wages) and landlords (who live from ground rent). For Marx, as indicated in our Preface, the violent separation 'in fire and blood' of the English peasantry from its means of production, in the process of primitive accumulation, was *the* original separation to be overcome in communism, and the 'more equal distribution of the population over the surface of the earth' (*Communist Manifesto*) would be the overcoming of the fundamental (and also largely forgotten) alienation between city and countryside.

---

38   Unbelievably, translated into English only in 1988 (Kautsky 1988).
39   Marx for example intensely studied the innovations in fertiliser of the German chemist Liebig, and their impact on higher crop yields in British and German agriculture.

Kautsky's book was, among other things, a polemic (without mentioning names) against some right-wingers in the SPD such as the Bavarian members David and Vollmar, who already in the early 1890s (following the re-legalisation of the party in 1890) were calling for a peasant programme.

Kautsky became known as the 'Torquemada'[40] of the SPD on the agrarian question, whose message was that the workers' movement had nothing to say to petty bourgeois peasants, a class doomed to disappear into the polarisation of a rural bourgeoisie and rural wage-labour proletariat. Peasants could at best look forward to being integrated into cooperatives after the working class seized power. A significant part of small peasant produce was for family consumption, and the sector was an important source of primitive accumulation for the system as a whole. In his early formulations, Kautsky strongly argued that in agriculture as in industry, bigger was better, and discounted the survivability of highly productive family farms. The task of socialists was to neutralise the peasantry as a social force, not to mobilise it.

Interestingly, the factions within the SPD on the question of a peasant programme were not aligned in the typical left-to-right spectrum that emerged at the end of the 1890s in the 'revisionism' debate or later. Left-wingers Bebel and Wilhelm Liebknecht both sided with Vollmar in advocating an agrarian programme at the 1895 party congress, but the party supported Kautsky. Ferdinand Lassalle's old formulation that all classes except workers are 'one reactionary mass' – a view attacked in Marx's *Critique of the Gotha Program* – was also a backdrop to the discussion.

In the long run, Kautsky's view of the inevitable disappearance of the smallholder peasant was refuted in the prospering modern farms of countries such as Austria and Denmark.[41] It was far more problematic when Lenin applied it to Russia.

In the 1890s, Lenin shared Kautsky's views on the peasants (and just about everything else). This is particularly curious, since he spent the years 1887–93 (after his older brother's execution for involvement in a plot to assassinate the

---

40   Tomas de Torquemada was a major figure in the Spanish Inquisition in the fifteenth
      century.
41   I am indebted in the preceding paragraphs to the Shanin/Alavi preface to the 1988 English
      translation of *The Agrarian Question*: Kautsky 1988, vol. 1, pp. xiii–xxxiii. Shanin wrote
      elsewhere of Kautsky's view, as applied to Russia, that it envisioned 'a "self-contradictory"
      revolution which must and can be bourgeois only. And yet, taking place in a period when
      in all the rest of Europe only a socialist revolution was possible'. Shanin 1986, p. 187. After
      1905, Kautsky actually hoped that the revolutionary élan of the Russian Marxists would
      rejuvenate the Second International (Shanin 1986, p. 253).

Tsar) in several provincial towns where apparently the last survivors of the Populist and terrorist group Zemla i Volya (to whom Marx had been sympathetic in their years of peak activity in 1878–81)[42] and Marxists mingled in rather comradely form. (It is significant that at this time, the term 'Narodnik', which later came to be known strictly and pejoratively as the term for a pro-peasant and subjective romantic, idealising the commune and downplaying the advance of capitalism in Russia, originally meant anyone concerned with the affairs of the common people; only after the polemics of the last phase of Populism did it acquire its negative overtones.) Lenin, opposing even his mentor Plekhanov, distinguished himself during the famine of 1891–2 by his attacks on humanitarian attempts in 'progressive' circles to help the stricken peasantry, reaffirming the supposedly Marxist position that the peasantry was a doomed social class and its disappearance should not be hindered, so that capitalism could complete its work.[43]

This is especially significant because there is no doubt that Lenin had read deeply in the Russian Populist tradition, going back to the 1850s/1860s writings of Chernyshevsky[44] and Dobrolyubov.[45] According to different people who knew him personally, Lenin read Chernyshevsky's proto-socialist realist novel *What Is To Be Done?* many times.[46] The turgid, intentionally anti-aesthetic novel tells the story of young people of the generation of the 1860s who break with their bourgeois families to live communally, supporting themselves with Fourierist artisanal collectives. It inspired tens of thousands of readers to follow that model for their life choices in the stifling oppression of Tsarist Russia. Of further significance is the character Rakhmetov, a veritable propotype of Lenin, a full-time, austere revolutionary. The title of Lenin's 1902 pamphlet *What Is To Be Done?* is an obvious homage to Chernyshevsky's book, however different the content.[47]

---

42   Marx called the late 1870s Russian terrorists 'the leading detachment of the revolutionary movement in Europe'.

43   300,000 peasants died in the famine: from 1889 to 1917 one year out of two were years of famine. See Kingston-Mann 1983, pp. 33–4.

44   Nicolai Chernyshevsky (1828–89) was a Populist writer who emerged in the 1850s with some of the first sociological studies of Russian society. In 1862 he was exiled for the rest of his life to Siberia.

45   Nicolai Dobrolyubov (1836–61) was a radical activist and literary figure of the 1850s. Like Chernyshevsky, he wrote for the most important oppositional journal of the day, *The Contemporary*.

46   See for example the account of Valentinov 1968, pp. 63–8.

47   Ingerflom 1988. Chernyshevsky in particular had developed the notion of 'aziatzvo', the

Lenin spent several years in the late 1890s in Siberian exile, during which he wrote his first major work, *The Development of Capitalism in Russia* (1899), which is often mistaken for his definitive views on the peasantry, whereas they later evolved considerably under the impact of events. Lenin in this book is at pains to show that, contrary to the lingering views of the Populists, capitalism had fully triumphed in Russia. The work is deeply flawed by a largely 'market' (as opposed to value) view of what capitalism is. The mir, which at the time constituted four-fifths of all cultivated land in European Russia, is barely mentioned, since for Lenin it was merely a 'juridical imposition' of the Tsarist state.[48] The large foreign loans and rapid industrial development under the management of Finance Minister Witte are also unmentioned.[49] Lenin winds up concluding that fully 51 percent of the Russian population consists of wage-labour proletarians, and that the polarisation of rich peasant capitalists and rural labourers in the countryside is largely complete.[50] Lenin includes all peasants 'almost' separated from their means of production in the category of poor peasants,[51] meaning that any peasant with a tiny plot, owning a horse and a cow, barely supporting himself and his family, and elsewhere performing occasional wage labour a few months of the year, was a 'proletarian'. The large estates, for Lenin, were rapidly becoming capitalist, when in

---

crushing 'semi-Asiatic' weight of the Tsarist state which atomised the entire Russian population and made impossible any coherent popular revolt, any conscious 'class for itself'. For Lenin, the working class which began to form and to rebel after the 1870s was the first force to form 'outside' of this atomisation, a view confirmed by the militant strikes of 1896 and thereafter. In Ingerflom's view, Lenin, with his own *What Is To Be Done?*, returns to elements of his Chernyshevskian roots in attacking the narrow point-of-production focus of the Economists, calling on revolutionaries, like the literary prototype Rachmetov, to go into all classes of Russian society, to denounce all oppressions, and to thus constitute themselves as a 'tribune of the people'.

48   Lenin's 1899 draft of the party programme did not deal with the mass of commune peasants except to claim that most of them were 'really' proletarians. See Kingston-Mann 1983, p. 48. Teodor Shanin points out, in the second volume of his key 1986 book *The Roots of Otherness*, that the formative period of Russian Social Democracy, from the mid-1880s to 1902, was a nadir of peasant struggle (Shanin 1986, p. 146).

49   The late 1890s, when Lenin was writing the book, were actually boom years for Russian industry under Witte's management. See von Laue 1963. Witte had become finance minister in 1892 and placed the tax burden for Russian industrialization on the peasantry.

50   After 1905, Lenin did admit that he was wrong about this polarisation (Kingston-Mann 1983, p. 53), but did not give up the basic view of the direction of development; it had merely been an error of timing.

51   Crisenoy 1971, p. 83.

fact the big landowners were alien to any idea of accumulation and profit-ability of capital.[52] Lenin also sees 'technological progress' where in fact the peasants were working with very simple, primitive implements long in use. If the manorial estates were largely capitalist, how to explain the restrictions on peasant mobility, tying them to one place, as had always been the case with serfs? Lenin's view of capitalism was limited to the sphere of circula-tion alone.[53] Already in his first text of 1893 ('New Economic Transformations in Peasant Life') Lenin had asserted that the mir was no obstacle to capital-ism:

> We are in no way interested in the form of landed property among the peasants. Whatever the form, the relationship between the peasant bour-geoisie and the rural proletariat is always the same.

During this period, according to Chantal de Crisenoy, individual peasant plots were actually in decline and the communes retained all their impor-tance.[54]

As Crisenoy puts it:

> By denying all specificity to the mir, Lenin shows himself more attached to preconceived ideas ... than attentive to existing social relations ... In his analysis, we find a total inversion of reality: everything that is a factor of primitive accumulation – mandatory services, taxes – is seen as a 'survival' blocking the emergence of capitalism; everything that is an obstacle to the appearance of capital – the handicraft industries, the rural commune – is designated as being 'its most profound basis'.[55]

In the 1897 article 'What heritage do we renounce?',[56] Lenin presents the mir as 'a village of small agrarians':

> ... when he wants to prove, against the populists, the existence of a work-ing class in the midst of the obschina, he advances the concept of the 'sedentary proletarian' and applies it to these same communal peasants ...

---

52   Ibid. p. 99.
53   Ibid. p. 103.
54   Ibid. p. 110.
55   Ibid. pp. 111–112.
56   In vol. 2 of Lenin 1960–70.

In 1899 he finds three times the number of wage workers generally accepted on the eve of 1914.[57]

Lenin, however, was (with Trotsky)[58] one of the few Russian Marxists who felt it necessary to devote any serious attention at all to the peasantry, against the dismissive attitude of Plekhanov. In 1902, several provinces rose up in response to famine, and Lenin at the same time drafted the first programme addressed to the peasantry, 'The Agrarian Program of Russian Social Democracy',[59] adopted by the party in 1903. He remained ambivalent on the peasants' future role, seeing them as either supporting a 'revolutionary democratic' party or lining up with the 'party of order'.[60] Many Russian Social Democrats condemned the entire programme, as Kautsky had done earlier in Germany. It called for cancellation of the debts from 1861,[61] free use of land for the peasants, restitution to the peasants of the 'otrezki', (choice strips of land that had been retained by the landowners in the 1861 reform) and cancellation of excessive rents and exploitative contracts. Lenin felt these changes would 'expand the internal market', and 'raise peasant livings standards and hasten the development of capitalism in agriculture'.[62]

After the 1902 uprisings, Lenin wrote 'To the Rural Poor', still maintaining his earlier views on the dynamic in the countryside. But in the article, as Kingston-Mann points out,

---

57   Crisenoy 1971, p. 115.

58   Trotsky said: 'In the coming revolution, we have to ally with the peasantry' (quoted in Lenin's 1904 *One Step Forward, Two Steps Back* [Lenin 1960–70, vol. 7]).

59   Lenin's 1899 draft of the party programme did not deal with the mass of commune peasants except to claim that most of them were 'really' proletarians. Kingston-Mann 1983, p. 48.

60   Crisenoy 1971, pp. 155–6. Just before this outbreak, Lenin had written: '"We will make a last effort (with the program) to stir up the remnants of the peasants' class hostility to the feudal lords". Scarcely had he written these lines when the peasants [in several regions – LG] destroyed 100 estates, seized the property of the big landowners, broke into barns to distribute food to the hungry ... for the first time, they showed hostility to the tsar, meeting the Cossacks with axes and pitchforks ...'

61   The 1861 emancipation of the serfs had been a patchwork of changes that saddled those freed serfs receiving land with decades of debts to pay for it.

62   Crisenot 1971, p. 159. Lenin went on, in the framework of his 1899 book, imagining that capital had largely conquered the countryside, saying that (in general) 'support for small property is reactionary, because it is aimed at the economy of a big capital ... but in the present case, we want to support small property not against capitalism, but against serfdom ...' (Crisenoy 1971, p. 160).

the repartitional commune, which had provided the institutional framework for so many of the outbreaks, was completely ignored.[63]

All in all,

> Peasant action could only be ... 'anti-feudal', and feudal survivals had to
> be the major concern of the Social Democratic agrarian program.[64]

In 1903, the Second Party Congress adopted Lenin's agrarian programme, without any mention thus far of a 'worker-peasant alliance'. Lenin warned against
such an alliance. To ally with the proletariat, in his view, the peasants must give
up 'their own class viewpoint' and adopt 'that of the proletariat'.[65]

3   1905–7: Ideology Meets Reality

In January 1905, Father Gapon, Orthodox priest and also Tsarist agent pro-
vocateur, led a mass worker demonstration in St. Petersburg to the tsar's palace
with petitions virtually begging the tsar to grant certain basic rights. The Cossacks fired on the crowd, killing hundreds, and the 1905–7 Revolution, the 'dress
rehearsal' for 1917, was on.[66] During those years, the Russian peasants revolted as intensely as did the working class, completely upsetting the schemas by
which Russian Marxism, under Kautsky's influence, had predicted that peasants would aspire to individual private plots of land and nothing more.

The peasants in 1905 themselves submitted, all told, 60,000 petitions to the
government. (The substance of numerous peasant demands for all land to
the mir was not taken seriously by any Russian Marxist at this time.)[67] The

---

63   Kingston-Mann 1983, p. 65. A 'repartitional' commune was one in which lands were
      periodically redistributed based on peasants' family size.
64   Ibid. p. 70.
65   Lenin's agrarian programme, quoted in Crisenoy 1971, p. 166. As she comments: 'Lenin
      remains close to the most orthodox positions of the Second International and the refusal
      of any alliance between workers and peasants' (p. 167).
66   In the interest of keeping the main theme of this text, the Russian peasants and the
      mir, I am skirting a blow-by-blow account of the 1905 revolution, which included, with
      prompting from no political party, the invention in praxis of the "soviet" by the working
      class. For an overview of the whole, see Trotsky's *1905* (original 1907–1908, English trans.
      1971).
67   Ibid. p. 98.

peasants invaded forests and grazing lands from which they had been excluded; they robbed stores, warehouses and manors, burning estates and killing the squires.[68] The large majority of rural strikes in Russia in 1905–7 were strikes of peasant smallholders, partly or seasonally employed. Most of these strikes were directed by the communal assemblies.[69] In 1905, the crops had failed again in 25 of Russia's provinces, closely linked to the locales of the uprisings.[70] As Shanin put it, 'Once the tsar's will could no longer be treated as a force of nature ... the whole social world of rural Russia came apart. Everything seemed possible now'.[71] The uprisings peaked initially in June 1905. The differentiations between wealthy, middle and poor peasants, which Lenin had so laboriously worked out in his 1899 book, seemed to recede in importance, as wealthier peasants helped poor neighbours with food.[72]

Under the impact of these events, Lenin, still in Zurich exile in the spring of 1905, prior to his return to Russia, proposed a 'revolutionary democratic dictatorship of the proletariat and peasants' to a establish a provisional government for the bourgeois-democratic revolution. 'This formulation was so inconsistent with pre-revolutionary Marxist programs that Lenin would be forced to prove again and again that he had not sacrificed his Marxist principles'.[73]

Lenin's peasant policy, during all the struggles of the summer of 1905, is summarised by Crisenoy as 'support the peasant movement, but above all don't tie one's hands for the future. It is necessary to advance and strike hard blows for

---

68   Shanin 1986, p. 84. Much of the following account of the countryside in 1905–7 is based on Shanin, Kingston-Mann and Crisenoy.

69   Shanin 1986, pp. 85–7.

70   Ibid. p. 88.

71   Ibid. p. 89. Crisenoy reports that '[o]f 7000 actions listed by the Okhrana between 1905 and 1907, 5000 are directed against the landed estates' (Crisenoy 1971, pp. 171–2). In April 1905, Lenin considered the transfer of all land to the peasants, to give agrarian capitalism 'a larger basis' and to hasten the transition to an 'American type' agriculture. But he continued to view the large landowners as capitalists and refused to come out clearly for peasant property. On the other hand, he was lucid enough to recognise the inadequacy of the agrarian program (ibid.).

72   'Lenin's intricate distinctions between farmhands, semi-proletarians, middle peasants, and the rural poor remained difficult even for his most loyal supporter to fully comprehend' (Kingston-Mann 1983, p. 167).

73   Kingston-Mann 1983, p. 79. The Menshevik conference of May 1905 criticised Lenin's idea of Social Democrats leading a bourgeois government. Plekhanov and his allies, themselves still within the classical Kautskyian framework, criticised peasant activism, saying it could only fragment large-scale capitalist enterprises (ibid. p. 82).

revolutionary bourgeois democracy ... to march separately and strike together, not hiding divergent interests, and to watch over one's ally as one would an enemy'.[74] There remained, she points out, still a sort of fear about peasant struggles, fear of their spontaneity, and great contempt for the peasant's 'lack of culture'.[75]

Meanwhile, the action of the peasants and the statements of their representatives 'were a striking refutation of (Lenin's) assessments'.[76] In the summer of 1905, the peasants created a central organisation with delegates from several provinces. The Pan-Russian Union of Peasants met for the first time clandestinely at the end of July and called for the abolition of private property and the expropriation of the big landowners; a majority favoured no indemnification.[77] The peasants did not limit themselves to the land question but also demanded free public education, amnesty for political prisoners, convocation of a Duma, and a Constitutional Assembly.[78] Lenin conceded that the peasant congress grasped its own interests well.[79]

The Social Democrats called for the formation of revolutionary peasant committees, but they played no role in the countryside. It was young peasants back from the factories who spread revolutionary ideas.[80] In the summer of 1905 the Bolsheviks held their Third Congress in London, with the peasant question as a major issue. They were divided, unable to foresee or control events. Lenin was torn; the party programme was unsatisfactory from a political viewpoint, but perfectly founded, in his view, from a theoretical viewpoint.[81] When the peasants went beyond the party slogan of taking over the otrezki (once again: the strips of land retained from the 1861 reform by the big landowners), and seized other lands, were they 'reactionary'? There was a constant contradiction between what Lenin saw as politically necessary and his economic ana-

---

74   'Social Democracy and the Revolutionary Government', March 1905, in Lenin 1960–70, vol. 8.

75   'General Plan of Resolutions at the III. Congress, Feb 1905', in Lenin 1960–70, vol. 8.

76   Crisenoy 1971, p. 174.

77   Ibid. p. 175.

78   Ibid. p. 176. Later, in November 1905, the peasants ran off the Tsarist civil servants and elected their own 'elders' (starost). Many directly attacked the whole system, the state and its representatives: police, army, and civil servants. The police reported 1041 actions of this kind between 1905 and 1907. 1000 manors were burned, and in several provinces, all estates were destroyed. There were peasant militias in the Ukraine, Lithuania, Georgia and the Volga Region. The mir retained all its influence.

79   Shanin 1986, p. 126.

80   Crisenoy 1971, p. 179.

81   Ibid. p. 180.

lysis; if he continued to defend points from his 1902 agrarian programme, it was because he remained convinced of the domination of capitalism on the large estates. In March 1905 he continued to assert that 'in Russia there are few vestiges of feudalism'.[82]

On 17 October the tsar issued a manifesto in response to the months of insurrection, 'speaking much about freedom and saying nothing about land – the one thing that mattered'.[83] It had no impact, and in October 1905 'attacks on estates erupted on an unprecedented scale and rapidly turned into mass destruction of manor houses in the Black Earth belt'.[84] This was no blind explosion; the peasants wanted to be rid of the squires and to ensure that they never returned; 2000 manor houses were destroyed. The government strategy consisted of heavy repression and ineffectual appeasement in the manifesto of 3 November, which abolished payments still due from the 1861 serf emancipation. State repression was, however, an 'orgy of brutality'.[85] It did manage to temporarily stanch the worker uprisings but the peasant revolts did not stop, climaxing only in July 1906. The June 1906 eruptions of rural violence had been so serious that the Emperor of Austria considered military intervention. In July 1906 as well, Lenin argued that the peasantry was 'revolutionary democratic', but that the Social Democrats would fight it when it became 'reactionary and anti-proletarian'. As Kingston-Mann put it, 'Despite the extraordinary incisiveness of his political insight into the problems of his adversaries, the deficiencies of Lenin's economics and sociology continued to render the concept of a Marxian peasant revolution a contradiction in terms'.[86]

---

82   'Revolution of a 1789 or 1848 Type?', March–April 1905, in Lenin 1960–70, vol. 8, quoted in Crisenoy 1971, pp. 180–1.

83   Shanin 1986, p. 92.

84   Ibid. p. 93. The Black Earth belt was the term for the most fertile lands.

85   Ibid. pp. 93–5. The original emancipation of the serfs in 1861 had scheduled decades of payments to the state for the redistributed land.

86   Kingston-Mann 1983, p. 100. Trotsky, who was the one Russian Marxist who agreed with Lenin on the importance of an alliance with the peasantry in 1903, took a different view after 1905–7, attacking Lenin's 'democratic dictatorship of the workers and peasants', and saying that peasants could not play an independent political role or form a party of their own. See Shanin 1986, p. 257. Trotsky felt that peasants did little of political significance in 1905, somewhat more in 1906, but that their role overall was meagre. He did not bother to consider the massive 1906 vote for the Social Revolutionaries in St. Petersburg. For Shanin, 'Trotsky's harsh anti-populism and and anti-peasantism put him with the most conservative of the Mensheviks' (ibid. p. 258).

Prior to these developments, the first Duma had met in April, and had not even considered peasant demands.[87] The movement finally ebbed, and the state and the squires regrouped. This did not prevent grazing lands from being invaded for a third time in the winter of 1906–7.

Meanwhile, in April 1906, the RSDLP held a Bolshevik-Menshevik 'unity conference' in Stockholm. There, Lenin called for the nationalisation of all landed property.[88] Lenin, then, favoured nationalisation as opening the way to capitalism; for the peasants, on the other hand, it meant *expanding communal property to the national level*. The Mensheviks feared that fragmenting large properties would slow down the development of capitalism. Plekhanov argued that transfer of land to the state would leave the autocracy with more land than ever before.[89] (Kautsky, in the Second International journal of record *Neue Zeit*, had come out once again against any Social Democratic programme for the peasantry.) Lenin quoted from Marx's *Capital* about transferring land to the state as a bourgeois measure which would create competition, as in the American West. The Congress ultimately voted to approve the Menshevik Maslow's plan for the municipalisation of land.[90] Lenin opposed this, saying it would only give power to local elites.

The initial slogans of the peasant uprisings were expressed in a language different from that of the urban revolts, expressing a desire for political power and civil rights, land reform, 'charitable government', 'liberty' and 'being listened to'.[91] In Shanin's view, many doubted the very existence of general peasant political goals in rural Russia in 1905–7, and Lenin said in 1917 that the problem with the peasant revolt of those years was that they did not finish the job, burning down only part of the manors.[92]

Other breakthroughs occurred in places such as Georgia, where in Guria province what Shanin called 'the first case in history of a peasant rule led by a Marxist elite' held out from 1903 to 1906, and news of which moreover travelled widely. The Latvian Social Democrats led widespread attacks on manors in the Baltic provinces in a 'mini-civil war' situation, during which 459 manor

---

87   The Tsarist regime responded to the mass uprisings by conceding a series of four elected Dumas, or legislatures, each one dissolved and reconvened with fewer powers than the preceding one.

88   Kingston-Mann 1983, p. 92. Crisenoy 1971, p. 192.

89   Crisenoy 1971, p. 93.

90   Ibid. p. 95.

91   Shanin 1986, p. 100.

92   Ibid. p. 101.

houses were destroyed in Latvia and 114 in Estonia.[93] The designated enemies
of the revolts throughout the Russian Empire were the state apparatus, the
kulak (wealthy peasant), 'commune eaters' who bought up communal lands
for themselves, and the reactionary bands of the 'Black Hundreds'. The Second
Duma met in 1907, was more radical than the first, and the peasants were
more anti-government. 'Peasants looked at their lives in ways unthinkable
before'.[94] They were very sophisticated, and the demand for transfer of land
to the peasantry and for the abolition of private land ownership was total.[95]

Under the impact of these cumulative events, Lenin called for the revision of
the RSDLP's 1903 Agrarian Programme[96] and said, in contrast to his 1899 book,
that 'the economy of the squires in Russia in based on repressive enserfing and
not on a capitalist system ... Those who refuse to see it cannot explain the
contemporary broad and deep peasant revolutionary movement in Russia'.[97]
Most Social Democrats now admitted that the 1903 programme was overly
pessimistic about the peasants' revolutionary potential. This change of attitude
was formulated as a call for a 'democratic dictatorship of workers and peasants'
that would promote an 'American road' of agricultural development under a

---

93   Ibid. p. 109.

94   Ibid. p. 131.

95   Ibid. p. 133.

96   As Shanin put it (Shanin 1986, pp. 152–68), after 1905 Lenin's practical orientation changed
      but theoretically little changed. He did not update *The Development of Capitalism in
      Russia*, on which his early agrarian programme was based. Shanin credits Lenin's 'on the
      spot' reporting in 1905–7 and 'the courage with which he championed new unorthodox
      tactics against his own comrades'. But he also points out that '70 years of research has
      not produced the name of one Bolshevik who was a peasant leader in 1905–7. 'At the
      peak of Russia's largest peasant revolt in centuries, the number of peasants within the
      cadres of the Bolsheviks was about zero, as was the number of the Bolsheviks elected to
      the 2nd Duma by the "electoral college" of the peasantry. Workers and peasants, on the
      other hand, learned from each other's struggles. The All-Russian Peasant Union rejected
      a Social Democratic worker delegation saying, "We have just got rid of self-appointed
      teachers and supervisors". The Congress then passed a resolution of full solidarity with our
      "brother workers in struggle". Peasant participation in political parties was remarkable by
      its absence. The utopianism of the SRs, formulated as the "socialization of all land", was
      attacked as naïve by the Social Democrats but was adopted in part or in full at the RSDLP's
      4th Congress ... When Lenin said Russia was not yet capitalist, he stayed within the earlier
      theoretical structure but just "moved the clock back"'.

97   Shenin 1986, p. 146. Plekhanov at the Fourth Party Congress said that 'Lenin looks at
      the nationalization of the land with the eye of an SR. He even begins to adopt their
      terminology, i.e. talks of popular creativity ... Nice to meet old acquaintances but it is
      unpleasant to see how Social Democrats adopt populist points of view' (ibid. p. 149).

revolutionary regime.[98] The forces of reaction also had to revise their views on the peasantry: 'As manors burned and the first and second Dumas heaped abuse on the government, the commune was singled out more and more as the reason for the peasant rebellion'.[99] This shift in perception presaged the post-1907 policy of Stolypin, who replaced Witte as Finance Minister in 1906, and attempted to undermine the communes by subsidising individual peasants who wished to leave them and farm their own plots.[100] The peasants did end the 1905–7 upsurge with more results than any other group. Rents went down and rural wages went up; most peasant debt was cancelled by the state. There had also been an important leap in peasant self-esteem.[101]

4   Years of Reaction: Stolypin's Attempt at a 'Prussian'-Style
         Revolution from Above

In 1906, P.A. Stolypin took over from the fallen Witte as the most powerful minister in the Tsarist government, carrying out harsh repression against the 1905–7 Revolution and simultaneously pursuing a policy of breaking up the peasant commune. His many executions of revolutionaries by hanging became known as 'Stolypin's neckties'.

Under the impact of the revolution, the government almost more than the Marxists had become aware that the commune, previously viewed as a pillar of the regime, was in fact the main source of peasant radicalism. Stolypin and his advisers looked back to the Prussian reformers of the 1820s who had carried out a revolution from above to prevent a revolution from below.[102] Private enterprise was to be promoted throughout the economy, and in agriculture this meant creating credits to enable individual peasants to leave the communes and acquire their own land, often by privatising communal land. Stolypin

---

98   Ibid. p. 150. Lenin was fascinated by two foreign models of agricultural development, the
       Prussian 'revolution from above' under Bismarck and his successors, and the American
       policy of free land for farmers to develop the west.

99   Ibid. p. 142.

100   In 1906 there were mass sales of land by gentry terrified of the insurrection in the coun-
       tryside; sales to peasants were facilitated by the Peasant Land Bank. See Atkinson 1983,
       p. 68.

101   Ibid. pp. 197–8.

102   Stolypin was remembered, in Shanin's view, as the 'last great defender of the autocracy.
       Stolypin was defeated by the Russian conservative lobby. He had been touted to be Russia's
       "second Bismarck" [the first having been Witte – LG]' (Shanin 1986, p. 236).

was assassinated in 1911, but his policy, aimed at breaking up the commune, remained in effect until 1917, in the hope of creating a Russian 'Vendée' against any future revolutionary movement.[103] As Crisenoy put it:

> the ruling classes were not mistaken ... After 1905–07, the mir become in their eyes one of the causes of peasant radicalism ... We have to say that, aside from the Social Democrats, this link between the mir, the revolutionary peasant movement and its demands for land was obvious to all. But Lenin was convinced of the opposite. For him the commune was still nothing but a "juridical envelope maintained artificially" ... For Lenin, the peasant's call for the nationalization of land was negative, and should not mask his instinct to be an "owner" ... In Lenin's view, the peasant did not know what he wanted, didn't even know what he was saying ... For Lenin, [there was] no uncertainty: the nationalization of the land necessarily brings with it a capitalist agrarian organization.[104]

In fact, Lenin and Stolypin had rather similar views on the entrepreneurial peasant as a promoter of capitalist development in Russia. To defend this change of orientation from the one he had held from 1899 until 1905, 'Lenin had to abandon his earlier claims that Russia was already capitalist'.[105] Lenin, like Stolypin, saw the role of the Russian government as similar to the earlier Prussian model. Stolypin's reform, in his view, would 'encourage the economically incompetent landlords to become Prussian-style bourgeois "Junkers"'.[106] Nationalisation would clear away feudal vestiges and make possible free competition, as in America.[107] 'Despite quotes from *Capital* and *Theories of Surplus Value*, Lenin was hard pressed to make the case that Marx "had taken pride in the economic virtues of the small farmer"'.[108] As Kingston-Mann put it:

---

103   Kingston-Mann 1983, p. 102. The Vendée was a region of western France whose peasants had joined counter-revolutionary forces against the Jacobins in 1792.

104   Crisenoy 1971, pp. 194–6.

105   Ibid. p. 103.

106   Ibid. p. 104. The Junkers were pre-capitalist landowners in Eastern Prussia who had reinvented themselves as capitalists while preserving quasi-feudal social relations on their estates. For a portrait, see Gershenkron 1943. Lenin also felt that American farmers in the west prospered because land there belonged to the state, hence creating no superfluous expenditures for rent or purchase.

107   Crisenoy 1971, p. 105.

108   Ibid.

His was a tactical move that reflected the strain which the complex real-ity of the Russian situation placed upon his Western-centered ideology ... The commune played no role in Lenin's plans and strategies ... Lenin ridiculed the idea that the 'medieval' commune retained any of its equal-izing functions.[109]

In 1907–8, Lenin argued that the process of rural differentiation had already destroyed the commune in all but name. A still functioning com-mune remained inconceivable to Lenin ... Certain that the peasantry lacked historically significant forms of social organization, Lenin inaccur-ately referred to commune peasants as only the tool of the village kulak ... Lenin had however moved far closer to a realistic approach than any other members of RSDLP.[110]

Under the auspices of Stolypin's agrarian reforms, between one-fourth and one-third of all Russian peasants, by some estimates, left the communes between 1906 and 1917. (Russia in these years became one of the world's biggest export-ers of cereals while also having terrible famines.) Communal peasants often responded to these desertions with violence.[111] Two to three millions peasants got property in the decade after 1906, or about one-fourth of the 12 million peas-ant households in European Russia.[112] Some of the obstacles to the reform were lack of roads, long winters, and the village assemblies proposing the worst and most distant lands to those who wished to leave.[113] In Crisenoy's view, Stolypin's reforms also ran up against overpopulation, the lack of land, and communal tenure.[114] She also sees Lenin's post-1905–7 break with Second International conceptions as 'very relative'; Lenin continued, as in 1899, to confuse capitalist

---

109   Ibid. pp. 106–7.

110   Ibid. pp. 107–10.

111   Most recent scholarship, according to Kingston-Mann, has emphasised the ephemeral character of the reform's impact; in 1915, two-thirds of 'new proprietors' were still plowing on scattered strips intermingled with communal lands (Kingston-Mann 1983, p. 123).

112   In 1913 agriculture made up 43 percent of Russia's national income, and grain exports sustained Russia's balance of payments. By comparison, in 1914 60 percent of the French population was still rural but national income per capita was four times higher than in Russia. By 1914, the Russian rural population was 37 percent higher than in 1897. See Atkinson 1983, pp. 102–4.

113   Thus does Crisenoy explain this 'meager result' (Crisenoy 1971, pp. 229–30).

114   Atkinson 1983, p. 81, arrives at a different estimate: by 1916 16 million dessiatins (1 dessiatin = 2.3 acres) were individualised; this represented 14 percent of the 115 million dessiatins of land in communes in 1905. Peasants in 1915 owned 35 percent of the 97 millions of dessiat-ins of privately owned land. But collective land ownership actually rose during this period.

agriculture and commodity agriculture. In 1915, he was still writing: 'The development of capitalism consists above all in the passage from natural economy to commodity economy'.[115] To recognise his error, Crisenoy writes, would mean breaking with what he had been saying for twenty years. 'By failing to recognize the attachment of the peasants to the mir, Lenin missed the reason for the failure of (Stolypin's) reform and one of the reasons for the 1917 revolution'.[116] In the revolutionary years 1917–19, serious violence was still being brought to bear against 'splitters-off' from the communes, and not, as Lenin's theory would predict, between rich and poor peasants.

5   Russian Peasants and the Commune in 1917 and Thereafter

Within a month of the February Revolution that overthrew the Romanov dynasty, the peasantry had risen en masse. They attacked the large landowners and the commune peasants attacked the separate farms. As in 1905, the commune was at the centre of peasant struggles, taking charge of confiscations and the redistribution of lands.

After 'reorienting' the Bolshevik Party following his return from exile and the famous 'April Theses', Lenin was arguing that the rural soviets had already shown far greater creative social imagination than the Provisional Government.[117] A Bolshevik rural Red Guard had formed in March–April 1917. In the 4 April edition of *Pravda*, Lenin wrote: 'If the revolution is not settled by the Russian peasant, it will not be settled by the German worker'.[118] Lenin's draft programme in April–May 1917 was 1) nationalisation of all land; 2) transformation of large estates into model farms, under soviets of agricultural workers and run by agronomists. But these formulations, observed Crisenoy, were deeply alien to the peasant movement.[119]

---

115   Lenin's article 'New Facts', from vol. 22 of his works, quoted in Crisenoy 1971, p. 248. In her view, both Lenin and Stolypin have the same dream of transforming the Russian peasant into a European peasant (p. 249). 'Lenin, like Stolypin, is a fervent defender of the disappearance of the rural commune' (p. 251). He remains convinced of the anti-commune sentiments of the peasant, as elaborated in his article 'Our Detractors' (January–February 1911), in Lenin 1960–70, vol. 27.

116   Crisenoy 1971, p. 253.

117   Kingston-Mann 1983, p. 141.

118   Ibid. pp. 142–3.

119   Lenin was aware of this. A few months later, before the October Revolution, he admitted that 'what (the peasants) want is to keep their small property, preserve egalitarian norms

The Bolsheviks, at this point, were still a minority, outnumbered by the Mensheviks and the sRs. Workers and soldiers had beaten up demonstrators carrying Bolshevik signs in April. By May, nonetheless, Lenin was telling the Congress of Peasant Deputies that peasants should at once seize all land, to the consternation of the Provisional Government and in particular of the sRs, who headed ministries and were prevaricating on the land question. The sR and Menshevik ministers were ready to defer any transfer of land to the peasants until a Constitutional Assembly could meet. Some sR observers noted with dismay the impact of Lenin's appeal for land seizures and the damaging political case the Bolsheviks made against the sR ministers in the coalition.[120] The leading sR political figure, Chernov, was assaulted by a peasant shouting, 'Why don't you take power, you s.o.b, when it's given to you?'[121] The Congress of Peasant Deputies in fact called for soviets of peasants everywhere, and attacks on individualised property accelerated.

As the Provisional Government and above all the front disintegrated in the summer of 1917, peasants were deserting the army in droves and returning to their villages to get their share of the land newly distributed from the gentry estates. This movement, like the soviets in 1905, was the work of no political party. Peasant disturbances peaked in October 1917. Immediately after over-throwing the Provisional Government, the Bolsheviks issued their Land Decree, recognising the *fait accompli* of land seizures in the countryside; under the decree, peasants were free to set up communes or artels (cooperatives). The Bolshevik Land Decree was essentially the sR programme. A wave of egalit-arianism had swept the countryside and in 1917–18 the peasant commune had extended beyond any previous historical frontier.[122] The peasants distributed gentry, church and monastery lands to families based on the traditional cri-terion of the 'number of eaters'; some independent peasants from Stolypin's reform were forced back into communes.[123] The confiscations were largely complete by the spring of 1918. 96.8 percent of all lands were in peasant hands, and three million landless peasants had received allotments. The commune at this point encompassed almost all rural households.[124]

---

and renew them periodically' (see 'Pages from the Journal of a Publicist', Septempter 1917, in Lenin 1960–70, vol. 25). Quoted in Crisenoy 1971, p. 273. But Lenin's realism made him admit the attachment of the peasants to the commune, and their desire to see it enlarged.

120   Ibid. p. 157.
121   Ibid. p. 162.
122   Atkinson 1983, p. 174.
123   Ibid. p. 176.
124   Ibid. p. 185.

Lenin, in Kingston-Mann's account, had always insisted that the dangers involved in peasant land seizures were always outweighed by benefits from attacks on bourgeois property. The land decree of October 1917, taken from 242 peasant mandates and from the SR agrarian programme, had abolished private property in land, and went against the Russian Marxist tradition in its respect for peasant communal traditions. Its terms were populist, and the non-Bolshevik left recognised its expedient, even opportunist character: 'The Russian Marxist tradition was rooted in a denial of the sociological insights which Marx himself had praised in the work of populists like Daniel'son'.[125] 'Unaware that peasants re-entered the communes in increasing numbers during the pre-war period, Bolsheviks and Mensheviks found no constructive socialist significance in the peasantry's successful efforts to return the otrubshchiki [the Stolypin-promoted 'splitters off' – LG] to the communes in the course of 1917'.[126] '... obsessions with capitalism in the countryside ... and awareness of the individualistic property fanatics and bigots among the peasants, had blinded Russian Marxists to much evidence about the agricultural economy, about the widespread resistance to the Stolypin reforms, and about the collectivist notions of peasants who demanded abolition of private property in land ... Fears of the kulak flourished in official circles, as peasant communes carried out an unprecedented equalization of land on behalf of the poor without any help from the Soviet authorities'.[127]

Early on, the Soviet government was interfering with the distribution of animals and farm materials, a policy aimed at leaving the poor peasants unable to farm and encouraging them toward the new state farms (sovkhoz). Once in power, the Bolsheviks had discouraged further destruction of estates, which the peasants, for their part, saw as a further guarantee that the former owners would never return. Bolshevik policy favoured specialists in the countryside (as sovkhoz directors). At the Seventh Congress of Soviets, there was already criticism of the privileges of the specialists. Sometimes the director of the sovkhoz was the former landowner! In these debates, Lenin again turned to the example of German (Prussian) state capitalism: its modern techniques were in the service of imperialism and the Junkers, but 'replace "state capitalism" with "the Soviet state" and you have all the conditions of socialism'.[128]

125   Ibid. pp. 173, 179, 183.
126   Ibid. p. 185.
127   Ibid. pp. 193–4.
128   Crisenoy 1971, pp. 277–9; the Lenin quote is from 'On Left Infantilism and Petty Bourgeois Ideas' in Lenin 1960–70, vol. 27, quoted in Crisenoy 1971, pp. 281–2.

But quarrels over administrative measures were soon to be greatly complicated by the drastic falloff in agricultural production. In November 1917, Russia
had still produced 641 million tons of wheat. Requisitions to feed the cities
began in early 1918, when already only seven percent of the grain planned for
Petrograd and Moscow was delivered. As the civil war intensified in the summer
of 1918, some fertile lands fell under the control of the Whites, and famine set
in. In response to requisitions, peasants cut back production to the basic needs
of their families; land under cultivation declined by 16 percent by 1919. The
Bolsheviks had counted on the support of the poorest peasants, but land distribution had moved many of them out of that category; the committees of poor
peasants had great difficulty functioning. The party cells in the countryside
had 14,700 members but were mainly made up of functionaries. By 1921, after
three years of civil war, harvests were at 40 percent of 1914 levels. Between 1918
and 1920, in the years of war communism, epidemics, hunger and cold killed
7.5 million Russians; four million had died in the civil war. People returned to
the land to survive; of the three million workers who made up the proletarian
side of the 'dual revolution' in 1917, only 1.2 million remained in the factories by
1922.

By 1921, furthermore, the proletarian democracy of 1917, embodied in the
soviets and workers' councils, had been destroyed or turned into rubber stamps
of the party. The left SRs, who shared power with the Bolsheviks for a few
months, were suppressed in July 1918 after they assassinated the German ambassador, in an attempt to undermine the Treaty of Brest-Litovsk.[129] Repression
against anarchist 'bandits' had begun in early 1918. The Bolsheviks crushed the
Kronstadt uprising in March 1921, and had earlier crushed the anarchist peasant
Makhno movement in the Ukraine. At the Tenth Party Congress, also in March
1921, internal factions within the party itself had been suppressed. That Congress also inaugurated the market-driven New Economic Policy (NEP). Oppositional currents within the Bolshevik Party, such as Miasnikov's Workers Group

---

129   The Treaty of Brest Litovsk was the treaty of Soviet surrender to the Central Powers on the
       eastern front, signed at the end of February 1918. Under its terms, Russia ceded 34 percent
       of her population, 32 percent of her agricultural land, 54 percent of her industry and 89
       percent of her coal mines. The Bolshevik Party decided to approve the treaty following a
       series of tumultuous meetings, in which a majority initially rejected it. For the basic story,
       see (among many other accounts) Deutscher 1980, pp. 359–94. From Lenin's viewpoint, it
       was a successful gamble which paid off months later when the Central Powers collapsed,
       nullifying the treaty. For those who opposed it, Brest-Litovsk was a first step whereby
       the Soviet Union placed national interests ahead of the international revolution. For an
       analysis of the treaty from this perspective, see Sabatier n.d.

or the Democratic Centralists, had been suppressed. By 1922, the remaining independent Mensheviks were offered the choice of execution or exile. From that point onward, the only open discussions remaining in Soviet Russia with any real influence over events involved a few hundred Old Bolsheviks at the top echelons of a party ruling uneasily over 150 million people, the great majority of them peasants. That party had also absorbed hundreds of thousands of new members after the October seizure of power, often people more interested in jobs and careers than in the real history and outlooks of Bolshevism.[130] A number of former bourgeois and even large landowners rallied to the new power, often becoming directors of sovkhozes, factories and mines.[131] The nucleus of a new ruling class was in place.[132] 90 percent of state functionaries were carried over from the Tsarist regime, and 90 percent of officers in the Red Army had been Tsarist officers.

The legacy of modernising Second International Marxism on the agrarian question remained the outlook of the Bolshevik Party in power. Thus the disconnect between the emerging factions of the regime – all of them – and the reality of the countryside, having the overwhelming majority of the population, remained as great as it had been prior to the Bolsheviks' arrival in power. As historian John Marot put it, to implement the development plans of all factions – the Trotskyist left, the Bukharinist right and the Stalinist 'centre' – meant 'to destroy the peasant way of life',[133] the commune. Lenin had recognised after 1905 that he had exaggerated the presence of capitalism in the Russian countryside, but, as indicated earlier, he merely set the clock back on the same dynamic.

---

130 Charles Bettelheim, not a source I like to quote, recounts the story of the group around Oustrialov, an ex-Cadet in Paris exile, known as the *Smenovekhovtsy*, from the name of their journal meaning 'new orientation'. This group called on any bourgeois intellectuals remaining in Russia to rally to the regime, which in their view had entered its Thermidor period. Bukharin analysed these 'friends' of a very special type, who hoped that under the cover of the 'monopoly of knowledge' bourgeois power might be restored in Soviet Russia. They believed that the October Revolution had accomplished an indispensable historic task, of which a new bourgeoisie could take advantage. The revolution had mobilised 'the most courageous and pitiless adversaries of the rotting Tsarist regime, crushing the corrupted strata of the intelligentsia which only knew how to speak of God and the devil ... they opened the way to the creation of a new bourgeoisie' (quoted in Bettelheim 1974, p. 263). (Bettelheim's book, despite insights of this kind, is vitiated by his numerous bows in the direction of Mao's China, in 1973 at the peak of its prestige in Paris.)

131 Crisenoy 1971, p. 332.

132 See Pirani 2008.

133 Marot 2012, p. 11.

The fundamental problem was that the peasant world, centred on the mir, was not on Lenin's timetable at all, belated, contemporary or otherwise; the owners of the newly-distributed private plots within the framework of the mir were not capitalist peasants producing for a market, but were participating in household economies, producing primarily for their own use, occasionally using markets to acquire the relatively few goods they could not produce themselves. Their surplus had previously gone to the Tsarist state through taxation to pay for industrialisation, and to the landlords for their consumption. With those two burdens removed, the sole external compulsion remained the modest taxation of the Soviet state. No industrialisation programme assuming a peasant capitalist rationality had any chance of achieving its goals. The peasant economy, as Marot put it, was neither capitalist nor socialist, and 'the peasants had little or no interest in the collective organization of production and distribution beyond the confines of the village'.[134]

By the spring of 1921, the ebb and isolation of the Russian Revolution, internationalist from the beginning in the strategic conceptions of Lenin and Trotsky (in their different theoretical frameworks; see below) could not have been more clear. The world revolution which had in 1917–18 seemed weeks or at most months away henceforth had to be reckoned in years. In quick succession the spring of 1921 saw the suppression of the Kronstadt uprising, the failure of the 'March Action' in Germany, the Anglo-Soviet trade agreement, the implementation of the market-driven New Economic Policy (NEP), the suppression of factions in the Bolshevik Party, the Treaty of Riga, formalising the Soviet defeat in the 1920 war with Poland, and the commercial treaty with Attaturk's nationalist government in Turkey, which a mere two months earlier (January 1921) had murdered the entire central committee of the Turkish Communist Party.[135] This general ebb of hopes for revolution in western Europe weakened the position of the internationalist, cosmopolitan wing of the Bolshevik Party and strengthened the position of the internal 'praktiki', the long-term veterans of the party apparatus from the years of clandestinity under Tsarist autocracy, personified of course by Joseph Stalin. The regime turned inward, and with famine still raging in the countryside, nothing had a higher priority than the peasant question.

For Lenin, the Bolshevik regime was a dual revolution, based on the 'democratic dictatorship of the workers and peasants', completing the bourgeois revolution of eradicating pre-capitalist agriculture. He wrote:

---

134   Ibid. p. 35.
135   See Chapter Two, 'Socialism in One Country before Stalin: The Case of Turkey, 1917–1925'.

> Yes, our revolution is a bourgeois revolution, *as long as we march* with the peasantry as a whole ... we have said it hundreds and thousands of times since 1905 ...[136]

This bourgeois revolution, in his view, could move to a socialist phase when aided, and only when aided, by revolution in the West. The alliance with the peasantry (the so-called 'smychka') remained crucial in Lenin's strategic perspective for the rest of his political life. He would have viscerally rejected Stalin's 1924 proclamation of 'socialism in one country'.[137]

My purpose here cannot be to put forward a specific theory of the 'class nature of the Soviet Union', harking back to the state capitalist/bureaucratic collectivist/degenerated workers' state debates of the 1960s/1970s. I merely signal my agreement with some variant of the class, as opposed to workers' state theories, but explaining my analysis in detail would further shift the focus away from my main purpose, namely tracing the impact of the agrarian question and the fate of the Russian peasant commune in shaping that outcome. I mention Trotsky and his theory of permanent revolution primarily to indicate the difference between his framework and Lenin's, who never accepted that theory,[138] however close they were in the spring of 1917.

---

136   Lenin, in 'The Proletarian Revolution and the Renegade Kautsky', quoted in van der Linden 2007, p. 16. Trotsky himself further elaborates on this in *Permanent Revolution*, Ch. 5: 'The Bolshevik slogan [of 'democratic dictatorship of the workers and peasants' – LG] was realized in fact – not as a morphological trait but as a very great historical reality. Only, it was realized *not before, but after October*. The peasant war, in the words of Marx, supported the dictatorship of the proletariat. The collaboration of the two classes was realized through October on a gigantic scale ... And Lenin himself estimated the October Revolution – its first stage – as the *true* realization of the democratic revolution, and by that also as the true, even if changed, embodiment of the strategic slogan of the Bolsheviks' (Trotsky 1931, Ch. 5).

137   Because Trotsky looms so large in the left-wing anti-Stalinist currents in the West, it is necessary at this point to signal his differences with Lenin's formulation in 1917–18; Trotsky's analysis of Stalinism also set down the framework for many would-be revolutionaries who later broke with him to declare Russia a class society (usually 'state capitalist'), such as C.L.R. James, Castoriadis, Shachtman, or Dunayevskaya.
        Trotsky's analysis of the revolution at the time of the NEP flowed from the theory of 'permanent revolution' he developed with Parvus at the time of the revolution of 1905. In this view, the weakness of the bourgeoisie in a backward country such as Russia made it possible for the working class there to lead a revolution which, in conjunction with a proletarian revolution in the West, would collapse the 'bourgeois stage' into an international proletarian revolution.

138   One good, and typical, example of a state capitalist analysis of the Soviet phenomenon

The Russian working class had its own thoughts about the NEP, built on the destruction of the soviets and workers' councils they had created in 1917, and the return of the managerial elite they thought they had overthrown in that year. It waged a series of militant strikes in August and September 1923. A second Workers' Group had formed in the spring of that year and played an important coordinating role in these strikes; according to Marot,

> [it] sought out alliances with elements of previous oppositions. Denouncing the New Economic Policy as the New Exploitation of the Proletariat by bureaucratically-appointed factory managers and directors of industry, the Workers' Group tried to recruit among party and non-party workers. It strove to lend political definition and direction to the massive strike wave ... It even looked for support abroad, among left-wing elements of the German Communist Party ... and among Gorter's Dutch Communists.[139]

And where was Trotsky while these strikes were going on? Marot is eloquent:

> Trotsky's political opposition toward the factional activity of the Workers' Group of 1923 outwardly expressed [his] firmly-held and ideologically internalized insistence on unitary, single-party rule ... Trotsky even refused public solidarity with the over two-hundred members who dared to participate actively in the workers' strike movement, and who had been subsequently expelled from the party ... Although Trotsky did next to nothing to lend political guidance to rank-and-file dissent outside the Communist Party, he was almost always prepared to respond favorably to invitations of political co-operation by one or another of the party leadership.[140]

Lenin was forced by rapidly declining health to withdraw from political activity in early 1923, and died one year later. In the last months of his very reduced activity, he had planned to 'throw a bomb' under Stalin at a forthcoming party

---

that breaks with Trotsky, but which emerges directly from Trotsky's framework, is Daum 1990. While generally superior to most other works in the state capitalism camp, Daum's book never mentions the mir, and it discusses the peasantry, like most other works in the genre, only in passing as a backdrop to the 1920s faction fight.

139   Marot 2012, p. 94.
140   Ibid. p. 95.

congress and, in his testament, called for Stalin's removal from the position of general secretary of the party.[141]

The fact that Soviet Russia emerged from the civil war in 1921 with the nucleus of a new ruling class in power still leaves open the fate of the mir, in which 98.5 percent of the peasantry – itself at least 90 percent of the Russian population – lived, up to its demise in 1929–30. It is thus important to sketch out the faction fight in the 'commanding heights' of the Bolshevik Party up to Stalin's collectivisations. There was nothing foreordained about what actually happened, which transformed Soviet Russia from the 'guided capitalism' of the NEP of 1921, conceived as a holding action prior to revolution in the West, into the mature totalitarian form consolidated under Stalin in 1929–32. No one in the three-way faction fight up to 1927, Stalin included, advocated the violent collectivisations that finally gave the Soviet Union the definitive contours through which it became known to the world as 'communism'.[142,143]

---

141 For a full account, see Lewin 1968a.

142 In taking this tack, I take my distance from some attitudes current in the libertarian or left communist milieu, in which I generally situate myself. I first of all reject the commonplace view one finds among anarchists, who see nothing problematic to be explained in the emergence of Stalinist Russia. Did not Bakunin already predict, in his 1860s struggle with Marx, that a Marxist-led revolution would result in the authoritarian rule of a centralising intellectual elite? I do not believe, further, that there exists a straight line, or much of any line, from Lenin's 1902 pamphlet *What Is To Be Done?* to Stalin's Russia, especially since Lenin admitted after 1905 that he had been wrong. Such a 'teleological' approach does not hold up in a close, month-to-month analysis of developments from the 1890s to the 1920s. I cannot fathom the mindset of a milieu in which it has long been fashionable to refer to C.L.R. James, or more recently, in certain circles, to Amadeo Bordiga, whereas it has been distinctly unfashionable to refer to Lenin, whom both James and Bordiga greatly admired.

143 *What Is To Be Done?*, briefly, is as much Lenin's anti-workerist anti-point-of-production (anti-'Economist', in the language of the day) polemic, arguing, against a narrow focus on workers' struggles alone, that revolutionaries should carry their denunciations of oppression into *all* classes of society, and be 'the tribune of the people', as it is about his use of Kautsky's notion of 'bringing consciousness from the outside' and his call for a tightly disciplined elite organisation of revolutionaries. It should not be forgotten that the Mensheviks, who rejected Lenin's narrower criteria for party membership at the famous 1903 'split' conference, calmly voted those very criteria into the party statutes in 1906. Further, under the impact of 1905, Lenin wrote that the '... working class is instinctively, spontaneously Social Democratic [i.e. revolutionary – LG], and more than 10 years of work put in by Social Democracy has done a great deal to transform this spontaneity into consciousness' (see 'The Reorganization of the Party', in Lenin 1960–70, vol. 10, p. 32; quoted in Daum 1990, p. 106.) C.L.R. James wrote, in *Facing Reality*, about the 'old type of Marxist organization' (by which he meant the vanguard party): 'All these beliefs led

Here is how Moshe Lewin (though offering statistics somewhat at odds with those cited previously) describes the situation of the mir, shortly before its destruction in 1929–30:

> On the eve of revolution, fewer than 50% of the peasants were still members of the mir … Eight million households held their land as private property, while 7.4 million holdings were still communally owned. The decay of this relic of the ancient peasant community was hastened by the increasing degree of social stratification within the peasantry. However, at the time of the revolution, the mir took on a miraculous new lease on life. The miracle can be explained by the fact that the agrarian reform, which freed the peasants from the bonds of feudalism, also evened out the differences between them to a very considerable degree. Having got rid of the pomeshchiki [the last descendants of the service aristocracy of the sixteenth to eighteenth centuries – LG] and some of the kulaks, the peasants reverted to the old egalitarian relationships of the mir, and by the same token to the institution itself … Ample evidence of the … communal form of land tenure is afforded by the agrarian code of 1922, which deals with it in great detail. The Party, however, appeared to take little account of this factor, and of its possible implications … between 1922 and 1927 the village society, by virtue of the general improvement in the economy, had grown considerably in strength, its budget had increased and, despite the efforts of the authorities to encourage the [rural soviets – LG] it was the mir which continued to be the 'sole organization in charge of the economic life of the village'.[144]

The 1921 turn to the NEP (New Economic Policy) did revive both industry and agriculture, in terms of the Bolshevik strategy of 'guiding capitalism' while marking time until revolution in the West. The NEP cannot be critiqued as a 'restoration of capitalism' because capitalism had never been abolished in the first place. To the charge of the Workers' Opposition, at the Tenth Party Congress in March 1921, that the Bolsheviks were creating state capitalism,

---

to the conclusion that the organization was the true *subject* … And if the organization, in philosophical terms, was the subject of history, the proletariat was the object … This conception of the organization is inherent in the extreme views that Lenin expounded in *What Is To Be Done?* He repudiated them later, but not with the force and thoroughness which were needed to prevent them from doing infinite mischief' (James et al. 1974, pp. 93–4).

144   From Lewin 1968b, pp. 85–6.

Lenin replied that state capitalism would be a major step forward for backward Russia, dominated as it was by petty producers.

Under the NEP, peasant food production by 1925 approached for the first time pre-World War One levels, in contrast to the famine conditions of 1921–2. The NEP, however, also led to the famous 'Scissors Crisis' of 1923 and 1925, in which the prices of industrial goods produced in the cities rose much higher than the prices for agricultural produce from the countryside, making it impossible for peasants to buy, and undermining the strategy of a controlled 'socialist primitive accumulation' off the peasantry advocated by the economist of Trotsky's left-wing faction, Evgeni Preobrazhensky.[145] This strategy, moreover, was doomed because, as indicated earlier, nothing, short of force, compelled the peasants to interact with the urban-industrial economy on the scale envisioned by the planners of the left, or for that matter by Bukharin and the 'socialism at a snail's pace' theorists of the 'right'.[146] By the mid-1920s, it was clear that the differences between the Trotskyist left and the Bukharinist right were more quantitative than qualitative, coming down to differences over the appropriate pace of 'pumping' the peasants, as Bukharin increasingly recognised the need to industrialise with a surplus taken from agriculture. Bukharin early on had prophetically written, against the left's industrialization plans,

> ... Taking too much on itself, [the proletariat] has to create a colossal administrative apparatus. To fulfill the economic functions of the small producers, small peasants, etc., it requires too many employees and administrators. The attempt to replace all these small figures with state *chinovniki* [see footnote – LG] – call them what you want, in fact they are state *chinovniki* – gives birth to such a colossal apparatus that the expenditure for its maintenance proves to be incomparably more significant than the unproductive costs which derive from the anarchistic condition of small production; as a result, this entire form of management, the entire economic apparatus of the proletarian state, does not

---

145 This strategy is spelled out in Preobrazhensky's 1926 book *The New Economics* (Preobraženskij 1965). Marot 2012 writes: 'In 1923 and 1925, factory managers and enterprising peasants respectively were redistributing the pie of goodies by gaming the market' (p. 39).

146 I put 'right' in quotes because no one was more reactionary than the leader of the 'centre', Stalin. I am here neglecting the important foreign policy debates that were intertwined with factional positions on Soviet economic policy, starting with the failure of the aborted 1923 uprising in Germany, the failed British general strike of 1926, and above all the disastrous Soviet intervention in China from 1925 to 1927, the latter two laid at the door of Stalin and Bukharin.

facilitate, but only impedes the development of the forces of production. In reality it flows into the direct opposite of what was intended, and therefore iron necessity compels that it be broken ... If the proletariat itself does not do this, then other forces will overthrow it.[147]

By the end of 1927, Stalin and his 'centre' had defeated, marginalised and expelled the Trotskyist left from the party, with the support of Bukharin and his faction.[148] Even then, the left remained largely clueless about the real danger represented by this 'centre'. Trotsky had said, prior to his own initial exile to Alma Ata (in Kazakhstan): 'With Stalin against Bukharin, perhaps. With Bukharin against Stalin, never'. What was ultimately at stake was the preservation of the 'smyshka', the worker-peasant alliance, the last pillar of Lenin's 'dual revolution', which would not survive any concerted attempt to squeeze the peasantry harder to pay for industrialisation. Many figures, across the political spectrum within the party, imagined the NEP lasting for years, perhaps decades, into the future.

The break in the situation occurred with two successive years of crop failure in 1928 and 1929. Breadlines were forming in Moscow by the end of 1928, and Stalin used the emergency to launch his infamous 'war on the kulak' (the wealthiest stratum of peasants, estimated at four to five percent of the total). Party cadre were ordered to confiscate whatever food they could find in the countryside, using 'Uralo-Mongolian' (i.e., violent) methods, in what amounted to military operations going beyond anything done in the confiscations during the civil war. The fine distinctions among the peasants, which Lenin had first laboriously worked out in his 1899 book and which had never been terribly successful for political purposes such as rousing the poor peasants against wealthier strata, were largely obliterated in the frenzy to meet quotas. Further, food confiscations were combined with forcing peasants into collective farms (the sovkhoz) or into the cooperatives (the kolkhoz).

The peasants resisted violently. Not only did they murder party cadre where they could, but, faced with no future but unremunerative wage labour on the collective farms, they destroyed their own crops and slaughtered something on

---

147   Quoted in Cohen 1973, p. 140. The *'chinovniki'* were originally Tsarist bureaucrats, strictly organised according to rank (*'chin'* in Russian). Bukharin accused the left of advocating a 'Genghis Khan' plan.

148   For a full account of the faction fight, see Marot 2012, Chs. 1–2. His book stands out, among left-wing anti-Stalinist accounts, for the devastating portrait of how the Trotskyist left (minus, it must be said, Trotsky himself) not merely capitulated to Stalin's 'left turn' beginning in 1928, but positively embraced it.

the order of 40 percent of all livestock (horses, cows and pigs), often in order not to appear as kulaks. In many situations, far from dividing along the 'class lines' predicted by misguided theory, peasants of all strata banded together in self-defence. Significantly, during a few months' breather decreed by Stalin in the spring of 1930, many peasants rushed back into the communes, but it was not to last. By 1932, an estimated 10 million peasants had died in forced collectivisations and relocations, and all communes, 98.5 percent of all Russian rural territory in 1918, had been destroyed.

Stalin, as he had done before and would do again, used the very real crop failures of 1927 and 1928 to achieve political ends, which in this case meant the destruction of the Bukharinist 'right'. The smyshka, which Lenin had seen as the foundation of the regime for the foreseeable future, was at an end, and 'bacchanalian planning', with tremendous speedup, piece work, and armed GPU units overseeing work in the factories, could begin.

In conclusion, it is important to note the reaction of the Trotskyist 'left' (minus, it must be said, Trotsky himself, already in exile) to Stalin's 'left' turn after 1927, in which he 'crudely and brutally' took over the bulk of the left's programme. The general attitude was: Stalin is implementing our programme; we must support him. Dozens, possibly hundreds of members of the left clamoured for readmission to the party so they could participate in the collectivisations. Typical was the case of Ivan Smirnov, former convinced Trotskyist, who capitulated in October 1929: 'I cannot remain inactive! I must build! The Center Committee is building for the future, barbarous and stupid though its methods may be. Our ideological differences are relatively unimportant compared to the building of major new industries'.[149]

6   From Five-Year Plan to Final Collapse

Soviet agriculture never fully recovered from Stalin's 1929–32 'war on the kulak', and thus became a permanent drag on the economy and society as a whole. The peasantry was permanently alienated from the regime. Quite apart from the huge loss of human life, the massacre of so many horses in a country with almost no metallic ploughs crippled the planting season for years into the future. Agricultural activity was henceforth organised in the wage-labour collective farm (sovkhoz) and the cooperative (kolkhoz), with additional small

---

149   Quoted in Lewin 1968b, p. 377. Smirnov was executed by Stalin in 1936. See Victor Serge's tribute: Serge 1936.

private plots, consisting of about one percent of all land under cultivation, and yet which over time produced a remarkable percentage of all food delivered to the cities.

The low productivity of the sovkhoz and kolkhoz sectors of Soviet agriculture played a large role in the ultimate collapse of the system in 1991. After the post-World War Two reconstruction period, the Soviet rate of growth was slowing from the late 1950s onward, from one five-year plan to the next. The so-called Liberman reforms of 1965 were an attempt to reverse the downward trend by a certain decentralisation of the planning process to the regions and to managers at the plant level; they failed against the resistance of the bureaucracy. The planners bent over their statistics to discover the obstacles in the system, only to discover that the 'plan' itself, and the bureaucracy promoting it, were the main domestic obstacles (quite aside from the fundamental alienation of the workers and peasants, and from the pressure of the capitalist world market and the Western embargo on key technologies). There was in reality no plan;[150] the plan was more like an ideological superstructure underneath which competition between firms – above all competition for skilled labour, scarce resources, and perhaps most importantly for spare parts – raged just as intensely as in any openly capitalist economy.[151] By the 1960s at the latest, corruption was endemic and also essential to the operation of the real economy. In some Eastern European (Comecon) countries such as Poland, if not in the Soviet Union itself, the U.S. dollar was indispensable for managers in need of key supplies. Over time, the underground economy was to a large extent *the* economy that worked at all. A further albatross was the very significant military sector, which drained the best technical workers and resources for this further sinkhole of unproductive consumption. (In addition to national defence, Soviet bloc arms sales were an important source of foreign exchange.)

The 1929–32 crippling of the agricultural sector, which still included almost forty percent of the work force (also involving huge hidden unemployment) when the system collapsed in 1991, was, however, a key factor in the overall crisis. In the West, the 1873–96 world agrarian depression, marking the entry into the world market of the major grain and meat exporters Canada, Australia, Argentina, the U.S. and Russia itself, combined with the transport revolution of steamships and trains, made possible the long-term reduction of the cost of

---

150   See Ticktin 1973 for an analysis which captures many aspects of the late Soviet system, and
         on the basis of which Ticktin predicted its collapse fifteen years before it took place.

151   Recalling, from another context, Bordiga's remark that 'The hell of capitalism is the firm,
         not the fact that the firm has a boss'.

food in the worker's wage from 50 percent c. 1850 to substantially lower levels. This new purchasing power of workers made possible access to consumer durables (radios, household appliances, and later cars) that was a fundamental part of the phase of real domination of capital, the reduction of labour power to its abstract interchangeable form. In the post-war World War Two boom in the West, the total wage bill of the productive work force (as opposed to the ever-growing population of middle-class unproductive consumers) declined as a percentage of the total social product while the material content of the average working-class wage rose.

Yet after World War One, it was precisely the impact of this nineteenth-century worldwide remaking of working-class consumption by the agrarian and transport revolutions that was sorely lacking in Soviet Russia. Hence the ever-increasing post-World War Two demand for consumer goods ran up a-gainst the barrier of generalised low productivity and hence higher prices for food. The only alternative was to import consumer goods from the West, at the cost of ever-increasing foreign indebtedness, which was $51 billion at the time of the Soviet collapse in 1991.

7   Conclusion

> The multiplication of human powers is its own goal.
> MARX, *Pre-Capitalist Economic Formations*

∴

The peasant question, almost 25 years later, is still with us on a world scale. Space does not permit an overview of its many contemporary forms, from the rural insurgencies in India to the Chinese regime's inability to meaningfully absorb its several hundred million remaining peasants, by way of Africa, Latin America, Southeast Asia and the Middle East. Today even more than one hundred years ago, the combined agricultural capacity of the U.S., Canada, western Europe, Australia and Argentina, in a global order producing for use, could feed the entire world several times over. That potential, blocked as it is by capitalist social relations, hangs over the agrarian subsistence producers of much of the rest of the world like a sword of Damocles; decades of world trade negotiations (such as most recently the so-called Doha round) have shattered upon it. U.S. and Canadian agricultural exports, after the conclusion of NAFTA[152] in 1993, swamped what remained of Mexico's peasant economy. Today's 'Fortress Europe' (the European Union), like 'El Norte' (the U.S.), are magnets attracting millions of people, including millions of peasants, from the devastated rural economies of Latin America, Africa and the Middle East, risking their lives to cross the Mediterranean or the Sonoran desert in hopes of joining the ranks of the sub-proletariat in the so-called developed world, providing the 'reserve army of the unemployed' for capital and conveniently, in the bargain, the perfect scapegoat for whipping up nationalist/racist populism in the indigenous working class.

In this reality, emerging from the rubble of the ex-Soviet bloc as the former apparent alternative to capitalism, Marx's decade-long fascination with the Russian peasant commune returns with all its urgency as the international left increasingly reconnects with the full dimensions of Marx's project, first suppressed by Engels, and lost for more than a century in the Second, Third and Fourth Internationals' confusion of the developmental tasks of the bourgeois revolution and those of the proletarian revolution. That latter revolution does not 'build socialism' but rather 'midwifes' a higher form of social organisation already present and implicit as the 'determinate negation' of the moribund old order, the 'real movement unfolding before our eyes', as the *Manifesto* put it.[153]

For four decades, since the 1970s, world capitalism, in fits and starts, has struggled against the growing evidence of its superannuation, both for truly developing global humanity and increasingly for avoiding environmental apocalypse. China and India may have, in those decades, given rise to some tens of millions (out of, let us recall, a combined 2.6 billion people) of a newly-affluent middle class striving for a 'Western life style' of consumption centred on the automobile. Nonetheless, the most elementary extrapolation of the resources and environmental destruction (pollution, atmospheric degradation, shortened life expectancy) involved in such a 'life style' to the world's 7.5 billion people (9 billion by 2050) shows its future existence as a grand 'fallacy of linear composition'. And this recognition takes us to the 'future past' of Marx's vision of the *re*appropriation of the world's productive forces, correcting, obviously on a far higher level, the fundamental 'schism' of the expropriation which began more than 500 years ago; to the overcoming of the separation of city and

---

152   The North American Free Trade Agreement, which in reality was mainly an agreement to dismantle Mexico's remaining barriers to untrammelled imports and investment.

153   See *Insurgent Notes* No. 1, 'The Historical Moment Which Produced Us' and the programme elaborated therein for a fuller view of the 'first hundred days' of implementing a communist programme today (Insurgent Notes 2010).

countryside and hence to the more even distribution of the world's population over the earth's surface (in the U.S., for example, 99 percent of the population currently lives on 1 percent of the land).

The coming revolution will not have as its goal the elaboration of a five-year plan in order to out-produce capitalism in 'steel, cement and electricity', to return to our initial quote from Trotsky (though it may do that, incidentally, as part of its realisation of more fundamental tasks). It will rather, for starters, dismantle worldwide the several hundred million jobs, from Wall Street's 'quants' to tolltakers, existing solely to administer capitalism, freeing that labour power for socially useful activity and combining it with the several billion people marginalised by capitalism altogether, to radically shorten the working day for all. With the dismantling of the car-steel-oil-rubber complex still at the centre of both capitalist production and consumption (not to mention capitalism's 'imaginary') the social labour time lost in commutes and traffic jams alone, in North America, Europe and East Asia, largely a product of the post-World War Two urban, suburban and exurban development schemes framed by real estate priorities, will be regained by society; similarly with the huge expenditure of fossil fuels made necessary by the conscious suppression of mass transit by the auto and oil industries, as a cursory tour of most American cities will reveal. Unravelling the full social, material and energy costs of urban, suburban and exurban space as it currently exists will already be a giant step toward the full de-commodification of human life. Or as Marx put it 150 years ago:

> ... When the narrow bourgeois form has been peeled away, what is wealth, if not the universality of needs, capacities, enjoyments, productive powers, etc. of individuals, produced in universal exchange? What, if not the full development of human control over the forces of nature – those of his own nature as well as those of so-called 'nature'? What, if not the absolute elaboration of his creative dispositions, without any preconditions other than antecedent historical evolution which makes the totality of this evolution – i.e. the evolution of all human powers as such, unmeasured by any previously established yardstick, an end in itself? What is this, if not a situation where man does not produce himself in any determined form, but produces his totality? Where he does not seek to remain something formed by the past, but is in the absolute movement of becoming?
>
> *Pre-Capitalist Economic Formations*

'Socialism in One Country' before Stalin, and the Origins of Reactionary 'Anti-Imperialism': The Case of Turkey, 1917–25

> All information on the situation in Khiva, in Persia, in Bukhara and in Afghanistan confirm the fact that a Soviet revolution in these countries is going to cause us major difficulties at the present time ... Until the situation in the West is stabilized and until our industries and transport systems have improved, a Soviet expansion in the east could prove to be no less dangerous than a war in the West ... a potential Soviet revolution in the east is today to our advantage principally as an important element in diplomatic relations with England. From this I conclude that: 1) in the east we should devote ourselves to political and educational work ... and at the same time advise all possible caution in actions calculated to require our military support, or which might require it; 2) we have to continue by all possible channels at our disposal to arrive at an understanding with England about the east.
>
> LEON TROTSKY, Secret memo to Lenin, ZINOVIEV ET AL., June 1920[1]

∴

Prefatory Note

The following article had its origin in a 'Letter to the Editor', c. 2001, to a Trotskyist group, inquiring about a commercial treaty signed by the Soviet Union with Kemalist Turkey in March 1921, a mere two months after 15 leading Turkish Communists were murdered just off the Turkish coast. Those who ordered and those who committed these murders were never identified and are the basis for numerous theories, but everything points to some person or persons in the Kemalist movement, up to the highest levels. What interested me was of course not a murder mystery but the fact that the Soviet Union entered into

---

1 Trotsky 1964–71, vol. 2, p. 209.

an alliance with a government that was patently killing and jailing pro-Soviet communist militants, and said and did little or nothing about it. That dynamic was of course familiar to anyone acquainted with post-1945 world history, as in the case of Nasser's Egypt or other 'progressive' Third World regimes, but here was the same pattern only four years after the Russian Revolution, i.e., in a period when almost everyone, myself included, thought that the dominance of Soviet national interests over 'proletarian internationalism' really emerged into full view only with the triumph of Stalin and 'socialism in one country' in 1924.

Some years later I began an email correspondence with a Turkish comrade, during which I inquired about the 1921 episode and to what extent it still figured in the historical self-awareness of the Turkish left. In due course I received a remarkable pamphlet answering my initial question, and more. For it emerged that the January 1921 murders and March 1921 treaty were merely one, very dramatic episode in a much longer and more complex process of ebbs and flows of the Soviet-Turkish relationship, and the intimately linked fate of Turkish communists during those shifts.

Not long after I first read this pamphlet, the group to which my Turkish correspondent belonged joined the International Communist Current. Not my crowd, of course, but during a two-week stay in Turkey in fall 2009 these same individuals received me with the fullest comradely hospitality and for many hours, and on several occasions, we discussed our agreements and differences.

On my last day in Istanbul, the chance discovery of a small bookstore on an obscure side street led me to the second source without which this article could not have been written: Paul Dumont's *Du socialisme ottoman a l'internationalisme anatolien* (1997), 500 pages of detailed history of Turkish communism of a quality (generally, political judgements aside) I would like to have for the major Western countries with which I am more familiar. To pre-empt the embarrassment of having quoted this book perhaps 70 times in the 140-odd footnotes, I can only say that the contents of a book, in French, from an Istanbul publisher, with such material about a communist movement in a country most people (myself included) know little or nothing about, deserve to be better known.

I begin with this personal account to ask the reader's forbearance for the perhaps excessive detail with which I have tried to nail down this political history. I felt at times like the Borges character who discovers the 'G–H' volume of the encyclopedia of a disappeared civilisation in a used bookstore and spends the rest of his life trying to find the other volumes. I knew next to nothing about Turkish history before this encounter and I still know very little. But I went to the lengths I did because if the tale these Turkish comrades have to tell is true, it represents a theoretical bombshell for the international revolutionary movement, such as it is, today.

In addition to the forty-odd pages of text, there are fourteen pages of footnotes and a thirteen-page 'Core Chronology'. I composed the latter, initially for my own benefit, to cut through the blur of unfamiliar names and places and events compressed into a relatively short time span; I append it for the reader who may experience the same confusion reading the text that I did in writing it.

> LG – New York City
> November 2009

Introduction

The 'anti-imperialist' ideology of the 1960s and early 1970s died a hard death by the late 1970s. Western leftist cheerleaders for 'Ho- Ho- Ho Chi Minh' in London, Paris, Berlin and New York fell silent as Vietnam invaded Cambodia, and China invaded Vietnam, and the Soviet Union threatened China. China allied with the U.S. against the Soviets in the new Cold War, and the other 'national liberation movements' that had taken power in Algeria, and later in Ethiopia, Angola, Mozambique, and Guinea-Bissau ... disappointed.

Today, a vague mood of 'anti-imperialism' is back, led by Venezuela's Chavez and his Latin American allies (Cuba, Nicaragua, Ecuador, Bolivia), more or less (with the exception of Stalinist Cuba) classical bourgeois-nationalist regimes. But Chavez in turn is allied, at least verbally and often practically, with the Iran of the ayatollahs, and Hezbollah, and Hamas, as well as newly-emergent China, which no one any longer dares call 'socialist'. The British SWP allies with Islamic fundamentalists in local elections in the UK, and participates in mass demonstations (during the Israeli invasion of Lebanon, summer 2007) chanting 'We are all Hezbollah'. Somehow Hezbollah, whose statutes affirm the truth of the Protocols of the Elders of Zion, is now part of the 'left'; when will it be 'We are all Taliban'? Why not, indeed?

Such a climate compels us to turn back to the history of such a profoundly reactionary ideology, deeply anti-working class both in the 'advanced' and 'underdeveloped' countries, by which any force, no matter how retrograde, that turns a gun against a Western power becomes 'progressive' and worthy of 'critical' or 'military' support, or for the less subtle, simply 'support'.[2]

---

2   Thereby reminding us of Kenneth Rexroth's quip (in Rexroth 1966) that Leninism had a genius

1   1921: The Soviet Nation-State Trumps Proletarian Internationalism

We find these anti-working-class origins, not surprisingly, in the defeat of the
world insurrectionary wave of 1917–21, a wave moving from Germany and Russia to ultimately affect dozens of countries. And we can date that defeat from
March 1921, highlighted (in the Soviet Union) by the crushing of the Kronstadt rebellion, the Anglo-Soviet trade agreement, the implementation of the
'New Economic Policy' (NEP) and, abroad, the defeat of the German 'March
Action', almost a year after most leading Bolsheviks had lost any hope, for
the near future, of proletarian revolution in the West, on which their initial
international strategy had been based. Less known, in the same conjuncture,
are the February-March 1921 friendship and commercial treaties signed by the
Soviet Union with newly formed authoritarian development regimes in Turkey,
Persia and Afghanistan, whereby those regimes' repression, imprisonment or
massacre of their respective communist or left oppositions were brushed over
for Soviet national interests in the post-World War One international order of
nation-states.[3] The aspirations and programmes of the Persian regime of Reza
Khan[4] (founder of the Pahlevi regime) and the Afghan regime of Emir Amanullah (1919–29)[5] were modelled on the new nationalist government of Turkey's
Kemal Pasha[6] (Attatürk), still, in 1921, fighting the first 'war of national liberation' against a Greece backed by British imperialism. Thus we begin with
the little-known (in the West) story of this arguably first 'development regime',
in which 'anti-imperialist' ideology first covered over the crushing of an anti-
CAPITALIST worker and peasant movement, and of a left-wing of a newly-

---

for coining terms such as 'critical support', 'democratic centralism', or 'revolutionary trade
unionism' whereby the noun always won out over the adjective.

3   These agreements, according to E.H. Carr, were 'a further stage in the process by which relations between Moscow and the outside world were placed predominantly on a governmental
basis'. See Carr 1952, p. 290.

4   On the sacrifice of the Soviet Socialist Republic of Gilan to Soviet-Persian relations, see
Chaquèri 1995.

5   On Attatürk's influence on an authoritarian modernising regime in Afghanistan, see Poullada
1973. Jemal Pasha, a Young Turk who had taken refuge in Germany after 1918, became an
adviser to King Amanullah (Carr 1952, p. 290).

6   Note to the unadvised reader (like myself prior to undertaking this study): the title 'Pasha'
in Turkish merely means 'commander', following the family name. Thus Mustafa Kemal
becomes Kemal Pasha. Later the term 'Attatürk', 'Father of the Turks', was coined; thus in
the following the names Mustafa Kemal, Kemal Pasha and Attatürk all designate the same
individual.

formed Communist Party committed to actual proletarian internationalism in wartime, rejecting the Third International's demand for military support of Attatürk.[7]

2   From Empire to Nation-State

The emergence of modern Turkey out of the collapse of the centuries-old Otto-man Empire, in the decade prior to 1921, is a geopolitical story with antecedents and aftershocks reaching from Sinkiang province[8] in northwest China in the east to Algeria in the west, by way of the Balkans in the north to Yemen in the south.[9] From their zenith in the sixteenth century to their senescence in the early twentieth, the Ottomans had loomed large in the European balance of power, finally disappearing in a few years at the end of World War One along with the three other empires (Hohenzollerns, Habsburgs and Romanovs) from which dozens of new nations and new, murderous nationalisms emerged, many of them still with us. This was for a century the arena of the 'great game' between Britain and Russia, now taken over by the contemporary 'great game' of U.S. foreign policy along the borders of Russia and China. Turkey and the extended 'Turkic region' is a 'techtonic plate' on which much of the modern history of Eurasia revolves.

It is too quickly forgotten, or sometimes not grasped at all, that nationalist consciousness is a distinctly modern phenomenon, a bit more than 200 years old, above all outside of the North Atlantic world (Britain, France, Holland, the U.S.) in which it first arose as part of the bourgeois revolution. Pre-modern king-doms and empires were dynastic, with dynastic marriages moving aristocrats indifferently around the courts of Europe. Bourgeois nationalism, above all with the French Revolution, asserted the 'nation' against this transcontinental dynastic elite in the supersession of the old, often supra-territorial structures.

While the Ottoman Empire was clearly dominated by descendants of the ethnic Turkic groups which erupted out of Central Asia in the eleventh century and thereafter to ultimately topple the Christian Byzantine empire, 'Turkish'

---

7   See the pamphlet of the International Communist Current, 'Left Wing of the Turkish Com-munist Party, 1920–1927' for the details of this little-known and highly significant story.

8   At the time of the 1911 revolution in China, Herder-inspired Turkic nationalism theorised by the Crimean Tatar Ismael Bey Gasprinski (see below) reached northwest China through Turkic traders and merchants. See Millward 2007, pp. 171–4.

9   For an overview of the Turkic linguistic and cultural area, see Çağatay et al. 2006.

national consciousness as such barely existed prior to the 1870s.[10] Whatever else one might say about it, the Ottoman Empire was truly multi-ethnic, a world in which Jews, Armenians, Hungarians, Arabs, Slavs, Greeks, Albanians, Kurds, Circassians and smaller groups co-existed, as second-class citizens, with the dominant Turks but with some significant local autonomy once they paid their taxes and fulfilled other obligations to the state. Nowhere was this multi-ethnicity more apparent and successful than in the city of Salonica[11] (annexed from the Ottomans by Greece in 1912), where such groups (with a Jewish working-class majority that was largely socialist by 1910), and above all the Europe-oriented Armenians and Jews, introduced a fair amount of modern economic practices and ideologies into the wider empire. (Salonica was perhaps not accidentally the city of Kemal Pasha, founder of the modern Turkish nation state.)

Karl Marx and Friedrich Engels followed the geopolitics of southeastern Europe, and hence of necessity the Ottomans, from the beginning of their collaboration in the 1840s. For more than thirty years, they were seized with a profound Russophobia, based on the belief that Tsarist Russia (which already achieved continental projection at the end of the Napoleonic Wars in 1815) would crush any democratic, not to mention socialist revolution in Europe, and that the ideology of pan-Slavism (also advocated by their anarchist rival Bakunin) would carry most Slavs (with the important exception of the Poles) in the Russian undertow. At times they argued that such a revolution would necessarily consolidate itself through a war on Tsarist Russia. The Holy Alliance of the Russian, Prussian and Austrian monarchs underwrote the continental reactionary 'balance of power' from 1815 to 1848, and virtually every European government had its 'Russian faction'[12] intent on appeasing the Tsar. Russian armies in fact crushed the Polish uprisings of 1831, 1846 and 1863, and the revolution of 1848 in Austria-Hungary.

This understandable (within limits) preoccupation with Russian reaction led Marx and Engels to look to the declining Ottoman Empire as a bulwark

---

10   Some early Turkish romantics such as Ahmed Midhad (1844–1912) were already attempting to create a more vernacular Turkish literary language in the 1860s. See Çağatay et al. 2006, p. 239.

11   Mazower 2004. An excellent historical view of the Salonica working class before World War Two is in Stinas 1990. Excerpts in English are available at: http://www.geocities.com/ antagonism1/stinas/index.html.

12   Marx even wrote a series of articles arguing that the British prime minister Palmerston was virtually a paid Russian agent. See his *Geschichte der Geheimdiplomatie des 18 Jarhunderts*, in Marx 1978.

against Russian expansion, and to often look askance on many anti-Ottoman rebellions and revolutions in the empire's Balkan possessions after 1848, as they weakened that bulwark. It further led them to something bordering on Slavo-phobia tinged with German nationalism where most Slavs (again, excepting the Poles) were concerned, disparaging any revolutionary potential of these 'peoples without history'[13] who would do well to integrate into the German area of influence and civilisation. Such a preoccupation only ended in the 1870s when the emergence of the Russian Narodniks, the early translation of Marx's *Capital* into Russian[14] and its impact in the Russian intelligentsia forced Marx to revise his views about the Slavic world, above all after his discovery of the Russian peasant commune.[15] (Nevertheless the dubious writings of Marx and Engels on the Slavic world provided a lineage in the European socialist move-ment for, e.g., German social patriotism against the Tsarist menace in World War One.)

For almost 200 years before its final dissolution in 1922, the huge Ottoman Empire, the 'sick man of Europe', was a major focus of Western imperialist penetration of the Balkans, the Near East and North Africa. Britain, France, Habsburg Austria, Tsarist Russia and later Bismarckian Germany jostled for places in the line – the 'feast of vultures' – to benefit from Ottoman decline. Although that decline dates from the late sixteenth century, Napoleon's 1798 expedition to Egypt was the signal event in awakening the Ottoman (and more generally Moslem)[16] world to the new dangers posed by European world hegemony. After the final defeat of Napoleon in 1815, Balkan crises in particular were the focus of this struggle for imperial advantage. Some of the highlights were:

Serbian National Uprisings (1804, 1815)
The Greek War of Independence (1821–30);
Serbian Autonomy (1839);
The Crimean War, pitting Britain, France and the Ottomans against
    Russia (1853–56);

---

13   See Rozolski and Himka 1986.

14   The Russian translation of vol. 1 in 1874 was the first translation of the book anywhere.

15   See Shanin 1983. Also Rubel 1972.

16   The Ottoman world was not merely an empire but also, for 500 years, the seat of the caliphate, 'direct successors of the prophet Mohammed', until Attatürk's abolition of the caliphate in 1924. For those centuries Ottoman power shaped Islam as had the Arab caliphates before it, and concealed the shift of power to the West from Moslems every-where; hence the shock of Napoleon's military superiority.

Great Eastern Crisis (Bosnian, Bulgarian Uprisings), Serbo-Turkish War (1875–78);

The Russo-Turkish War of 1877–8; Bosnia's annexation by Austria-Hungary;

The Berlin Conference of 1878, called by Bismarck to adjudicate the ongoing Balkan crisis (and rob Russia of its most recent territorial gains);[17]

The Bulgarian crisis of the early 1880s, Serbo-Bulgarian War (1885);

The Armenian massacres of 1896 and 1908, prefiguring the Armenian genocide of 1915;

The Turk-Greek War of 1897;

The 1911–12 war following Italy's annexation of Libya;

The two generalised Balkan Wars of 1912–13

Such were, in succession, some of the eruptions of this lingering fatal illness. This process culminated in the assassination of the Austrian archduke in Bosnia in June 1914, setting off World War One. (In the Balkans, World War One appeared as little more than a generalised extension of the two earlier wars.)[18] These Balkan revolts, state creation and Ottoman repression set off domestic political crises in England and France throughout the nineteenth century.[19] The geopolitical convergence of Islam, Catholicism and Eastern Orthodoxy in this relatively small corner of southeastern Europe created an unusually acute international dimension to this vortex of peoples and states. The supra-territorial character of Ottoman social organisation scattered different ethnicities in crazy-quilt fashion. Like the 'prison house of nations' (as Lenin called Tsarist Russia), the 1918 collapse of the Ottoman Empire, the Austro-Hungarian empire and the Hohenzollern dynasty gave way to often unstable small new nations, underscoring the precarious and often artificial character of 'national identity' from Central Europe, via the Middle East, to the eastern reaches of Russia and northwest China.

The 'Eastern question' (as this long, slow Ottoman decline and Western rivalry over the spoils was called) also overlapped with the Anglo-Russian

---

17   It was in December 1876, prior to the conference, brokered by Bismarck, that he declared to parliament that the Balkans were 'not worth the bones of a single Pomeranian grenadier'. In the revised (1878) revision of the Treaty of San Stefano, the only remaining Ottoman holdings in the Balkans were Macedonia and Albania. Glenny 2000, p. 156, called the Macedonian question 'the unyielding philosopher's stone of Balkan nationalism'.

18   Ibid.

19   See R.W. Seton-Watson 1972.

'Great Game' along the borders of Russia, all the way to Kamchatka. British foreign policy in Asia was built around a deep fear of a Russian invasion of its prize colony India through Afghanistan, making the latter country, along with Persia, the object of intense Anglo-Russian rivalry right through the end of World War Two, after which the u.s. took over the British role. Military clashes between tiny British and Russian forces in remote, little-known border areas near the Himalayas on several occasions became the stuff of international crises and war scares.[20] Protection of the Suez Canal against any hostile naval power in the eastern Mediterranean, before the additional emergent centrality of oil, was ultimately based on the same preoccupation,[21] as was (in part) British backing of anti-Soviet forces in Central Asia after the Russian Revolution. While Russian expansion to the west was (relatively) contained in Europe, Tsarist eastward expansion in Central Asia (the conquests of Bukhara and other old khanates) in the eighteenth and nineteenth was viewed by Britain with the same unease. Hence were the internal politics of many small nations or would-be nations, of little significance in themselves, conjugated with the largest Eurasian geopolitical issues.

3   From Folklore Studies to the Authoritarian Development State

The emergence of nationalist particularisms out of the decay of Ottoman rule occurred over a matter of decades. Ethnic groups with little self-awareness as such, sometimes with little or no corresponding territorial concentration, and which had co-habited (happily or not) with other such groups, were transformed by this process into rival nationalities, vying to create ethnically-based and territorial nations. And, unfortunately, they came to this awareness and this nationalist agenda 'too late' in the world history of capitalism, too late, that is, to constitute viable nations as the western European originators had done.[22]

---

20   See the books of Peter Hopkirk, in particular Hopkirk 1992. Also Meyer and Brysac 1999.
21   See Cooper Busch 1971.
22   Consider for example that France, one of the classic nation states effectively unified by the seventeenth century, still in the late seventeenth century had to struggle to impose French as a national language in many regions of the country, and to impose French national identity on diverse provincial groups (see Weber 1976). Germany and Italy, which both completed their national unification in 1870, featured regional dialects well into the twentieth century, many of them still the first language of daily life today; Spain, also a creation of the 'first wave' of national unification, in the late 1970s had to recognise wide

Modern nationalism came to the Turkic world[23] through Russia, and the Turkic populations scattered along the southern borders of Russia. Germany by the early nineteenth century had elaborated the first 'romantic populist' nationalism in the work, above all, of Herder, which during the Napoleonic Wars was turned against the universal pretensions of French nationalism.[24] This nationalism, in contrast to France's Enlightenment version and its civilising mission, emphasised the uniqueness of language, folklore, and myth against abstract universalism. Herder was still rooted in eighteenth-century cosmopolitanism and located German romantic populism within a European framework, but those who followed him were not so careful, from Fichte's *Speeches to the German Nation* (1813) onward. This German romantic populism spawned replicas in Scandinavia and the Slavic world, where it issued in Pan-Slavism. It was against the pretensions of Russian Slavophilism that, beginning in the 1870s, a pan-Turkic or pan-Turanian ideology first appeared[25] in the Turkic populations of the southern perimeter of the Tsarist empire, hearkening back to a mythical Ur-Turkic nation in Central Asia ('Turan') and holding out the chimera of a revived pan-Turkic nation to succeed the dying Ottoman Empire. While this 'pan-Turanism', even, in some fertile imaginations, attempted a reconstruction of the shamanic cosmology[26] of the Turkic peoples prior to their conversion to Islam, and influenced mainly the small educated middle classes, it nonetheless spawned larger real world developments. Kemal Pasha (Attatürk, 'Father of the Turks') and the new statist elite pragmatically rejected pan-Ottomanism and pan-Turanism,[27] but strongly embraced the new nationalist ideology of the 'National Pact' for the reduced Turkish state after 1923 after

---

regional political and linguistic autonomy for diverse groups. Given these realities, Marx and Engels's pre-1870s blindness to the 'peoples with without history', where most Slavs and particularly south Slavs is concerned, is almost comprehensible. They certainly never had to think about nation-state formation of the peoples of Chechnya or the Khanata of Bukhara.

23   Çağatay et al. 2006. The Young Turks, who gathered in exile in Paris, were preceded by the Young Ottomans, with a somewhat similar agenda, based on their reading of Montesquieu, Rousseau, Smith and Ricardo. See Lewis 2002, p. 173.

24   On the passage of German romantic populism to the colonial and later Third World, see Tibi 1980 for a classic case.

25   'Pan-Slavism was the father of Pan-Turanism'. See Kohn 1960, p. 259.

26   One such work in this debate was Köprülü 1929.

27   In the Turko-Soviet friendship and commercial treaty of March 1921, the Kemalist government agreed to crack down on pan-Turanian agitation aimed at Russia, and the Soviet government agreed not to promote anti-Kemalist agitation in Turkey.

pan-Ottomanism and pan-Turanism proved to be chimeras.[28] Enver Pasha, one of the main figures of the Young Turk attempt (1908–18) to reform the dying Ottoman state and later a defeated rival of Attatürk, conferred with Radek and Lenin after World War One, urging them to back his dream of a great Turkic nation and finally turning against the Soviet state in an attempt to found it (see below).[29]

Modest Ottoman reform had focused on the education system, from an awareness, after decades of unique preoccupation with the military, that generalised knowledge was a key to a viable economy and hence armed forces.[30] The University of Istanbul, the first university in Turkey, opened in 1900. As early as 1885, foreign capital had financed a railway boom. The telegraph centralised power as nothing before and made possible a centralising shakeup of both the civil service and the military. The real social base of Ottoman reform was in fact the educated civil service. After 1908, the Young Turks intensified this programme, building drains, reorganising the police and fire brigades, and building public transportation and utilities. They opened education to women. Inspired to some extent by pan-Turkic and pan-Turanian ideas, some Young Turks, after the February Revolution in Russia in 1917, had high hopes of a 'great new destiny' in the east.[31] Pan-Turanism had had its first exponent in Ismael Gasprinski (1841–1914), a Crimean Turk, who in 1878 founded the first newspaper in Turkish, *Tergüman*. (The Crimea was the most capitalistically-developed Turkic zone in Tsarist Russia, with a developed Crimean Tatar middle class, and Kazan was the undisputed cultural capital of Turkic Russia.)[32] Another

---

28   Pan-Islamism also haunted the Western governments in the late 19th century, fearing a general Muslim revolt against the West. After the Bolshevik Revolution, these fears were augmented by the spectre of a Bolshevik-Muslim alliance. See Paul Dumont 1997, p. 225.

29   See Heyd 1950; Hostler 1957; and virtually all the writings of Alexandre Bennigsen, especially Bennigsen 1986. On Enver Pasha's misadventures after leaving Turkey in 1918, see Hopkirk 1985, Ch. 11.

30   A French writer, Edmond Demolins, had published in 1897 a book entitled *A quoi tient la superiorite des Anglo-Saxons?* (*What Is the Basis of Anglo-Saxon Superiority?*). The book, emphasising the education of individualism as the key, had a significant impact in both the Turkish and Arab world (Lewis 2002, pp. 303–4).

31   Ibid. p. 238.

32   This primacy of the Tatars, for the Turkic populations of Russia, was also noted by Bennigsen 1986, pp. 16 ff. By 1900, Tatars even dominated the fur trade in New York City, and had a 20 percent literacy rate, higher than the rate in European Russia at the end of the nineteenth century. But after 1878, 'from the Bosporus to the borders of China, Moslems ... realized that without a profound modification of society, the whole of the Moslem world was condemned' (p. 26). Until 1905, according to Bennigsen (p. 33), this

Tatar intellectual, Sihabäddin Märcani (1818–89) had also articulated the idea of a 'Tatar nation', possibly the first ideology for a modern territorial nation in the Turkic world (in contrast to the supra-territorial institutions of the Ottomans). As early as the 1850s, Märcani had had contact in Kazan with Russian and European scholars. His book 'was a well-formulated ideology for a Kazan Tatar territorial nation',[33] and the 'Young Tatar' movement in the 1890s competed with Gasprinski in a 'Turk or Tatar?' debate, as many Tatars were taken with Herder's idea of a common language as the basis for a nation. Gasprinski's newspaper, on the other hand, had been a response to the Ottoman defeat in the 1877–8 war with Russia, which had ruined forever what was left of the myth of Ottoman invincibility. Gasprinski's brother-in-law in 1911 founded a journal *Türk Yurdu* [*The Turkish Homeland*] in Istanbul. Gasprinski's Tercüman argued for the emancipation of women and for technical education along Western lines, reporting on such topics as technological advance in the United States, the modernisation of Japan, Balkan wars and women's rights in the West. His conservatism made him argue against any confrontation with Tsarist Russia, and only a few Turkic intellectuals were moved by membership in a larger 'Turkic nation'.[34]

Nevertheless, the most important founding theoretician of Turkish nationalism was Ziya Gökalp (1875–1924) who used Herderian and broadly German

---

Tatar ferment remained pro-Tsàr, but this was shaken by the Japanese military victory over Russia. By 1906, an Islamic left had appeared. Sufi brotherhoods also became part of this ferment through the colonial world, reviving the idea of holy war. Russian Muslims were the first to discuss Marxism, before the Ottoman Turks, the Iranians or the Arabs (p. 40). A group in the oil capital Baku (Azerbaijan) affiliated with the Russian Social Democrats (RSDLP), the first and only time the Bolsheviks authorised a group that was both national and confessional. The Pan-Turkic nationalists in Russia saw Marxism above all as a theory of organisation. Yusuf Alecura (1876–1933) was another Tatar nationalist figure who was educated in Europe and who started a Tatar newspaper published from 1906 to 1917. After the rise of Attatürk, Alecura became more prominent than ever and dominated the first Congress of the Turkish Historical Society in 1932. Çağatay et al., p. 238.

Another key Tatar nationalist intellectual was Abdureshid Meddi, a theoretician of the Young Tatars. In his speeches, writes Brian Glyn Williams (Williams 2001, pp. 319–20), 'we hear for the first time, language that defines the Crimea not as a province of the Russian Empire, a segment of the Dar al-Islam or adjunct of a larger Turkic homeland, but as the patrimony of the Crimean Tatar nation. In a speech given in 1910 ... Meddi uses allegories of blood mixed with soil that evokes the language of classic German nationalism'.

33   Çağatay et al., p. 235.
34   Williams 2001. p. 312.

romantic cultural ideas to create a Pan-Turkic equivalent[35] of Pan-Slavism. Gökalp, like many who followed him, also wanted to purge the Turkish language of its abundant Persian and Arabic vocabulary. Though not himself a politician, he elaborated much of what became the programme of the Young Turks in power.

French influences had long dominated the emergence of Turkish modernism. As the creaking Ottoman Empire attempted to modernise its military forces during the nineteenth century, French officers and French military doctrines were imported wholesale. The growing educated elite spoke French, and was educated in French. German influences as such only began to have an impact in the last decades before World War One, again through military advisers and joint projects such as the Berlin-Bagdad railway. Gökalp himself knew only French, but absorbed German ideas through the *Année Sociologique*, the journal of the French sociologist Emile Durkheim (himself a neo-Kantian after years of study in Germany) which discussed the work of Herder, Fichte, Hegel, Nietzsche, Toennies and Treitschke.[36] (Another key figure for emerging Turkish nationalism was Mazzini, for his role in Italian national unification 1860–70).[37] Gökalp looked to Durkheim's 'solidarism' as a 'third way' beyond capitalism and socialism. From Comte's positivist sociology, Gökalp learned that 'the inborn mysticism of St. Simon's school had definitely overthrown the democratic ideal in favor of a new autocracy of scientific leadership',[38] a precursor to the authoritarian statism of the Attatürk period and the Kadro ideo-

---

35   According to Heyd, the Turkish national renaissance of the second half of the nineteenth
      century 'sprang from the researches of European Turkologists who showed the Turks
      that they belonged to a great nation with a cultural tradition that went back centuries
      before Islam' (Heyd 1950, p. 105). The French writers Lamartine and Loti also praised
      Turkish culture. The mediator of German cultural nationalism was Hüsenzade Ali, from
      the Caucasus, who encountered both socialism and pan-Slavism at the University of St.
      Petersburg in the 1890s. After the Turk-Greek war of 1897, Ali went to Baku and attempted
      to unite Sunnis and Shiites in a closer union with Turkey. He later became, like Gökalp, a
      member of the CUP, which itself had copied the model of the Russian secret societies.

36   Heyd 1950, p. 165.

37   Mazzini was also a figure of import in the Balkans, where the Italian unification process
      had been followed closely by various nationalists, and where Serbia fancied itself in the
      role of a 'Balkan Piedmont' in an eventual Balkan unification.

38   Heyd 1950, p. 168. For Heyd, there is little doubt 'that Gökalp's conception of society, the
      elite and the Leader prepared the way for Attatürk' (p. 140). Gökalp was also an admirer of
      the German mercantilst Friedrich List. Under Gökalp's influence, People's Houses were
      established in every Turkish town for the study of local folklore. 'The appreciation of
      Treitschke by Durkheim seems in every way applicable to Gökalp' (p. 163).

logy of ex-Communists who theorised the role of a scientific elite in the early
1930s.[39] Durkheim also provided Gökalp with a theoretical justification for the
pre-eminence of society over the individual.

Gökalp arrived in Istanbul in 1896 and was immediately received into the
Young Turks' Committee of Union and Progress (CUP) which would domin-
ate politics in the last phase of the Ottoman Empire (1908–18) and whose
very name echoed its positivist technocratic (and St-Simonian) programme,[40]
like that of the Brazilian technocrats of the same period. After World War
One, Gökalp was accused of having helped foment the anti-Armenian agitation which had led to the 1915 genocide, a genocide whose existence he
moreover denied. Beginning in 1923, after the founding of the Turkish Republic, he became a propagandist for the Kemalist regime, substituting the 'nation'
for the primacy of 'society' he had taken from Durkheim, and used the German
sociological counterposition (from Tönnies) of 'culture' and 'civilisation' in his
vaunting of Turkish culture. He identified Bolshevism as the 'Red Danger'. As a
Kemalist ideologue, Gökalp founded museums of Turkish folkore, ethnography,
archaeology and libraries, as well as a central institute of statistics. After his
death, other linguistic purists did eliminate foreign elements of grammar and
syntax from Turkish to the point that 'a Turkish youth today has to use a dic-
tionary to understand fully the work of Gökalp',[41] written only decades earlier.
(In Soviet Russia, on the other hand, the state encouraged Turkic intellectuals

---

39   In Turkey as in a number of other developing countries in the interwar period (e.g. Brazil,
      Argentina) ex-Communists played an important role in building the development state.
      In Turkey this was best exemplified by the Kadro (from cadre) group of the early 1930s.
      Vedat Nedim Tör, a former secretary general of the party, became a theoretician movement
      in the early 1930s. Other key figures had originally been part of the Aydinlik (Clarity)
      group c. 1919, directly modelled on Henri Barbusse's – another future Stalinophile – French
      journal *Clarte*. As one historian of the Turkish CP put it: 'Their central idea remained that
      the elite in Turkey must awaken to its historic role as the revolutionary force in society
      and "overcome the inertia of the masses"'. See Harris, 1967, p. 146, and his later book *The
      Communists and the Kadro Movement* (Harris 2002), showing that all the key figures of that
      movement came from the Aydinlik group.

40   'Later cataclysms of the 20th century have obscured the contemporary impact of the
      Young Turk revolution. Yet its importance is comparable with the Russian Revolution of
      1917 and the collapse of communism in the Soviet Union and Eastern Europe in 1989. The
      speed with which the sultan's power crumbled astonished the great powers, and took the
      revolutionaries themselves unawares' (Glenny 2000, p. 216). These later cataclysms have
      also obscured the 1917–21 events in Turkey, Persia and Afghanistan as the source of 'anti-
      imperialist' alliances with the national bourgeoisie.

41   Ibid. p. 120.

among the Azeris, Crimean Turks, Turkomans, Kinghis, Uzbeks and Kipchuks to build a literary language from their spoken language as a way of weakening pan-Turanian appeals in books imported from Istanbul to Russian Islamic centres. For the Ottoman Turanists, World War One had been an opportunity to free the 'northern Turks' from Tsarism.)

The Young Turk period, extending to the end of World War One, wrought some changes in the Ottoman state and society, prefiguring the more thoroughgoing reforms of the Attatürk period after 1923. The rule of the CUP initiated a period of freedom of the press and political association. While Ziya Gökalp shied away from holding active political power, many of the CUP's reforms up to 1918 grew out of his proposals. Following a conservative counterattack by the religious establishment in 1909, the CUP pushed through constitutional reforms severely reducing the power of the sultan and the cabinet and increasing those of parliament. Bureaucracy was reduced, tax collection was rationalised and the armed forces were modernised. Public transportation in Istanbul was improved. But all in all the CUP reforms fell far short of their 1908 programme, or the necessities of a modern capitalist state. Starting in 1911, the disastrous war in Libya and the two Balkan wars overwhelmed domestic reform, and in 1913, at the conclusion of the Second Balkan War, the Ottoman Empire had lost 83 percent of its land and 69 percent of its population in Europe. War had nonetheless brought the CUP to 'almost absolute power within the councils of the state'.[42] It used this power to accelerate secularisation and the modernisation of the state apparatus. The tax system was drastically revised. In 1915–16, courts, schools and religious foundations were completely secularised. Under the pressures of war, women's rights were extended, as in the secularisation of the marriage contract, and expanded education for women.

The Ottoman Empire's entry into World War One on the side of the Central Powers, most strongly advocated by the mercurial figure of Enver Pasha, also brought to the fore the German influence on institutions where it had previously been overshadowed by the British and the French. General Liman von Sanders took over direct command of the First Army even before the war, with many German officers as advisers in the further modernisation and reorganisation of the armed forces. Naval reorganisation had occurred before 1914, through British involvement, because of a delicate balancing act among the powers. Until August 1914, Britain, France and Germany were all directly involved in the affairs of the Ottoman state, including the Ottoman Public

---

42   Shaw and Shaw 1976–7, vol. 2, p. 300.

Debt Commission and the Ottoman Bank, the latter two controlled by Britain and France. Enver Pasha and his allies in the CUP, however, in September 1914 pushed through the abolition of the onerous Capitulations,[43] taking over control of customs duties previously controlled by the Western powers. German General von Seeckt became chief of the Ottoman general staff, and other top German officers took over other key posts, including departments of Operations, Intelligence, Railroads, Supply, Munitions, Coal and Fortresses in the Ministry of War.[44] German strategic concerns also dominated Ottoman military deployment during the war itself.

At the Ottoman surrender in October 1918, Enver Pasha and other top CUP members were forced to flee to Germany, and were condemned to death in absentia in July 1919.

4   Socialism and Communism in the Ottoman Empire and in Turkey to 1925

The Young Turk[45] revolution of 1908 was accompanied by a certain working-class ferment. Strikes erupted in Istanbul, Salonica and Smyrna among longshoremen, tobacco and glass workers, public transport and railway workers. Between 1876 to 1908, there had been important strikes in the naval shipyards, at the tobacco monopoly and on the railroads. But, according to one historian of the period,[46] c. 1908 a true working-class or proletarian population, numbering perhaps 200,000, was still emerging from a much larger number of artisans in decline. Such labour organisation as existed was very much locally oriented. The kinds of organisations which emerged in the early workers' movement in Europe, such as mutual aid societies and unions, were absent, even as the industrial revolution took hold. The emerging working class was employed

---

43   The Capitulations were grants of partial Ottoman state sovereignty to Western powers during the centuries of Ottoman decline, giving Britain and France (first of all) control of different aspects of finance, fiscal policy and the customs house.

44   Shaw and Shaw, 1976–7, vol. 2, p. 313.

45   The term 'Young Turks' is here used interchangeably with their formal name, the Committee for Union and Progress (CUP).

46   See Dumont 1997, pp. 15 ff. All quotes from Dumont, an essential source for this article, are my translations. Dumont's book is second only to the ICC pamphlet as a guide to this story. The book, for all its wealth of detail, nonetheless misses the left wing of the Turkish communists and gives excessive weight to the right wing of Sefik Hüsnü and the Aydinlik group.

in the state armament industry, mining, by foreign firms and other industrial companies.

Socialist ideas entered the Ottoman Empire through the more European-oriented minorities: Armenians, Jews, Greeks, Serbs, Bulgarians.[47] The Socialist Workers' Federation of Salonica (then a city of 150,000 and a key transportation hub) which maintained a correspondence with the Second International, was the sole mass-based organisation in the empire at the time. (After Salonica was annexed by Greece in 1912, it ceased to have a decisive impact on the movement elsewhere in the empire.) Italy's 1911 invasion of Libya gave rise to a demonstration of 10,000 workers in Salonica, and the Second International condemned Italian imperialism. 20,000 Salonica workers turned out for the May Day demonstration of that year. The Ottoman and Balkan adherents of the Second International had attempted a confederation at a conference in Belgrade in 1910, but the effort was exploded by the two Balkan wars. With few exceptions, such as the Serbian Social Democrats who voted against war credits in September 1914, these Second International parties succumbed to nationalism in both the Balkan wars and in World War One.[48]

Jews, Armenians and Greeks, in keeping once again with the multi-ethnic character of Ottoman society, also played important roles in the socialist and later communist groups in Istanbul.

Enver Pasha and other Young Turks discredited by the military debacle approached the Bolsheviks[49] in 1919 in the hope of financial and political support against Kemal Pasha, whose military triumphs during the world war had quite eclipsed them. The Bolsheviks initially saw in Enver Pasha a useful ally in the Sovietization of the Transcaucus, where British-backed military activity against the Russian Revolution continued until 1920, and where he, as a Turk, could appeal more directly to the 'Islamo-Communist' currents there (see below).[50] While the exiled Young Turks pursued these machinations, Kemal Pasha was rallying the military forces in Anatolia which would ultimately ruin the Unionists' plans.

---

47   Ibid. p. 35.

48   See the issue of *Revolutionary History*, vol. 8, no. 3, *The Balkan Socialist Tradition and the Balkan Federation, 1871–1915*.

49   Enver Pasha's credentials, in addition to being the commander in some disastrous military defeats in the World War, also included involvement in the massacres of Armenians. Grigori Zinoviev became his main Bolshevik sponsor (Carr 1953, p. 265).

50   On Enver Pasha in the years 1919–1922, see Carrere d'Encausse 1981, pp. 263–6. More generally on Islamo-Communism, see Bennigsen 1986.

Kemal Pasha, because of his marginalisation from the top CUP leadership in the intense rivalry with Enver Pasha, as well as his commanding role in several Ottoman military victories during World War One (above all Gallipoli), was not discredited in the fashion of Enver Pasha and others (Enver having been the commander during several disastrous defeats). After the Central Powers surrendered in October-November 1918, the Allied armies occupied Istanbul along with Greek troops, the latter being in pursuit of their 'Great Idea' of annexing Istanbul and western Turkey and rebuilding the Byzantine Empire lost to Islam in 1453. After Britain and France had divided up the extensive Ottoman territories in the Middle East, they pursued plans to reduce Turkey proper to a small rump state in Anatolia, and to divide the rest into Greek, Italian, French and British spheres of interest. Kemal Pasha rejected such a dismemberment[51] and rallied nationalist forces in Anatolia for a three-year war that expelled the Greeks and made him into the undisputed leader of the new reduced nation. This Allied and Greek occupation, and the successful Kemalist counter-attack, are the backdrop to the 1919–22 developments described below.[52]

5   Misadventures of Enver Pasha

In the immediate postwar years, moreover, there was throughout the collapsing Ottoman Empire a tendency to amalgamate Bolshevism and Islam,[53] further

---

51   A huge national mythology surrounds the rise of Mustafa Kemal, embalmed in the large Attatürk ('Father of the Turks') mausoleum in Ankara. After his military victories as Ottoman commander in World War One came his May 1919 move to Samsun, where he began to mobilise resistance to the Allied and Greek occupation.

52   Readers unfamiliar with this period in Ottoman and Turkish history should keep in mind that until the Kemalist nationalists turned the tide against the Greek invasion in autumn 1921, the Ottoman Empire (finally abolished in 1922) was still the internationally-recognised government and with its capital in Istanbul. Mustafa Kemal turned the small town of Ankara in the centre of Anatolia into the new capital in December 1919 in order to deflate the prestige of Istanbul in the new Republic. The Grand National Assembly moved there in April 1920. Hence references in this text to Kemal's government should be understood as meaning the as-yet unrecognised breakaway nationalist revolt against the Allies, the Greeks and the punitive Treaty of Sèvres (1920) – more punitive to the Ottomans than the Versailles Treaty was to Germany – that the Kemalist revolt undid.

53   One manifestation of the power of Islam in the immediate postwar political conjuncture was the creation of the 'Green Army' c. May 1920. Various Muslim groups in the former Russian Empire used green, the colour of Islam. Some of these militias fought in the

evidenced at the notorious[54] Baku Congress of the Toilers of the East in September 1920. Enver Pasha had first contacted the Bolsheviks through Karl Radek in Radek's Berlin prison cell, which doubled as a political salon frequented by members of the German High Command,[55] corporatist and AEG Telefunken CEO Walter Rathenau (later an architect of the German-Soviet Treaty of Rapallo in 1922) as well as various German Communists. General von Seeckt, with links to the Freikorps and one of Radek's contacts, had already in the spring of 1919 proposed sending Enver Pasha to Moscow.[56] In conversations with Enver Pasha, Radek proposed significant Soviet aid to the burgeoning movement in Anatolia, in exchange for which the CUP would spread Bolshevik propaganda throughout the Moslem world.[57] Enver Pasha summarised his agreement with Radek saying that he would embrace socialism, 'on the condition that it was adapted to the religious doctrines governing the internal functioning of the Moslem countries'.[58]

A second step in the rapprochement between the CUP and the Bolsheviks took place in October-November 1919, in negotiations with the CUP organisation Karakol around the figure of Shal'va Eliava. A retired military officer, Baha Sait, went to Baku in late 1919, and in January 1920 signed an agreement

---

Transcaucasus and participated in the capture of Baku in September 1918. The Kemalists used the rumours of such a 'Green Army' to quell suspicions about its secularism in Turkish public opinion, suspicions fanned by the Sultanate in Istanbul. The actual Green Army saw as its task the struggle against reactionary Islamic opponents of the Kemalists (Dumont 1997, p. 349). The Green Army's pan-Asianist, possibly pan-Turanist call was 'Asia for the Asians'. At the Second Congress of the Comintern in July 1920, Lenin denounced pan-Asianism as serving the interests of 'Turkish and Japanese imperialism' (ibid. p. 351). When Cerkes Edhem emerged as a strongman of the Green Army and showed potential of becoming a rival to Mustafa Kemal, a break with the nationalists occurred in 1920, and Kemal attempted to dissolve the organisation. In October 1920, the law on associations was amended to give the government the right to ban organisations it deemed dangerous to state security (ibid. p. 355).

54   'Notorious' because of the presence of many Muslim delegates who today would rate as little more than Islamic fundamentalists, who responded in particular to Grigori Zinoviev's call for a 'jihad' against the West. The Baku Conference was attended by 235 Turks, 192 'Persians and Parsees', 8 Chinese, 8 Kurds, 157 Armenians and 100 Georgians (Carr 1953, p. 260).

55   This included Col. Max Bauer, chief of staff of Ludendorff, and later military adviser to Chiang kai-chek.

56   Vourkoutiotis 2007, p. 36.

57   Dumont 1997, p. 139.

58   Ibid. p. 140.

for an offensive alliance against European imperialism and to support revolutionary efforts in Moslem countries. As in the agreement with Enver Pasha, these CUP elements would promote revolution where they could in exchange for Soviet arms and money. The Soviets guaranteed the political and ideological independence of the Islamic countries that joined the anti-imperialist struggle, while the Unionists agreed to recognise Soviet power in Turkestan and Dagestan and help establish it in Georgia, Azerbaijan and Armenia.[59]

Following this rapprochement, an initial so-called 'Turkish Communist Party' was founded in Baku[60] at the beginning of 1920. Most of the founders were 'notorious Unionists'[61] who had fled to Azerbaijan. Through this grouping, the first contacts with the Kemalists in Turkey were also established.[62] Nuri Pasha,

---

59 Ibid. p. 141.

60 The Turkish CP thus began as an exile party. Baku, the oil-rich capital of Azerbaijan, underwent a tumultuous Sovietisation involving a myriad of ethnic groups in the significant working class (including many Moslem workers from other Turkic regions of the Tsarist empire). The city had had a rich history of working-class activity well before 1917. Before World War One, strikes in Baku were longer, more frequent and more successful than in any Russian city. See Grigor Suny 1972, p. 47. Baku was not accidentally a centre of Soviet revolutionary strategy. The Azeri language could be understood by Istanbul Turks, Persians in Tabriz, Kurds, the Turkic peoples of the Transcaucasus, Georgians and Armenians. Azerbaijan was, as Paul Dumont put it, 'one of the main revolutionary crossroads of the Near East', a 'Mecca of anti-imperialist struggle' (Dumont 1997, p. 286).

61 Ibid. p. 142. These founders included Halil Pasha, uncle of Enver Pasha, an Ottoman officer in World War One; he had been ordered by Mustafa Kemal in August 1919 to make contact with the Bolsheviks for the nationalist movement. Salih Zeki, former Ottoman bureaucrat, had organised a massacre of Armenians in his district in 1916. Dr. Fuad Sabit had been dispatched by Mustafa Kemal to Azerbaijan in July 1919, where he made contact with the Bolsheviks as well. Their creation of a 'Turkish Communist Party' in Baku was intended to ingratiate them with the Russians.

62 In addition to the exiled founders of the CP in Baku, there were numerous socialist and communist groupings active in the Ottoman Empire after the Allied occupation of November 1918. There were also important strikes in Istanbul, such as the tramway strike of May 1920 organised by the (Second International) Turkish Socialist Party. The TSP at that time had 5000 members. Earlier strikes in 1920 had swelled party membership, such as those at the naval shipyards of the Golden Horn. 1 May 1921 saw the biggest May Day demonstration in Istanbul's history. French intelligence services were also anguished by the appearance of Russian agitators. In February 1919 they uncovered a propaganda group in Istanbul using the name 'Turkish Communist Party', made up of Russian émigrés, Jews, some Moslems and some Greeks. (This information in gleaned by Dumont 1997, pp. 197 V. Vourkoutiotis 226.) Other radicalised elements appeared in exile in Germany, some developing ties to the Spartakusbund at the end of the war (ibid. p. 231) and were in the

half-brother of Enver Pasha, was a key figure. In reality, one major objective of the group, in addition to creating a communist party in Turkey, was to infiltrate the local Baku administration (then in the hands of the Musavatist Party)[63] either to incorporate Azerbaijan into the new Turkey or even to launch the much-touted pan-Turkic state. But first of all, as Paul Dumont puts it

> the Sovietization of Georgia and Armenia, like that of Azerbaijan, presented the advantage of countering English machinations in the Transcaucasus ... Here, the Unionists of Baku were applying the directives of the Anatolian government: the establishment of a common border with the Bolsheviks constituted, in effect, one of the main ideas of Kemalist strategy in this region.[64]

Both the Soviet Union and the Kemalist government saw this Sovietisation as key to preventing any encirclement by the British.

In the summer of 1920, the CUPers in the new 'Communist Party'[65] held further negotiations with the Bolsheviks, obtaining arms and gold for the Kemalist resistance. Enver Pasha, who dreamed of supplanting Mustafa Kemal with a Soviet-backed invasion of Anatolia, argued in August 1920 for the creation of

---

streets with them in January 1919. A number of them perished in the murder of the 15 communists off Trabzon in January 1921.

63   The Red Army entered Baku only in April 1920, putting an end to the annexationist dreams of the Unionists.

64   Ibid. p. 143 n. 1. Attatürk had noticed the defeat of the 1919 Hungarian Revolution of Bela Kun and how the absence of a common border with the Soviet Union had been a major factor in its isolation.

65   The main figure of the first phase of the Turkish CP was Mustafa Suphi (1883–1921). After studies in Paris, he had worked in the opposition to the CUP in Turkey and was imprisoned. He escaped to Russia, where he entered into contact with the Bolsheviks. After the revolution, he became the key figure in contact with the Turkish interior and worked under Stalin's Commissariat of Nationalities. He represented Turkey at the founding Congress of the Third International in March 1919. He arrived in Baku in May 1920 and undertook the reorganisation of the exile party founded earlier that year. He returned to Turkey at the end of 1920 to request legalisation of the TCP from Mustafa Kemal. He and his entourage were greeted by anti-communist demonstrations organised by the nationalists of the eastern provinces, and he and fourteen other communists were murdered at the end of January 1921. Ibid. p. 143 n. 3.

According to the ICC (International Communist Current n. d., p. 5), Mustapha Suphi had also been influenced by the Islamo-Communism of Sultan Galiev, an influence he never entirely shed.

a 'Union of Islamic Revolutionary Societies' to fight for the Communists' anti-imperialist programme, in exchange for further Soviet military and financial support. In the course of these negotiations, Enver wrote in a muted letter (not mentioning his larger scheme) to Kemal Pasha that

> In principle, the Russians agree to support revolutionary movements directed against England, even if these movements are not communist ...[66]

In a speech at the Baku Congress, Enver Pasha again reiterated that

> ... It is not merely a desire for support that pulls us toward the Third International, but also close ties that unite its principles with ours.[67]

A long programmatic statement, *Mesai* [*Labor*], also written in September 1920, and with the participation of Enver Pasha,

> seems to want to define a specifically Turkish line, taking into account both national and religious realities. National independence is presented as an indispensable step toward internationalism. The teachings of Islam are assimilated to socialism; among other things, the califate is maintained, as well as the sovereignty of the sultan.[68]

These statements seem to indicate both a real commitment to working with the Bolsheviks and an attempt to create a left alternative to Kemal Pasha.

Comintern chairman Grigori Zinoviev, despite his call at the Baku Congress for a 'jihad' against the West, was for his part not convinced, and warned that the Congress would need to be circumspect about 'the leaders of this movement which not long ago were killing workers and peasants in the interest of a group of imperialist powers ... The Congress proposes that they prove by their actions that they are ready to serve the people and erase their previous faults'.[69]

---

66   Ibid. p. 145. Dumont interprets this letter as an attempt to assure Kemal that this collaboration would not pull him to the left.

67   Ibid. p. 147. Both the Bolsheviks and the Muslim revolutionaries at Baku played a careful verbal game of not 'dotting the i's' about their true divergent perspectives, for the purpose of the momentary alliance (ibid. p. 299).

68   Ibid. p. 149.

69   Ibid. p. 151.

Nevertheless, Enver Pasha persisted and in the following months established, with Soviet agreement and financial support, his 'Union of Islamic
Revolutionary Societies' and its Turkish branch, the 'party of popular soviets'.[70] Most Communist-oriented groups in Anatolia, morever, by 1921 were
well infiltrated by Unionists.[71] In late July 1921, a Greek victory over the Kemalists seemed close at hand, and Enver, with Soviet backing, sensed that his
moment had arrived. Mustafa Kemal, however, rallied the Turkish forces and
after his victory at Sakarya began the offensive that expelled the Greeks in
1922.[72] Once the Soviet government realised it would be dealing with a Kemalist government in Turkey,[73] Enver Pasha's pro-communist dalliance was near-
ing its end. He went to Bukhara initially as a Soviet representative but broke
with the Bolsheviks and enlisted the Turkmen Basmachis in his earlier pan-
Turanian dream, now fighting against the Red Army, and was killed in battle in
1922.[74]

---

70   Ibid.

71   Ibid. p. 157.

72   Both the ICC pamphlet and Dumont make the important point that Greek Communist
      agitation against the war was an important factor in the Kemalist victories. Dumont
      writes, basing himself on a Soviet source (p. 392 n. 2): 'The Greek Communists rose up
      against the war in Asia Minor starting in mid-1920. It seems that they, by their active
      anti-militarist propaganda, significantly contributed to the undoing of the troops sent to
      Anatolia. Starting at the end of 1920, desertions in the Hellenic army multiplied and there
      is every evidence that a certain number of mutinies took place in the barracks around
      Smyrna. According to N. Dimitratos, the delegate of the Greek Communist Party at the
      Third Congress of the Comintern, more than 100,000 "workers and peasants" had deserted
      during the first two years of the war. This figure may seem a bit Homeric, but it nonetheless
      gives a certain idea of the extent of the phenomenon'.

73   The Soviet government wanted close ties with Mustafa Kemal in their battle against
      British intervention, which in late 1919 was still backing anti-Soviet forces in Armenia,
      Georgia and Azerbaijan. The Soviets also hoped that such an alliance would strengthen
      their appeal to the Turkic populations within Russia. Chicherin, at that time in charge
      of Soviet foreign relations, made a direct appeal to the 'workers and peasants of Turkey'
      in September 1919, just as Mustafa Kemal was imposing himself as the leader of the
      nationalist movement, to continue the struggle against the Greek invaders. Kemal, for
      his part, was already using the prospect of a Soviet alliance to alarm the Western powers,
      while clearly demarcating himself from communism. At the same time he realised that
      Soviet military aid was essential to his survival. The tradeoff was Kemal's assistance in the
      Sovietisation of Armenia, Georgia and Azerbaijan (ibid. pp. 169–70).

74   Carrère d'Encausse 1981.

6   The Main Factions of Emerging Turkish Communism

a   Turkish 'Spartakists'

A group of Turks in exile in Germany during the war, organised in the Party of Workers and Farmers of Turkey, were won over to Marxism and some of them were in the streets with the Spartakusbund in January 1919. They emerged from the several thousand Ottoman citizens then studying or working in Germany. The intellectual core, with their leaders Ethem Nejat and Sefik Hüsnü, returned to Turkey in mid-1919 after publishing one issue of their journal *Kurtulus* [*Liberation*] in exile, an issue strikingly remote from the explosive issues of the time. In reality, this group was known as 'Spartakists' mainly because they had been in Germany. But the Spartakusbund's influence was overshadowed, in this largely intellectual group, by the French influence of Henri Barbusse's journal *Clarté*. That latter current saw intellectuals as 'spiritual inventors who mark the unfolding of progress', a view wholly embraced by the Kurtulus group.

Back in Turkey, they added the word 'socialist' to their name and acquired legal existence. They had pretensions of rivalling the much larger and much more working-class based Turkish Socialist Party (TSP), but in their first phase of existence did not get very far, turning out only a few hundred people at the mass demonstration organised by the TSP on May Day 1921. In reality, their programme differed little from that of the TSP.[75] They received authorisation to resume publication of *Kurtulus*. Ethem Nejat and Sefik Hüsnü were, again, the main editors. Both issued from middle-class backgrounds and had studied abroad, Hüsnü being strongly influenced by Jaurèsian socialism in France. By early 1920, some members rebelled against the elitist bent of the group, and left Istanbul for Kemalist territory. Sefik Hüsnü and Ethem Nejat moved toward communism, leaving the leadership to its moderate fraction.

In late 1920, Sefik Hüsnü and Sadrettin Celal resumed control, now applying the Comintern line under the influence of the Baku Congress of the Toilers of the East, benefitting from the increasing debacle of the TSP. The group's new journal was named, not accidentally, *Aydinlik* [*Clarity*] after Barbusse's journal in France, and an affiliated 'Workers' Association of Turkey' had several hundred worker militants. Nevertheless, in 1921, despite the application of the Comintern line of a 'united front against the coalesced forces of the bourgeoisie', they failed to match the dynamism of the working-class base of the

---

75   The programme featured the eight-hour day, a legal minimum wage, abolition of child labour, the creation of village cooperatives, the nationalisation of public transport, mines, forests, etc. Ibid. p. 325.

PST in Istanbul. An Allied intelligence report on left-wing activity in Istanbul did not even mention *Aydinlik*. But its ties to the Comintern caught the attention of the Kemalists, and in spite of the group's November 1922 telegram to the Grand National Assembly congratulating it on the abolition of the sultanate.

We shall return to the career of Sefik Hüsnu and the *Aydinklik* group momentarily, when Hüsnu, with these elitist origins, emerges as the leader of the right-wing of the Turkish communist movement under the Turkish Republic, and ultimately becomes a Stalinist.

b   *The Left Wing of Turkish Communism, 1920–25*[76]
More obscure, and little discussed in Western-language literature on Turkish socialism and communism in this period, is a distinct left-wing, with its main initial base in Anatolia, whose best known figures were the Bashkir Sharif Manatov and Salih Hacioglu.[77] They emerged in 1920 out of the ferment fol-

---

76   I am indebted for what I know about this left wing to Turkish comrades who sent me their pamphlet Left-Wing of the Turkish Communist Party, prior to their adhesion to the International Communist Current (ICC). The pamphlet is not online but is available from the ICC. E-mail communication and subsequent conversations with these comrades have been invaluable in writing this article. The pamphlet is hereafter referred to as 'ICC pamphlet'.

77   Sharif Manatov was the son of an imam of Bashkir, in the southern Urals. According to Dumont, he began his political career as a militant on the far right of the Bashkir assembly. Manatov had come to Constantinople in 1913. 'In 1914, his anti-war position forced him to emigrate to Switzerland where he met and became a friend of Lenin ... [After 1917] ... he went back to Bashkiria ... and was even elected as chairman of the Bashkir Soviet ... He was initially part of the Bashkir national liberation movement but when its leader went over to the Whites, Manatov broke with the movement and was imprisoned' (ICC pamphlet). He went over to the Bolsheviks and in 1918 Stalin (Commissar for Nationalities) made him vice-chairman of the Central Muslim Commissariat. He worked into the Bashkir nationalist movement and was sent to Baku to the Musawat government there. By April 1920 he was in Ankara as Bashkir representative at the government of the Grand National Assembly. He then became one of the most active Bolshevik propagandists in Anatolia, and quickly built an impressive network of militants. In Ankara he began giving lectures on the ideas of the October Revolution. Through his influence on the workers and notables of Eskisehir, that city became the main bastion of Anatolian communist ferment (Dumont 1997, pp. 374–5). George Harris describes him as 'the first voice on Turkish soil to proclaim that Lenin "had invented a doctrine that differs from Marxism". He apparently attempted to convert Attatürk to Bolshevism. In June 1920, he wrote the General Statutes of the Turkish Communist Party which called for soviets, the abolition of private property, and nationalisations' (Harris 1967, pp. 70–2).

lowing the Ottoman surrender, the soviet movement in northeast Anatolia, and a regroupment of disparate forces in the 'red bastion' of Eskisehir, in western Anatolia. Hacioglu in particular was from the beginning opposed to the ideology of 'national wars of liberation', but through the 1919–22 war the Turkish communists mainly followed the Comintern position on the question. Through the 1919–22 years of struggle, war, repression and prison, and ultimately until its defeat and eradication by 1927, this faction evolved to broadly 'left communist' positions. It had far more real depth in the working class and allied groups than the Istanbul-based, elitist *Aydinlik* group, top-heavy with intellectuals, even though the latter had the sponsorship of the Comintern and, with the triumph of Stalinism, ultimately prevailed as the left-wing was dispersed and liquidated, often physically. The Turkish left communists even had an ally in a Comintern official, Grigori Safarov. Safarov worked in the Comintern's Eastern office and had already clashed with Lenin on the national question. He joined the Bolsheviks in 1908, had been with Lenin in Switzerland, and returned to Russia on the same train. He was affiliated with the Russian left communists and wrote a book, *The National Question and the Proletariat* (1923). He did everything in his power to support the left-wing of the Turkish communists against Hüsnü and the *Aydinlik* group, but was removed from his position as a member of the anti-Stalinist opposition.[78]

After his expulsion from Turkey in autumn 1920, he returned to the Soviet Union and was later murdered (ICC pamphlet). Salih Hacioglu, born in 1880, was a veterinarian. In World War One, he served as a military veterinarian on several fronts and was revolted by the experience. He made his way to Ankara and encountered Manatov and his seminars. He and Manatov took over the local organisation of the Turkish Socialist Party in Eskisehir and launched the short-lived newspaper Emek. After the repression of the People's Communist Party in January 1921, he was one of the figures condemned to 15 years at hard labour. (He was however amnestied by the end of the year.) Both he and Manatov, in the previous fall, had warned Mustafa Suphi of the dangers awaiting Turkish CP members (ICC pamphlet).

78   ICC pamphlet, pp. 15, 22. Safarov heard the plea of Salih Hacioglu in November 1925 to depose the right-wing Aydinlik leadership of the Turkish party. Safarov's role, over and against the Soviet press and various Comintern Congress resolutions on support for bourgeois revolutions in the semi-colonial and colonial world, shows that in spite of the Soviet treaties with Turkey, Persia and Afghanistan, the Comintern did not speak with one voice. Safarov later went to Germany and worked with the Communist opposition group the Leninbund, then returned to Russia and was subsequently shot.

7   Vicissitudes of the Soviet Rapprochement with Kemalist Turkey
         and the Fortunes of Turkish Communists

Kemal Pasha was clearly a pioneer among leaders of authoritarian development regimes outside the West in many ways, and not least of all in his strategy
of frightening the Western powers by mercurial relations with the Soviet Union,
as well as in the alternation of his tolerance and repression of internal Communist activity in Turkey itself. What interests us above all is Soviet tolerance
of that repression when it suited Soviet foreign policy.

Mustafa Kemal's original mission in Anatolia naturally had a class dimension
as well as a nationalist one:

> ... the reason Mustafa Kemal went to Samsun, which has become the
> beginning of everything in the mythology of national liberation, was
> because British imperialism wanted to send an Ottoman commander
> there ... [this] ... was due to the fact that, following the suppression of the
> soviet movement in the cities of Erzurum, Erzincan, Bayburt and Sivas at
> the hands of the Ottoman army, they wanted the region to be examined
> and they wanted precautions to be taken against similar possible events
> in the future if necessary. The soviet movement, centered in the city of
> Erzincan, was a development from the revolutionary propaganda made
> by Russian soldiers in the region, and while the Russian army was retreat-
> ing after the revolution, the Armenian, Kurdish and Turkish laborers in
> the region, moving beyond sharp national divisions, came together. This
> movement was crushed by the Ottoman Army in January 1918.[79]

The Turkish working class, though small, and with its ties to rural labour, was
definitely a force to be reckoned with in the political calculations of contending
parties in the post-world war social climate.

Worker ferment also emerged in the western zones under Allied occupation,
above all Istanbul. In 1920–1, the Turkish Socialist Party, with a real working-
class base and affiliated with the Second International, took a militant turn in
occupied Istanbul with the threat of a general strike (January 1921). Another
strike was threatened at the gas works in April, followed by a May Day demonstration of unprecedented size. Largely unsuccessful struggles against foreign
companies followed. The Socialist Party went into decline through these stale-
mates, but a militant tramway strike erupted in January 1922. The SP threw itself

---

79   ICC pamphlet, p. 3.

into the struggle in order to regain momentum, but the strike ended in a disaster for the workers. New worker organisations arose to fill the void.

Mustafa Kemal's movement was a reconfiguration of the old military and CUP elite into a new proto-state (known until the 1923 declaration of the Turkish Republic as the Grand National Assembly):

> The Kemalist movement was led by previously mid- to high-ranked members of the military and political bureaucratic bourgeoisie ... the ruling cadres of the movement either came from the Ottoman Army or from the (CUP) ...[80]

Mustafa Suphi, a key figure in the very early history of the Turkish CP, arrived in Baku (Azerbaijan) in May 1920, with full backing of the Comintern. His assignment was a delicate one. The ex-Unionists who had founded the self-styled 'Turkish Communist Party' a few months earlier were on the one hand suspected of being more Islamic socialists than communists, but on the other hand, they still maintained powerful connections with CUP figures in the Turkish bureaucracy and military and could be of great use as contacts with the Kemalist movement.[81] Suphi thus reconstituted the group as the 'Baku section' of the Turkish CP, and expelled some of the more dubious figures. He dispatched an envoy to Mustafa Kemal in July asking the Ankara government 1) if the Turkish Bolsheviks would be allowed to create a legal organisation in Anatolia; 2) what changes might be made in the current Bolshevik programme to make it applicable in Anatolia; and 3) what were the views of the Grand National Assembly on the application of the Bolshevik programme? The envoy was also instructed to tell the Ankara government that the Baku organisation would provide it, for the time being, with 50 cannons, 70 machine guns and 17,000 rifles.[82] It amounted to an offer to exchange these arms for legal toleration of Bolshevik activity in Anatolia.

An initial conference of Turkish communists had taken place in Moscow in July 1918 and had revealed serious factional disagreements; Mustafa Suphi hoped to heal these differences and qualify the party for membership in the

---

80   Ibid.

81   The Kemalist representative in Moscow, for his part, was under strict instructions to seek weaponry and munitions from the Soviet government, but to do everything in his power to prevent an intervention of the Red Army in regions disputed with the Turkish nationalists.

82   Dumont 1997, p. 276.

Third International, which held its Second Congress in July 1920.[83] The founding congress of the party, superseding the organisation created in the spring, took place in Baku in September, immediately after the (above-mentioned) Congress of the Toilers of the East. 74 delegates participated, in contrast to the 20-odd delegates two years earlier. Following in the spirit of the just-concluded international Congress, many of these delegates, in the view of Dumont, 'saw in communism nothing but an extremist variant of the teachings of Islam' whereas perhaps ten had any real Marxist background.[84] The Unionists were eliminated from the central committee. In discussions at the congress, a majority of delegates argued for maintaining Islamic traditions and vigorously opposed the party's programme for secularising the state administration and judiciary. There was approval for the abolition of the caliphate, but all other anti-religious measures were soft-pedalled. The congress also approved the decisions taken by the Comintern's Second Congress on support for national liberation movements which included bourgeois elements. The delegates' 'Appeal to the Workers in Turkey' argued for a series of political and social measures[85] but not for a radical social transformation.

Contacts and concertation between the Kemalists and the Soviet government had, up to the turn of Turkish fortunes at Sakarya, hardly been without its frictions. The Soviet backing of Enver Pasha had not helped. A further major sticking point had been Armenia, where the Bolsheviks had committed themselves to the right of self-determination,[86] and where Kemal Pasha wanted three provinces for Turkey previously lost to Tsarist Russia. Kemalist forces to that end had pushed beyond the pre-1914 Turkish borders with the apparent goal of annexation. Chicherin (then in charge of Soviet foreign policy) and the Soviet government were suspicious of a secret agreement between Kemal and

---

83   The Second Congress, after serious debate, ratified the idea of supporting bourgeois nationalist 'anti-imperialist' struggles. Attending the conference from the colonial and semi-colonial world were delegates from Georgia, Armenia, Azerbaijan, Bukhara, India, Turkey, Persia, China and Korea (Carr 1953, p. 251).

84   Dumont 1997, p. 272. The ICC pamphlet is much more hard-hitting: 'The majority of the congress, just like the majority who participated in the People's Congress of the East, had not managed to break from nationalist ideology, and some of them had feelings toward Westerners that were arguably quite racist' (p. 9).

85   The programmatic points of the 'Appeal' included recognition of the right to strike, universal suffrage, replacement of the standing army by popular militias, fiscal reform, mandatory and free primary education, distribution of land to poor peasants and improvement in the conditions of workers (Dumont 1997, p. 275).

86   Lenin had aleady attacked Tsarist Russia's occupation of the three eastern Turkish provinces (Kars, Ardahan and Batum) before the 1917 Revolution.

the Allies enabling Britain to open a new anti-Soviet front.[87] On one hand, in a speech in Baku in November 1920

> Stalin extolled the third anniversary of the Bolshevik revolution and laud-
> ed the friendship between Soviet Russia and Kemalist Turkey, declaring
> that the Turkish revolutionary movement, although bourgeois in char-
> acter, was resisting the Entente imperialists and creating such ferment
> in the Caucusus and the Near East as was unimaginable three years
> earlier.[88]

But Chicherin warned of a possible armed conflict with Turkey if Kemal pushed too far,[89] and both the Soviets and the Armenians suspected that Kemal wanted all the territory awarded to the Ottoman Empire at the Treaty of Brest-Litovsk and might possibly 'have been encouraged by representatives of the Entente powers to press beyond Kars in the hope of driving the Red Army out of Azerbaijan'.[90] After the collapse of General Wrangel's White Army in the Cri-mea in November 1920, and the subsequent transfer of thousands of Red Army soldiers to the Caucusus, the Kemalists calmed down, stopped referring to Brest-Litovsk, and focused on annexing parts of Armenia.

Mustafa Kemal, himself obviously no communist, had his own reasons to be dubious of the Soviet-Turkish entente. At the time of the arrival of Mustafa

---

87   See O'Connor 1988. Chicherin considered Turkey to be 'crucial' to Anglo-Soviet relations
      (p. 121) and later conceived of a defensive alliance of the Soviet Union with Turkey,
      Persia and Afghanistan (p. 142). Chicherin in June 1920 in a diplomatic note had called
      for a plebiscite for Kurdistan, Lazistan, the area of Batum, eastern Thrace and various
      Turco-Arab locales, many of them areas coveted by the Kemalists. But the following day,
      Kemal was informed of a large shipment of Soviet weapons and munitions (Dumont 1997,
      p. 293).

88   Hovannisian 1971–96, vol. 4, p. 343. Stalin also communicated to Kemal, through the newly-
      established leader of the Turkish CP in Baku, Mustafa Suphi, that the Soviet government
      'considered the movement of nationalist resistance in Anatolia to be a model for all
      peoples of the East ...' Suphi added to Stalin's message the assurance that the party would
      'avoid any initiative of an extremist character' while the war against the Greek forces
      continued (Dumont 1997, p. 181).

89   On 7 November 1920, 'Chicherin instructed that the Turks should be cautioned that future
      military aid was dependent on their acceptance of a Soviet-mediated armistice with
      Armenia and on their commitment to eject any Entente force that might attempt to
      occupy Batum. Stalin, then still in Baku, was given the authority to suspend the shipments,
      if necessary' (ibid. p. 344).

90   Ibid. p. 347.

Suphi's envoy seeking legal recognition of the Turkish CP, moreover, 'the hypothesis of a possible Bolshevization of Anatolia ... was in no way particularly extravagant'.[91] Pro-Soviet sentiment in the nationalist milieu was at a high pitch, and Kemal himself had issued a manifesto calling on Muslims to form a bloc with the Communists against the Western powers. Another important Kemalist leader, Kazim Karabekir, commander of the Army of the East, imagined the possibility of 'acclimatizing Bolshevik theories to Anatolia' once certain modifications were made.[92]

Significant Soviet aid in the form of gold shipments began to arrive in August 1920; more would follow in December. The vindictive Allied peace treaty of Sèvres (among other things depriving Turkey of the three disputed Armenian provinces that would cause the serious problems discussed above) was imposed on the surviving Ottoman government in Istanbul on 10 August, and four days later Mustafa Kemal addressed the (rebel) Grand National Assembly in Ankara on the similarities between the communitarian spirit of Islam and Bolshevism,[93] a speech aimed, once again, at winning the trust of the Bolsheviks while frightening the West. At this juncture, Kemal had to walk a very fine line between offending the Soviets and allowing the Baku-based Turkish CP to operate in Turkey itself, as the party delegate had requested in July. Kemal used the occasion of the rout of the Red Army in Poland in August 1920 to harden his attitude toward communist activity in Anatolia and to steal the populist rhetoric of a left-opposition group, the People's Party (see below) that seemed to be outflanking his government in parliament. With the Soviet government distracted elsewhere, Mustafa Kemal in September replied to Suphi that

> we should abstain from untimely and useless initiatives, as these could become a factor of disunity and in that way bring about the failure of the national struggle for independence.[94]

---

91   Ibid. p. 176. At the same time, it is important to keep in mind that communist militants in Turkey in the period under consideration (1917–25) numbered no more than 20,000 (ICC pamphlet).

92   Ibid. Karakebir, commander of the Army of the East, in August 1920 suggested to Kemal Pasha putting some Turkish Communists in 'honorific posts' to appease them (ibid. p. 276). In his view, the communist movement should be neutralised because 'an uncontrolled agitation could only benefit the British, who would not hesitate to exploit the anti-communist sentiments of forces faithful to the Caliph' (ibid.).

93   Ibid. p. 177.

94   Ibid. p. 277.

At the same time, to avoid pushing Suphi and the CP into clandestine activity, Kemal reiterated that he and they were pursuing the same objective (national liberation) and asked the Baku organisation to send an accredited representative to Ankara 'so that the Turkish communist organization and the national power could collaborate fully'.[95]

This was, once again, complicated by the situation in Armenia, as indicated. Nonetheless, at the beginning of November 1920, Suphi replied to Kemal's letter announcing that the accredited mission was preparing to leave for Ankara, adding that

> his party was committed to fully supporting the national government and would do nothing to weaken or divide the fighting forces.[96]

In early December, Mustafa Suphi and 20 comrades left Baku for Turkey, apparently convinced by Kemal's letter that they were welcome there,[97] and arrived in Kars on 28 December, where they received an official welcome from Kazim Karabekir, despite the latter's suspicions about their intentions. The timing could hardly have been worse, since at that very moment Kemalist forces were engaged in violent confrontation with the armed bands of Cerkes Edhem (see below), a former supporter of the Grand National Assembly who had turned against Kemal in the hope of rallying 'extremist' elements against him in the name of 'Bolshevism', and who thereby showed the latter's potential for sowing disunity.[98] At this juncture, the government had decided that the communists should return to Russia. Kazim Karabekir ordered the governor of Erzurum, Hamit bey, to whip up a press campaign and 'appropriate demonstrations' against Mustafa Suphi and his comrades to dissuade them from remaining in Turkey. In this way, Karabekir (and presumably Kemal Pasha) hoped that this negative reception would appear to be due to the recklessness of the communist group and not directed against the Soviet Union. On 22 January, an angry crowd in Erzurum prevented Suphi and his comrades from leaving the train station, and they returned toward the coast, everywhere encountering crowds shouting anti-communist insults and hurling rocks. Six days later, on 28 January, they finally arrived in Trabzon where they immediately accepted the offer

---

95   Ibid. p. 278.

96   Ibid. In October, Kemal had tried to foment an 'official Communist Party' to co-opt ferment to the left, but the serious militants remained underground.

97   Salih Hacioglu, the left spokesman, had warned Suphi at the party's founding congress in Baku of the dangers of returning to Turkey.

98   Ibid. p. 279.

of a motorboat to depart. They were overtaken by another boat, murdered, and thrown into the sea.[99]

Activities of the Turkish Communist Party were not entirely paralysed by these murders. But they were part of a larger crackdown on the left by the Kemalists. In December, measures had already been intensified against 'extremists' and by January 1921, according to Paul Dumont, 'most left-wing organizations in Anatolia had disappeared'.[100] The Trabzon murders had merely been the culmination of a wave of repression.[101] A few days later (1 February 1921) the 'People's Communist Party of Turkey' (see below) was forced to disband and its leaders charged with spying for a 'foreign power' and sentenced to long years in prison.

Paul Dumont is eloquent on the Soviet reaction:

> The repressive measures of January 1921 were noted in Moscow without the slightest murmur. Only much later did Pravda mention the 'crimes' perpetrated in 1920 and 1921 by the Ankara government. At the time, quite to the contrary, the emphasis was on the progress of Turko-Russian friendship.[102]

---

99   Paul Dumont, for his part, does not think that Karabekir or Hamit bey organised the murders. Telegrams between them specified that no violence should befall the group. Yahya, the local ferryman who suggested the motorboat, and with a local reputation for ferocity, has often been suspected, if only to relieve Suphi of the funds he was carrying to finance communist activity in Anatolia. But doubt is cast on the idea that he acted on his own because, after he was arrested and murdered in turn, he had threatened to 'spill the beans'. Whose beans? Dumont suggests as possibilities the Unionists for whom he worked in Trabzon, some local notables, or an agent of the Ankara government. Kazim Karabekir accused the Unionists of being behind it. But nothing ever went beyond conjecture (ibid. p. 282).

100   Ibid. p. 183.

101   As E.H. Carr 1953, p. 301, dryly puts it: 'For the first, though not for the last time, it was demonstrated that governments could deal drastically with their national Communist Parties without forfeiting the goodwill of the Soviet government'. The treaty preamble, signed on the same day as the Anglo-Soviet trade agreement was signed in London, mentioned 'solidarity in the struggle against imperialism'. For Turkey as for the Soviet Union, it meant 'the exclusion of foreign interlopers from Transcaucasia and from the shores of the Black Sea ... These advantages outweighed for both parties any differences about the treatment of Turkish communists' (Carr 1953, p. 303).

102   Ibid. p. 185. Dumont continues in a footnote to this passage: 'The first article hostile to the Ankara government we found in this newspaper was on Oct. 26, 1922 ... Fifteen days earlier, Turkey had signed the armistice of Mudanya with the Allies. Thereafter, the

In this climate, Turkish negotiators arrived in Moscow on 17 February 1921. The Armenian question was still a central source of tension. A military confrontation also seemed possible in Georgia, where both Red Army and Turkish troops were present, the latter in provinces lost to Russia in 1878. The Turkish Minister of Foreign Affairs, Bekir Sami, was making anti-communist speeches in the capitals of Europe.

In order to retain the alliance with the Kemalist regime, the Soviet government signed a 'treaty of friendship and fraternity' with Turkey on 16 March 1921. Turkey retained the three provinces occupied in 1920, and other concessions.[103] The Kemalists agreed to crack down on groups in Turkey attempting to propagate pan-Turanism in Russia, and the Soviet government agreed not to back activities aimed at the Kemalist government in Turkey. Nevertheless, mistrust reigned on both sides and many questions of implementation dragged on into 1922. But the Kemalists' repression of all communist groups in Anatolia never intruded.[104]

After the repression of 1920–1, the ebbs and flows of an organised left independent of Mustafa Kemal paralleled the ebbs and flows of the Turkish-Soviet relationship. On May Day 1921, there were in fact massive worker demonstra-

---

Bolsheviks would multiply attacks against the Kemalist government. The first mention of the murders of Mustafa Suphi and his comrades appeared in Soviet newspapers in May 1921' (Carr 1953, p. 304). An article about Suphi in another Soviet publication in July 1921 by the Islamic Communist Sultan Galiev scarcely mentions the circumstances of Suphi's death (Dumont, p. 283). Chicherin had raised the matter with the Turkish delegation negotiating the friendship and commercial treaty in February, but the latter professed innocence of involvement by the Kemalist government. The ambassador argued that the arrests of communists in the December-January crackdown had resulted from their own 'tactical errors', because they had attempted to prematurely launch a 'social revolution in Anatolia' (ibid.).

103   The treaty also settled the disputes over the Caucusus (Armenia, Azerbaijan and Georgia). O'Connor 1988, p. 142.

104   The Third Congress of the Communist International, which met in June–July 1921, issued a call to support the Kemalists, in general alignment with the new strategy of 'conquering the masses'. Harris 1967, p. 102. In a letter from the Comintern Executive Commission secretary, the ambassador Aralov was instructed to 'govern' the local communists who they feared would 'scare the national intellectual circles with pointless "left communist" blows' (ICC pamphlet). Aralov did more than 'govern'. In his memoirs, he reports that in 1922 Nazim Bey, a Communist leader, told him that he was in a position to establish a pro-Bolshevik government in Ankara, if the Soviet government would support him, and that he was supported in this goal by 120 deputies. Aralov claims that he rushed to inform the Kemalist authorities of what was afoot (Dumont 1997, p. 395).

tions in Istanbul. In December 1921 – January 1922, M.V. Frunze, commander-in-chief of Soviet forces in the Ukraine, made an extended visit to Ankara that was a high-water mark in relations. Some of the Communists who had received long sentences had already been amnestied in September 1921, and in March 1922 several of them were authorised to reconstitute the 'People's Communist Party of Turkey'. The Soviet ambassador kept Kemal Pasha well apprised of their activities.

A pamphlet of the Turkish CP in February 1922, a month before the party returned to legal status, pulled no punches:

> The purely bourgeois and despotic group [the Kemalists – LG] … has already begun to try to block the danger it fears the most: the young communists secretly organizing in the country … The Kemalist movement started throwing them into its dungeons at the first opportunity.[105]

But the pamphlet did not stop there:

> But the point that matters to us is that all the acts of betrayal and murder were committed while in a close alliance with Russia … While representatives in Russia declared that Anatolia was communist in their long articles in the Moscow newspaper, a horde of police and soldiers chased the real communists in Anatolia.[106]

Relations between the Soviet Union and Turkey, despite the re-legalisation, went downhill from there, however; in April 1922 the Cheka accused the Turkish embassy in Moscow of espionage and Kemal Pasha recalled his ambassador. Worse still, from the Soviet viewpoint, Kemal refused to condemn the Basmachi revolt led by Enver Pasha. With the final crushing of the invading Greek troops in September 1922, the chill became manifest.[107]

---

105   Quoted in ICC pamphlet, p. 12.
106   Ibid.
107   Interestingly, and tellingly, the Comintern executive on one hand issued an appeal at this very moment entitled 'Workers, oppose a new war in the East!', thereby overturning the 'anti-imperialist' support for Kemalist Turkey of the previous three years. They foresaw the Turkish working class returning to struggle against the 'caste government' in Ankara. On the other hand, Radek for his part called on Turkish workers to continue to support the 'legitimate demands' of the national liberation movement. '"You must understand that the time has not yet come for the final struggle and you will for a long time

Further repression of communist groups intensified in October 1922. The Ottoman sultan, who had not yet formally handed power in Istanbul over to the Kemalists, banned several worker organisations. However, thousands of worker militants did attend congresses in the Curukova region, with an important presence of the communist left. Then, during the negotiations for the Treaty of Lausanne (November 1922 – July 1923), which formally recognised the Kemalist victory in Turkey and scrapped the punitive Treaty of Sèvres, Kemalist-Communist relations warmed yet again. By early 1923, various communist groups were at liberty to have a public existence and publications. The Soviet press blew hot and cold (as shall be documented below) praising the alliance with Turkey while attacking the Turkish rapprochement with the Allies. But once the Allies had conceded control over the Straits to Kemal Pasha, the Kemalists unleashed a police operation against communist militants in Istanbul. This time, *Pravda* ran the headline 'White Terror in Turkey'. Be that as it may, numbers of workers struck on May Day 1923, above all in Istanbul. Further strikes involving 30,000 workers occurred in a July–November 1923 strike wave (see below).

8   Other Currents of the Turkish Left, 1918–25

In addition to the 'Spartakist' group and the Turkish communist left described above, which became the two main factions of the Turkish CP, it is necessary to parse out the different currents and organisations on the scene in these decisive years, some of whom muddled the clarity of the CP.

Outright repression such as the murder of Mustafa Suphi and fourteen other communists in January 1921 was only one dimension (albeit the most brutal) of the difficulties that confronted militants in Turkey under the Kemalist regime. Mustafa Kemal also was masterful in mixing co-optation and repression, as illustrated in the fates of other currents in the years leading up to the creation of the Republic (October 1923) and thereafter.

---

have to act in concert with the bourgeois elements ...”' (Dumont 1997, p. 195, quoting the Comintern's International Correspondence of 30 September 1922). Radek went so far as to assert that the arrests of Turkish communists were ordered by the 'conservative faction' of the Kemalist movement, and absolved Attatürk from blame. Harris 2002, p. 55.

a   *The Green Army*

One manifestation of the power of Islam in the immediate postwar political conjuncture was the creation of the 'Green Army' c. May 1920.[108] Various
Muslim groups in the former Russian empire used green, the colour of Islam.
Some of these militias fought in the Transcaucasus and participated in the
capture of Baku in September 1918. The Kemalists used the rumours of such
a 'Green Army' to quell suspicions about its secularism in Turkish public opinion, suspicions fanned by the Sultanate in Istanbul. The actual Green Army
saw as its task the struggle against reactionary Islamic opponents of the Kemalists.[109] The Green Army's pan-Asianist, possibly pan-Turanist call was 'Asia
for the Asians'. At the Second Congress of the Comintern in July 1920, Lenin
had denounced pan-Asianism as serving the interests of 'Turkish and Japanese
imperialism'. When the above-mentioned Cerkes Edhem emerged as a strongman of the Green Army, with 3,000 fighting men under him, showing the potential to become a rival to Mustafa Kemal, a break with the nationalists occurred,
and Kemal attempted to dissolve the organisation. In October 1920, the law on
associations was amended to give the government the right to ban organisations it deemed dangerous to state security.

Matters were complicated by the influence of the Bashkirian Bolshevik,
Sharif Manatov, on the Green Army. Manatov was undoubtedly one of the most
interesting figures on the left-wing of the emerging communist movement. He
was giving lectures in Eskehir, a centre of radical agitation, and much of the
Green Army press coming out of Eskehir was showing 'through various theo-
logical subtleties, that the precepts of Bolshevism were identical to those of
Islam'.[110] A Comintern influence on the Green Army meant that outright repression of its militants, at this delicate juncture for Mustafa Kemal, could create
problems with the Soviet Union. Kemal's solution was to create, in late October,
an 'official' Communist Party sponsored by the state. Having integrated some
Green Army militants (including Cerkes Edhem) into the official party and
moved its press to Ankara, Kemal then dissolved the Green Army. A number

---

108   According to Harris 2002, some 'more or less conservative politicians in Anatolia were
      drawn to this rough-hewn Islamic Communism in the spring of 1920' (p. 45).

109   Ibid. p. 349.

110   Ibid. p. 354. In fact, the declarations emanating from Eskehir in the summer of 1920
      were more radical than the programme adopted at the founding congress of the Turkish
      Communist Party in Baku in the following September. The Eskehir group stated that the
      national liberation movement was 'in the hands of the bourgeoisie'. It pointed to the
      prominence of former CUP (Young Turk) members in the Kemalist regime and said that
      it supported neither the Ottoman government in Istanbul nor the Kemalists in Ankara. It
      denounced conscription, religion and the family (ICC pamphlet, p. 8).

of Edhem's irregulars were integrated into the Kemalist army. Edhem, catch-
ing the drift of events, tried to provoke a resistance, which proved futile. The
government issued an edict prohibiting the recruitment of irregular forces by
anyone, for whatever reason. Completely outflanked, Edhem's troops disbanded or were crushed as part of the general repression of early January 1921, and
Edhem fled. The Kemalist government then integrated the publishing operations of the former Green Army into the official state press.[111] On 8 January,
as part of the wave of repression of December 1920 – January 1921, Kemal violently denounced Edhem and the 'propagators of communism' before the Grand
National Assembly.

b *The People's Party*

The People's Party (Halk firkasi) was another means by which Green Army
militants could adapt themselves to Kemalist institutions, even though some of
its members refused such integration. In the summer of 1920, it made up more
than one-fourth of the deputies in the Grand National Assembly in Ankara, the
largest opposition to the Kemalists. It took over wholesale the Green Army's
mix of Bolshevism, Islam and Pan-Asianism. Few people at this juncture had
any clear idea of what Bolshevism meant, beyond popular resistance to the
Allies. Cheik Servet, a major party spokesman, argued in the wake of the Baku
Congress that the task was allying with the Bolsheviks for a jihad against the
West. For Servet, Bolshevism's principles were those of Islam, namely 'charity
and generosity'.[112]

The People's Party was powerful enough in the Grand National Assembly to
defeat a Kemalist candidate for the powerful post of Minister of the Interior
(in charge of political surveillance) and elect one of its members, Nazim Bey.
Mustafa Kemal was not pleased, and forced his resignation.

Then, in early September, the People's Party presented a programme of
somewhat radical measures that would clearly lead to a divisive debate in
the assembly. These included an assertion of popular sovereignty, specified
intellectual and manual workers as the real source of power, and affirmed the
'sacred precepts of Islam', above all fraternity, as the means for struggle against
the vices of the West. It argued for democratic assemblies at every level of
public life, a struggle against alcoholism and criminality, free and mandatory
public education, land distribution and the easing of tax burdens.[113]

---

111 This account of the dismantling of the Green Army and its absorption by state organs is
     from Dumont 1997, pp. 354–8.
112 Ibid. p. 360.
113 Ibid. p. 362.

Kemal Pasha met this threat by lifting much of the People's Party programme into his own, in less provocative language. Outflanked, the People's Party acquiesced and Kemal's programme, instead of theirs, went to the constitutional commission. The new constitutional law of 20 January 1921 affirmed fidelity to the person of the sultan-caliph, to Islam and to the institutions of the Ottoman monarchy.

c   *The 'Official' Turkish Communist Party*

Created as a grab-bag to defuse the Bolshevik influenced elements of the Green Army, the official Turkish Communist Party was founded in late October 1920 as a prop to Kemalist power. All communist groups were ordered by the Ministry of the Interior to cease activity or join the new party. For the government, the official TCP was the only form of Bolshevism appropriate for Turkey since, in contrast to Russia, all strata of Turkish society were subjugated to the oppression of Western imperialism.[114] To avoid the confusion of workers' and soldiers' soviets, Kemal ordered Ali Fuad Pasha, Kemalist commander of the Western front, to become a member of the party's central committee, so that the party would be 'in the hands of the highest commanders of the army'.[115] The arrival, also in October, of an important Soviet mission in Ankara was the occasion for a wave of pro-communist articles in the nationalist press, as a gesture to the Soviet Union.[116] Much of the new party's programme strangely echoed the People's Party programme co-opted by Mustafa Kemal. The party statutes stated that those arguing for the suppression of property were 'supporters of imperialism and capitalism', reasserted the identity of communist principles with Islam, and the party's complete independence from Moscow. Nevertheless, the party's newspaper was suppressed by the government in January 1921 in the general crackdown on all left organisations, and the party, with no public presence, faded away.

---

114   Ibid. p. 369.

115   Ibid.

116   G.S. Harris, on the other hand, identifies October 1920 as the moment at which the communist presence in Anatolia became truly worrisome to the bourgeois-dominated Grand National Assembly. Kemal had 'based his whole movement on the existing bourgeois elite'. In that month the Minister of Economics presented a report on the practical difficulties of cooperation with the Soviet Union. In the debate following that report, most deputies' attitudes turned to suspicion of Soviet motives. On the following day, Attatürk announced the creation of the 'official' TCP (Harris 2002, pp. 27–34).

9   The People's Communist Party: The National Question Point-Blank

The serious Turkish communist party which survived, and emerged from, these ideological shifts and dubious fellow-travellers such as the Islamo-Communists ultimately polarised between the right-wing, Sefik Hüsnü's Aydinlik group, and the left-wing, the Anatolian current represented by Sharif Manatov and Salih Hacioglu, and, following Manatov's expulsion from Turkey, Hacioglu.

The People's Communist Party (Türkiye halk istirakiyyun firkasi) was created in the summer of 1920, possibly in contact with Mustafa Suphi's organisation in Baku.[117] It emerged from a network of propaganda groups in Istanbul, Eskisehir and the ports of the Black Sea, as well as militants of the Green Army who had gone underground rather than be co-opted. It included, as indicated, Manatov and Hacioglu, the latter destined to be the left's spokesman right up to its liquidation in Turkey and in Russia. The party programme was strikingly similar to that of the Green Army, with the important exception of an assertion of the separation of religion and state. On 14 July 1920, a proclamation published in Eskisehir announced 'to the peasants and workers' of Anatolia the creation of a Turkish Communist Party affiliated with the Third International. The party militants even managed to organise demonstrations against forced conscription in Eskisehir. Financing for a party press and other activities arrived in October with the Soviet mission in Ankara.

Mustafa Kemal quickly attacked this clandestine party through the 'official' Communist Party and expelled Manatov from Turkey in October 1920. Most militants of the clandestine party refused to bend and launched their counterattack in November. Salih Hacioglu and others from the core group fused with some deputies of the left-wing of the People's Party and founded the Türkiye halk istirakiyyun firkasi, with Hacioglu playing a key role. They issued a circular announcing the creation of the new party and insisting that it alone was the real continuity with the now co-opted Green Army, while denouncing the 'official' Communist Party[118] in the name of the Third International and of Bolshevism. The party statutes and programme were nonetheless recognized by the Ministry of the Interior at the end of December 1920 and the party briefly became legal.

---

117   Ibid. p. 374.

118   The Manatov-influenced newspaper *Seyyare-I Yeni Dünya*, published in Eskisehir, had in the summer launched the slogan 'Workers of the World Unite!' In a speech to the Grand National Assembly, 'Attatürk said that "this organ alone had broken its promise to follow instructions to support his revolutionary movement"' (Harris 2002, p. 27).

It was, to put it mildly (as Paul Dumont underscores),[119] a bad time to emerge from clandestinity. As has been shown previously, at the end of 1920 and the beginning of 1921 the Kemalist regime was bent on liquidating the Anatolian left. The party nonetheless forged ahead, launched its daily newspaper, *Emek* (*Labour*) in mid-January, and created an uproar. The editorial of the first issue argued that the Koran was hostile to private property and to capitalism. It made no concessions to others' attempts to tailor communism to any special Turkish conditions. A major effort, however, during the paper's brief existence, was to reconcile Bolshevism with the Islamic tradition. The paper was banned after it reprinted an article from a Bulgarian communist newspaper attacking the dictatorial nature of Kemalism and predicting civil war in Anatolia. On 8 January, as indicated earlier, Mustafa Kemal had made his violently anti-Communist speech.

Salih Hacioglu was arrested on 11 January, and, shortly thereafter, Muslim clerics issued a fatwa calling on believers to avoid communist groups. At the end of January, most party leaders were arrested, excepting only three who had parliamentary immunity. The party was dissolved on 2 February. In April 1921, even the parliamentary deputies were stripped of immunity, convicted of attempting to overthrow the government, and sentenced to 15 years of hard labour. Less prominent figures received shorter sentences.[120]

This heavy repression did not, however, snuff out the activities of communist militants in Anatolia. The new rapprochement between Turkey and the Soviet Union, marked (as indicated previously) by Frunze's visit in December 1921, was preceded by amnesties of many of those arrested, including Salih Hacioglu.[121]

---

119   Dumont 1997, p. 379.

120   This account is, yet again, drawn from Dumont 1997, pp. 380–1. On 29 September 1921, however, two weeks after the military victory at Sakarya which turned the tide of the war against the Greeks, the Grand National Assembly voted to amnesty the communists arrested in the previous January, in a new rapprochement with the Soviet Union motivated by a need for money and arms. In this juncture, the Kemalist government decided to wipe the slate clean on Soviet support for Enver Pasha (for whom the victory at Sakarya had been the swan song), to provide aid to victims of the famine in Russia, and to sign, on 13 October, the Treaty of Kars, which put an end to border disputes in the east (Dumont 1997, p. 384).

121   Dumont interprets this amnesty as a gesture toward the Soviet government at a time when the Kemalists were badly in need of arms and funds to continue the campaign against the Greeks after the victory at Sakarya (ibid. p. 383) A new crisis emerged in mid-1922. 'The relations between the government and the Anatolian communist movement would, of course, follow a strictly parallel evolution. When, on one hand, when it was necessary to cultivate the Soviets, the Turkish militants would benefit from a benevolent

The following is Paul Dumont's interpretation of the situation of Turkish communism at this juncture, in a passage worth quoting at length:

> The dissolution of the People's Communist Party ... marks a turning point in the history of the Turkish 'left'. For nearly a year, various groups of militants scattered around Anatolia would be forced to slacken their activity. When the PCPT arose again from its ashes in March 1922, it had lost a large part of its vitality and spontaneity. Thereafter we find a doctrinaire movement, cut off from active political life and completely domesticated by the Communist International.

> Compared to this cautious and drab left, of the later period, the 1920 left was characterised, overall, by its combativity, its candor in matters of doctrine, and also by its wiliness. Further ... we are not talking about one left, but several, which are inextricably interpenetrated. Through the multiplicity of individual positions, we can distinguish, with a little benevolence, three major currents. A nationalist, even ultra-nationalist current, whose main idea seems to have been exploiting communist effervescence to create a Greater Turanian Turkey reaching from Constantinople to Bukhara. A moderate current, represented by Hakki Behic, careful above all to avoid a social upheaval, and an advocate of reforms granted and managed by the state. Finally, there was an 'extremist' current, in thrall to the ideas of the October Revolution, but in no way ready to throw overboard the cultural and social traditions of the country.

> What strikes us, in these three currents, is the central role they assign to Islam. With their eyes on the West, Ottoman socialists before the First World War cheerfully ignored the Islamic phenomenon. For the Turkish left of 1920, based in the heart of Anatolia, its eyes fixed on the East, Islam was on the contrary a permanent obsession ...

> Once the Third International succeeded in integrating the Anatolian communist movement, this concern with justification by Islam disappeared totally from the ideological baggage of the Turkish militants. After 1922, we see a garden-variety Marxism take hold in Turkey, one that

---

indifference. When, on the other hand, when peace with the Entente seemed within reach, the Communists would on the contrary have to deal with harassment, reprimands and, finally, with repression. In short, the same scenario as 1920–1921' (ibid. p. 384).

was certainly convincing, but somewhat oblivious to the economic, cultural and social realities of the country. This transformation of ideas was accompanied by a change in recruitment. The Green Army, the Populist group, the official Communist Party and the People's Communist Party had been infiltrated by a mass of former members of the Committee for Union and Progress. After the failure, in September 1921, of the putsch planned by Enver Pasha against the government of Mustafa Kemal, these Unionists definitively turned away from the ideas of the left, which had shown themselves to be inoperative in the confrontation with Kemalist nationalism. These 'extremists' found themselves left to their own devices, not knowing very well what to do with the doctrine provided by the Comintern, and aware of having missed the train of the revolution.[122]

Such, at any rate, is Dumont's learned but ultimately academic view. He is, however, seemingly oblivious to the explicit left-wing opposition coming from Anatolia to Sefik Hüsnu and the Aydinlik group, and the debate that erupted in the party over support to bourgeois national liberation, i.e., the Kemalist movement. The anti-nationalist stance of Salih Hacioglu and the left-wing base was hardly 'drab'.

The PCPT was allowed to resume legal existence in spring 1922, but repression tightened again and it was forced to hold its party congress in September in clandestinity, in Ankara.[123] The congress voted, in line with the directives of

---

122   In this characterisation of the pre- and post-1922 period, Dumont (ibid. p. 384) is talking about the dominance of Sefik Hüsnu and the Aydinlik faction. His portrait seems to totally omit the left wing described in the ICC pamphlet. Harris 2002, p. 40, also notes three streams in early Turkish communism: 'unlike almost all other Communist movements'. At the Third Congress of the Comintern in June–July 1921, one Turkish Communist had called for purging the PCPT of all undesirable elements, including the 'provocateurs' working for the Ankara government, the followers of Enver Pasha and the pan-Turanists of the Green Army (Dumont 1997, p. 385). Apparently the Balkan parties, led by the Bulgarians, were involved in this rectification, but many local organisations were in no hurry to rid themselves of 'heterodox' elements such as the Enverists and members of the 'official' Communist Party. This was part of the new strategy of the 'conquest of the masses' laid down by the Third Congress.

123   Dumont 1997, p. 400, seems to acknowledge the presence of the left wing at the clandestine conference, without providing details: 'Confronted with the new attitude adopted by the authorities [i.e. repression – LG] shouldn't the party resolve itself to stop supporting the Kemalist movement? There is every reason to believe the discussion was intense. But Zorine and the other delegates from the Comintern were there to make sure the directives of the International were respected. In spite of the climate of repression which

the Third Congress of the Comintern, to support the Kemalist revolution for the time being. It also announced a certain orientation to the Turkish peasantry, the great majority of the population.

Party militants, with the left predominating, did manage to get a significant worker confederation off the ground in Cilicia, in southeastern Turkey. The confederation's congress, attended by the full Central Committee of the PCTP and 40 proletarian delegates, called in early October 1922 for the eight-hour day, a guaranteed minimum wage, paid vacations, and collective bargaining contracts. The congress attacked the anti-worker policies of Kemalist anti-communist Prime Minister Rauf bey, declaring that 'the working class, which lost so many sons in the struggle against Western imperialism ... would be compelled to no longer offer its support'.[124]

Be that as it may, on 11 October, the contending armies signed the Armistice of Mudanya ending the Turko-Greek war, and a new shift to the right was imminent. In the midst of national celebrations of the military victory, the PCTP was dissolved by the government, which accused it of treason and of espionage on behalf of the Soviet Union. Sixty-odd party militants, including a number of working-class sympathisers, were arrested in Ankara on 20 October, and a few days later further arrests followed throughout Anatolia. The new Cilician confederation was also banned. All in all, 200 people had been arrested. Salih Hacioglu and a handful of party leaders escaped the dragnet because they were en route to the Fourth Congress of the Comintern in Moscow.

Once again, for the Soviet government and the Comintern, the importance of the relationship to the Kemalist government trumped solidarity with the political prisoners. The French Communist Party newspaper *l'Humanité* simply ran the headline 'Hands Off Turkey'. Izvestia and *Pravda* continued to hail Turko-Soviet friendship and fretted about whether the Soviet Union would be included in the Lausanne Conference, where the terms of the peace would be finalised in spring 1923. The Kemalist abolition of the sultanate on 1 November was widely commented upon in the international communist press, but not the political prisoners.

---

was setting in, the congress decided that the ... [party] ... would continue to support the actions of the government'. The ICC, again, paints a rather different picture, saying that the Aydinlik faction of Sefik Hüsnü boycotted the congress because of the left's position against national liberation movements, and that the left dominated the central committee. With the significant presence of Comintern officials, the left failed to get its opposition to national liberation movements ratified (ICC pamphlet, p. 14).

124   Dumont 1997, p. 408.

Only on 15 November did long articles on the repression in Turkey appear on the front pages of *Izvestia* and *Pravda*. In the interim two weeks, the Kemalists had continued various anti-communist harassments. The Soviet embassy in Ankara had been forced to close its commercial outlet and a Soviet courier's diplomatic pouch had been confiscated. In Paul Dumont's estimate, these harassments, combined with the preoccupation over the Lausanne conference, were the pinpricks that brought about the change in tone.[125]

A new silence on the repression descended on the international communist press in late November. The Lausanne Conference opened on 20 November with Soviet participation, and the settlement of the status of the Straits loomed large in the offing. On 22 November, a major article by Karl Radek in *Pravda* asserted that the Soviet Union would 'support the legitimate demands of Turkey' at Lausanne and that critics in the West of the inconsistencies of Soviet policy

> did not understand that, at bottom, our position is absolutely independent of tactical maneuvers or the internal policy of the Turkish government … But in spite of all deviations and zigzags, Soviet Russia is following the great historical road on which the international industrial proletariat can march together with the liberation movements of the peoples of the East in the struggle against international capital.[126]

The Fourth Congress of the Comintern dotted the i's by reaffirming the decisions of the Third Congress, inviting communists of the colonial or semi-colonial world to collaborate with 'bourgeois democracy'. Communists, in contrast to what Lenin had said in 1920, might even collaborate with the pan-Islamists.[127] This support for the nationalist bourgeoisie in the semi-colonial and colonial world was reiterated in a speech by Karl Radek. Salih Hacioglu sent the following reply to the Comintern delegates:

> … the latest attack and assault, which was directed at the Turkish Communist Party by the national bourgeoisie, which acquired its class consciousness thanks to the financial and political aid from the Soviet government …[128]

---

125   Ibid. p. 411. The entire back-and-forth between the arrests and the official Soviet and Comintern attitude is recounted in Dumont 1997, pp. 408–15.

126   Quoted ibid. pp. 414–15.

127   Ibid. p. 415.

128   ICC pamphlet, p. 16.

would, he said, neither beat the Turkish communists into submission nor stop the social revolution.

With the end of military hostilities and the reunification of the country, the focus of communist activity shifted from Anatolia to Istanbul,

> with its countless artisanal shops, food industries, tanneries, tobacco processing plants, its textile industries, soap manufacture, naval shipyards and its port and railway installations, the most important 'proletarian' agglomeration in the Near East.[129]

Following the Anatolian crackdown of October 1922, Sefik Husnü's group in Istanbul was the only legal left-wing organisation in the new Turkey. The sultan, in the last days of Ottoman power, had indeed carried out similar arrests in Istanbul, forcing a number of militants to flee abroad. But tensions between the Allies and the Kemalist regime during the Lausanne negotiations provoked yet another shift in Turkish-Soviet relations. Following the Fourth Congress of the Comintern, Hüsnü, with a base in Istanbul, and Salih Hacioglu, back from Russia and representing Anatolia, faced each other as the two key figures of Turkish communism. As a disciplined Comintern party, its task was to continue supporting the Kemalist regime while at the same time preparing for the coming proletarian revolution, a support which Hacioglu and his base rejected. Hüsnü's journal *Aydinlik* (whose 'Spartakist' origins have already been discussed) became the party's theoretical expression in Istanbul. Hüsnü and his followers applied the new Third International tactic of 'conquering the masses' and sought a mass organisation to 'enter', but they were excluded from the only real worker-based organisation in Istanbul, the General Workers' Union of Sakir Rasim, a seasoned union militant. Rasim and his militant followers had real success in a campaign against foreign enterprises, to the approval of the Kemalists and the Turkish employers, while leaving the *Aydinlik* group on the margins.

The Hüsnü faction of the TCP, however, got its chance when the 'official' Communist Party announced a nationwide economic congress in Smyrna, to convene in February 1923. The congress was to group peasants and farm hands, business people, workers, industrialists and artisans to draw up ambitious economic reforms for the new regime. Huge local energies went into drawing up

---

129   Dumont 1997, p. 419. The Turkish CP, in addition to its recognition of the role of the agitation of the Greek Communists in determining the outcome of the 1919–22 war by provoking significant desertions from the Greek armies, also called on communist workers in Allied-occupied Istanbul to fraternise with the British, French and Italian soldiers there (ICC pamphlet, p. 18).

proposals and programmes. Sefik Hüsnü drew up a programme for a workers' commission that called for, among other things, the eight-hour day, an absolute ban on child labour, three days' leave per month for women, sixteen weeks' maternity leave, a weekly rest period, abolition of all legal limits on the right to strike and to association, a health care system and even 'factory committees' for communication between workers and bosses.[130] A further text with a programme for the entire Turkish economy, appearing in *Aydinlik*, called for the modernisation of Turkish agriculture and a series of measures improving the situation of the Anatolian peasantry, as well as dealing with other sectors. This document was notable by its recognition of the necessity of accepting, for the interim, the inevitability of dealing with foreign capital. *Aydlinlik*, echoing its elitist Clarté origins discussed earlier, was in effect calling for the state-sponsored creation of a Turkish capitalist class:

> ... the State should favor the creation of cooperatives aimed at serving the internal market and take charge of all foreign commerce ... most urgent was the nationalization of the railway companies or at least partial nationalization through the purchase of shares ... and finally the creation of a real public service dedicated to opening up Anatolia.[131]

The congress began in mid-February 1923, lasting ten days. The Soviet ambassador as well as the ambassador from Azerbaijan arrived on the same train as Mustafa Kemal and caused a sensation by their presence on the congress's tribunal of honor. 'Anti-imperialism', during the negotiations at Lausanne, was the order of the day. The authorities had taken care to choose 'worker' del-

---

130   Ibid. p. 430. At times, Hüsnü even went so far as to deny the existence of classes in Turkey, because the entire nation was oppressed by imperialism.

131   Ibid. p. 431. Dumont points out that these anti-foreign ideas were 'in the air', to be found in any number of Turkish newspapers at the time. Hüsnü's programme stood out by its call for a fundamental shakeup of Turkey's socio-economic structures. G.S. Harris documents that Hüsnü had already argued as early as 1921 in Aydinlik for the 'need to support state capitalism' and that 'support of the petty bourgeoisie in Turkey's case was likely to provide a more efficient transition to the eventual classless society'. Hüsnü also 'opposed measures that would discourage artisans and small entrepreneurs from investing or modernizing their enterprises' (Harris 2002, p. 53.)

   By 1930, various former Aydinlik associates had gravitated toward the openly statist Kadro group, which conceived itself as a 'think tank' for Kemalism. These included Sevket Süreyya Aydenir, already Minister of Education by the late 1920s, and Vedat Nedin Tör, former Communist Secretary General (Harris 1969, pp. 142–3.) All the key figures of the Kadro group came from an Aydinlik background.

egates (187 total, many of them having no working-class credentials) with an eye to sidelining potential subversives. The congress was divided into four working groups: agriculture, commerce, industry and labour. The more circumspect General Union of Workers from Istanbul presented a more moderate programme than Hüsnü's, more oriented to petitioning the employers for benevolence. Despite hostility from the commerce and industry sections, which introduced their amendments, the worker delegation managed to get its programme forwarded to the government. The ability of the small worker minority present to expedite its platform against serious hostility inspired Sefik Hüsnü to congratulate the Turkish worker delegation on its maturity and its ability to make itself heard by the other social classes present.[132] Hüsnü and the Socialist Party of Workers and Farm Laborers, with the war over and a significant impact at the national conference, thought their moment, after the chill of the fall arrests, had arrived.

Once again, Hüsnü and the *Aydinlik* group made their calculations without anticipating the pendulum swing of Turko-Soviet relations. They failed to reckon with the fact that after their triumph at Lausanne, the Kemalists no longer needed the Soviet alliance. Some propaganda volleys had been exchanged during the Lausanne peace talks, over real or apparent Turkish concessions to the Allies. Then, the masks came off. Kemalist 'health inspectors' raided the offices of Hüsnü's party and proceeded to arrest Salih Hacioglu. On 17 March, an ad hoc tribunal launched the trial of the militants arrested the previous October, as well as Salih Hacioglu and a number of radical workers. During the Lausanne détente, the Russians had tried to obtain the freedom of those arrested through official channels. Suddenly Hüsnü's group, reeling from the newest shock, and having itself presented candidates in the December 1919 elections, could only manage to issue a minimum programme to ferret out the 'progressives' among those running. Hüsnü merely urged supporters to vote for the Kemalists, barring the way to 'reaction'. The Soviet and Turkish newspapers exchanged propaganda volleys. On 21 April, a new wave of harassment and then arrests followed, this time netting Sefik Hüsnu and other party leaders. Aralov, the ambassador in Ankara, was asked to take a leave, and several employees of the Soviet consul in Istanbul were expelled from Turkey.

Now the international communist press rose to the occasion, with *Pravda* headlining 'White Terror in Turkey' in May. But mere weeks later, those arrested during the 'white terror' were acquitted and released at the end of May. Those

---

132   Dumont 1997, p. 436.

arrested in October 1922, charged under a law prescribing the death penalty, were condemned to three months imprisonment plus a fine.

Numbed by these experiences, Sefik Hüsnü and his militants were unable to take up the challenge of mass work (which had never been their strong suit) when the climate between Russia and Turkey improved again, following their release. Instead, it was the opportunist, moderate General Union of Workers that was able to take advantage of the strike wave in the summer of 1923. The signing of the Treaty of Lausanne on 24 July 1923 gave the signal. A wave of nationalism and even xenophobia, based on the long humiliations of the past, made foreign companies the targets of preference. Moslem workers demanded the firing of Christian blue- and white-collar workers, and the expulsion of European managers. Greek and Armenian emigration intensified. The intensity of anti-foreigner feeling among the strikers and the resulting militancy at foreign companies made it possible for Kemalist officials to publicly sympathise. In some locales, Turkish workers turned against the non-Turkish and non-Moslem minorities. A wave of measures followed in October, enforcing Turkish as the sole public language, not only in commerce and industry, but in everything from advertising to the sub-titles of films. Foreign companies were required in October 1923 to employ only Turkish Moslems. The General Union of Workers, which had earlier already tried its hand at nationalism and xenophobia, rode the wave, even as it cultivated ties with the British Labour Party and the Second International. At the proclamation of the Turkish Republic on 29 October 1923, Sefik Hüsnü's group, unable to go against the nationalist and xenophobic mood of many strikers and never as strongly rooted in the working class as the Anatolian faction, was again an isolated sect.

On 3 March 1924, the caliphate was abolished and education in Turkey was fully secularised. In the wake of the strike wave, 1924 proved to be a good year for expansion of unions. Sefik Hüsnu's journal *Aydinlik* expanded its base in the Istanbul intelligentsia. On 26 November 1923, during the railway strike, Sakir Rasim and the General Union of the Workers of Istanbul had convoked a congress with 250 delegates representing 19,000 workers. The organisation was renamed the General Union of the Workers of Turkey. A figure close to the Kemalists and a member of their People's Party was chosen as vice-president, and made overtures to the government as well as anti-communist statements. The Kemalist government remained suspicious of the Union's ties to the Second International, and ordered it to disband on 18 December. Well-placed friends of the Union's Kemalist vice-president, however, issued a counter-order, and its fate remained in the balance until May. In January 1924 there had also been a push for a new labour law, as had been promised the previous year at the economic conference. Sakir Rasim, the Union leader, attempted to get traction with a letter of 2 February from Kemal promising such a new law. The dead-lock dragged on, during which Sefik Hüsnü had a rapprochement with Rasim. After another large May Day rally, in mid-May a court finally ordered the Union to cease its activities. Workers, however, responded during the summer of 1924 with spontaneous actions at foreign companies. A tramway strike erupted in July. The police were called, several strikers were wounded, and 30 people were arrested. A postal strike followed, answered by a lockout, and was defeated by the use of scabs. Worker agitation spread to Anatolia, first of all with railway strikes, including in Eskisehir, from which so much anti-Kemalist politics had emerged. The government responded by bringing in French, Greek and Bul-garian (Christian) strikebreakers.

In September 1924, the dissolved Union was reborn under the name 'Associ-ation for Worker Relief', attempting to appear as a Kemalist organisation. But Rasim and Hüsnü had other ideas. Socialists and Communists worked together to infiltrate and control the organisation. Hüsnü himself joined as an agitator. The same sectors as in 1923 mobilised around the same demands, and, as in the previous year, defeat followed defeat.

In February 1925 a vast Kurdish revolt broke out in eastern Turkey, led by one Chaikh Said. On 4 March, the Grand National Assembly voted full powers to the government and a state of emergency was declared. In this climate, the worker militants retreated.

The Kurdish revolt pushed the Kemalists back toward a rapprochement with the Soviet Union. Turkey's international position looked serious, with a possible military threat from Iran and tension with Britain over Mosul. The Soviet Union and Turkey once again needed each other.

Once again, the dialectic of rapprochement with the Soviet government, coupled with internal repression, marked a new swing of the pendulum, and Hüsnü's journal *Aydinlik* was suppressed in February 1925. The final issues had been evolving in a more and more openly pro-Soviet direction. In May 1924 Hüsnü had expressed disappointment with the 'bourgeois' Republic, even as he continued to urge support for Kemal against the 'imperialists'. He criticised the liberal economic tendencies in the regime and called for more statist policies. He was in effect evolving a theory of a state capitalist 'stage' for Turkey.[133] After the mid-1924 suppression of the tobacco monopoly, controlled by foreign capital, Hüsnü called for more state monopolies. Statist measures

---

133   This state capitalism would become fully explicit, once again, in the ideology of the Kadro group in the early 1930s, formed, as previously indicated, of ex-Aydinlik collaborators. See Harris 2002.

were supported in *Aydinlik* in industry, foreign trade, communications, and the tertiary sector. Articles on agriculture called for 'expropriation of large properties' and free distribution of land to the poor peasants.

At the Fifth Congress of the Comintern in 1924, Hüsnü and *Aydinlik* were attacked by the Ukranian Manuilsky and accused of class collaboration, even though the Turks had only been rigorously applying the Comintern line of support for bourgeois national liberation against imperialism. Manuilsky was simply making an example of the Turks for the benefit of all the parties of the colonial and semi-colonial world. Sefik Hüsnü in reply argued that Turkey was only at the beginning of its national liberation. The critique did push Hüsnü and the party militants to pay more attention to the worker milieu.

In January 1925, the Turkish Communist Party held a clandestine Third Congress in Hüsnü's house in Istanbul, with a large contingent of Comintern officials again present. Salih Hacioglu, freshly out of prison, attended, but was now in a distinct minority against the *Aydinlik* faction, fully in control with Stalinist backing. The Congress undertook an assessment of the charges made the previous year by Manuilsky, and Sefik Hüsnü, while retained as secretary general, had to make his self-criticism. The new central committee was identical to the editorial board of *Aydinlik*. The party's agitational journal was revived, and closer ties to the Union for Worker Relief were planned. The left later blasted the right-wing leadership:

> The ruling group of the Central Committee means nothing other than the editorial board of ... Aydlinlik ... This board consists of sectarian writers who have no connection to the proletarian masses ... This newspaper tells the workers to increase the national accumulation of capital ...[134]

In mid-May, in the ongoing repression following the Kurdish revolt, forty party members were arrested. Hüsnü had taken precautions – the left hinted that he was forewarned by friends in the regime – and fled to Germany. The above-ground organisation in Istanbul was crushed, with virtually all members in hiding or in exile. The trials began in mid-August, after the Kurdish revolt had been put down. Sefik Hüsnü and others who had gone into exile got 15-year sentences at hard labour in absentia. From that time on, the party, with 500–600 members at most, had to remain underground.

The left took a rather different view of the whole affair:

---

134 Quoted in ICC pamphlet, p. 20.

> The class basis of this central committee became obvious after the government closed down Aydinlik ... Of course all the other members of the Central Committee found the magical time to take refuge in the houses of their royal relatives in Constantinople and Germany. Perhaps they had been warned by someone from the government before the arrests.[135]

Salih Hacioglu in November 1925 made a last appeal at the Eastern office of the Comintern to have the *Aydinlik* group demoted from party leadership, but Stalin was now fully in control and Hacioglu got nowhere. By this time, the left-wing of the party was dispersed, in prison, in exile and increasingly in the camps in the Soviet Union:

> For every critical remark made, our worker comrades are exiled to the far corners of the USSR. There our worker comrades are not left with any choice other than starvation, freezing to death or committing suicide. For this reason we declare that the royal hands of the current members of the Central Committee are red with the blood of our comrades who died or committed suicide.[136]

With Salih Hacioglu's removal from the party's Central Committee (1926) and his expulsion from the party itself (1928), and finally his arrest and deportation to the camps (1929), culminating this process of dispersion and disappearance of many lesser known figures, the Turkish communist left's real historical existence came to an end. It has been worthwhile telling their story as a remarkable example of a current which, at the earliest possible moment, saw the reality of 'anti-imperialism' in the Soviet government's rapprochement with bourgeois regimes (above all, Turkey and Persia) while communist militants in those countries were shot and imprisoned, in the Turkish case with Soviet arms and money. Today's 'anti-imperialist' cheerleaders would do well to understand the anti-working class thrust of their own ideology and see capitalism in the 'advanced' as in the 'developing' world as a seamless whole, posing the same tasks for those who would truly go beyond it, and not merely reorganise it. This was true in Turkey in the early 1920s and all the more true in Venezuela, Bolivia, Iran and Afghanistan today. It was the great merit of the Turkish communist left

---

135   Quoted from ibid. 'A list of the social class backgrounds of those in the party leadership and those involved with the opposition was added at the end of the declaration; indeed there was not a single person in the Central Committee made up of the ex-Aydinlik editorial board who came from the working class'.

136   Quoted in ICC pamphlet, p. 20.

of the earlier period to reject 'critical support' for national liberation in order to embrace internationalism, and we can best pull their story out of the history books and into living reality by doing the same.

Appendix: Core Chronology

While assembling the material for this article (October–November 2009), I myself found the complexity of the narrative and the simultaneity of interrelated events hard to keep straight. To remedy this for the reader, I append this more or less straightforward chronology.

- 1876 to 1908: occasional important strikes in the Ottoman naval shipyards, at the tobacco monopoly and on the railroads.
- Pan-Turanism has its first exponent in Ismael Gasprinski (1841–1914), a Crimean Turk, who in 1878 founded the first newspaper in Turkish, *Tergüman*.
- Tatar intellectual, Sihabäddin Märcani (1818–89) also articulated the idea of a 'Tatar nation', possibly the first ideology for a modern territorial nation in the Turkic world (in contrast to the supra-territorial institutions of the Ottomans)
- The most important founding theoretician of Turkish nationalism, Ziya Gökalp (1875–1924) used Herderian and broadly German romantic cultural ideas to create a Pan-Turkic equivalent of Pan-Slavism.
- 1908: Young Turks (Committee for Union and Progress, CUP) seize power.
- 1909: Conservative counter-attack on Young Turks by the religious establishment.
- 1909: In response, the CUP pushes through constitutional reforms severely reducing the power of the sultan and the cabinet, increasing those of parliament, reducing bureaucracy, rationalising tax collection and modernising the armed forces.
- 1910: Ottoman and Balkan adherents of the Second International attempt confederation at a conference in Belgrade.
- 1911: Gasprinski's brother-in-law founds a journal, *Türk Yurdu* (Turkish Homeland).
- 1911–12: Ottoman Empire's war with Italy following Italian annexation of Libya.
- 1911: Italy's invasion of Libya sparks demonstration of 10,000 workers in Salonica; the Second International condemns Italian imperialism. 20,000 Salonica workers turn out for 1911 May Day demonstration.

- 1912–13: Two generalised Balkan Wars; Greece annexes Salonica; Ottoman Empire loses 69 percent of its population and 83 percent of its territory in Europe.
- pre-1914: Naval reorganisation under British auspices.
- 1914: German General Liman von Sanders takes over direct command of the Ottoman First Army.
- September 1914: Ottoman Empire joins WWI on side of Central Powers.
- September 1914: Serbian Social Democrats vote against war credits.
- September 1914: Enver Pasha and his allies in the CUP push through the abolition of the Capitulations, taking over control of customs duties previously controlled by the Western powers.
- 1914: German General von Seeckt becomes chief of Ottoman general staff, other top German officers take over other key posts, including departments of Operations, Intelligence, Railroads, Supply, Munitions, Coal and Fortresses in the Ministry of War.
- 1915: Armenian genocide; over one million people killed.
- 1915–16: courts, schools and religious foundations completely secularised.
- 1915: Kemal Pasha commander of Ottoman forces at Gallipoli.
- February 1917: Revolution in Russia creates bourgeois provisional government.
- November 1917: Bolshevik Revolution.
- January 1918: Ottoman army suppresses the soviet movement in the northeast Anatolian cities of Erzurum, Erzincan, Bayburt and Sivas. Soviets are multi-national and inspired in part by radicalised Russian Army troops following Russian Revolution.
- July 1918: Initial conference of Turkish communists in Moscow.
- September 1918: capture of Baku.
- October 1918: Ottoman surrender. Enver Pasha and other top CUP members forced to flee to Germany (condemned to death in absentia in July 1919).
- October–November 1918: Allied armies occupy Istanbul with Greek troops.
- November 1918: Germany, Austria-Hungary surrender; revolution erupts.
- January 1919: Group of Turks in exile in Germany during the war, in the streets with the Spartakusbund; won over to Marxism and organise in the Party of Workers and Farmers of Turkey (PWFT).
- Mid-1919: Intellectual core of PWFT, with their leaders Ethem Nejat and Sefik Hüsnü, return to Turkey; receive authorisation to resume publication of their journal *Kurtulus*.
- 1919: Enver Pasha and other Young Turks in exile approach the Bolsheviks in 1919 in hope of financial and political support against Kemal Pasha.

- March 1919: Enver Pasha first contacts the Bolsheviks through Karl Radek in Radek's Berlin prison cell.
- Spring 1919: General von Seeckt, with links to the Freikorps and one of Radek's contacts, proposes sending Enver Pasha to Moscow.
- March 1919: Mustafa Kemal goes to Samsun because of social agitation there at urging of Ottoman government and the British occupational forces; mythical beginning of nationalist revolt.
- October–November 1919: Second step in rapprochement between the CUP and the Bolsheviks, in negotiations with the CUP organisation Karakol around the figure of Shal'va Eliava. Retired military officer, Baha Sait, goes to Baku in late 1919, and in January 1920 signs an agreement for an offensive alliance against European imperialism and support to revolutionary efforts in Moslem countries.
- 1919–22: Turko-Greek War; Greece backed by Allies. Elements constituting the Turkish Communist Party (founded September 1920) support the 'war of national liberation'.
- Early 1920: initial so-called 'Turkish Communist Party' founded in Baku at the beginning of 1920; mostly CUP figures.
- May 1920: Mustafa Suphi, key figure in the very early history of the Turkish CP, arrives in Baku (Azerbaijan) with full backing of Comintern.
- May 1920: creation of the 'Green Army'.
- June 1920: Sharif Manatov writes the General Statutes of the Turkish Communist Party which calls for soviets, the abolition of private property, and nationalisations.
- Summer 1920: CUPers in new 'Communist Party' hold further negotiations with Bolsheviks, obtaining arms and gold for the Kemalist resistance.
- Summer 1920: Mustafa Suphi reconstitutes Baku group as the 'Baku section' of the Turkish CP, expels some more dubious figures.
- Summer 1920: People's Communist Party of Turkey (PCPT) (Türkiye halk istirakiyyun firkasi) created in Anatolia, possibly in contact with Mustafa Suphi's organisation in Baku.
- Summer 1920: Sharif Manatov gives lectures in Eskehir, which emerges as a centre of radical agitation.
- July 1920: Mustafa Suphi dispatches envoy to Mustafa Kemal asking Ankara government if Turkish Bolsheviks can create a legal organisation in Anatolia.
- Summer 1920: Cerkes Edhem emerges as a strongman of the Green Army, with 3,000 fighting men, shows the potential to become a rival to Mustafa Kemal. Edhem breaks with Kemalists, and Kemal attempts to dissolve the organisation.

- 14 July 1920. Proclamation in Eskisehir announces 'to the peasants and workers' of Anatolia the creation of a Turkish Communist Party affiliated with the Third International. Party militants organise demonstrations against forced conscription in Eskisehir. The Manatov-influenced newspaper *Seyyare-I Yeni Dünya*, published in Eskisehir, in the summer launches the slogan 'Workers of the World Unite!' In a speech to the Grand National Assembly, 'Attatürk said that "this organ alone had broken its promise to follow instructions to support his revolutionary movement"'.
- July 1920: Second Congress of Third International. Lenin denounce a pan-Asianism as serving the interests of 'Turkish and Japanese imperialism'.
- Summer 1920: People's Party (Halk firkasi), another means by which Green Army militants could adapt themselves to Kemalist institutions, makes up more than one-fourth of the deputies in the Grand National Assembly in Ankara, largest opposition to the Kemalists.
- August 1920: Enver Pasha, dreaming of supplanting Mustafa Kemal with a Soviet-backed invasion of Anatolia, argues for the creation of a 'Union of Islamic Revolutionary Societies' to fight for the Communists' anti-imperialist programme, in exchange for further Soviet military and financial support.
- August 1920: Significant Soviet aid in the form of gold shipments begins to arrive in Anatolia; more follows in December.
- 10 August 1920: Vindictive Allied peace treaty of Sèvres (among other things depriving Turkey of three disputed Armenian provinces) imposed on the surviving Ottoman government in Istanbul.
- 14 August 1920: Mustafa Kemal addresses the (rebel) Grand National Assembly in Ankara on the similarities between the communitarian spirit of Islam and Bolshevism.
- August 1920: Kemal uses occasion of rout of Red Army in Poland to harden his attitude toward communist activity in Anatolia and steal the populist rhetoric of the People's Party (see below).
- August 1920: People's Party powerful enough in Grand National Assembly to defeat a Kemalist candidate for powerful post of Minister of the Interior (in charge of political surveillance) and elects one its members, Nazim Bey. Mustafa Kemal not pleased, forces Nazim Bey's resignation.
- September 1920: Baku Congress of the Toilers of the East. Comintern chairman Grigori Zinoviev, calls for 'jihad' against the West.
- Cheik Servet, a major Islamic-Communist, argues in the wake of the Baku Congress that immediate task is allying with the Bolsheviks for a jihad against the West. For Servet, Bolshevism's principles are those of Islam, namely 'charity and generosity'.

– September 1920: Founding congress of the Turkish Communist Party, super-seding the organisation created in the spring, takes place in Baku imme-diately after Congress of the Toilers of the East. Salih Hacioglu in minority opposing national wars of liberation.

– September 1920: Mustafa Kemal replies ambiguously to Mustafa Suphi's request for legal recognition of Communist activity in Anatolia. Salih Hacio-glu and Sharif Manatov warn Mustafa Suphi of the dangers awaiting Turkish CP members returning to Turkey.

– Early September 1920: People's Party presents a programme of somewhat radical measures with potential for divisive debate in Grand National As-sembly. Kemal Pasha meets this threat by lifting much of People's Party programme into his own. Outflanked, People's Party acquiesces and Kemal's programme, not theirs, goes to the constitutional commission.

– October 1920, the law on associations was amended to give the government the right to ban organisations it deemed dangerous to state security.

– October 1920: Arrival of important Soviet mission in Ankara the occasion for wave of pro-communist articles in the nationalist press, as gesture to the Soviet Union.

– October 1920: Creation in late October of an 'official' Communist Party spon-sored by the state. Having integrated some Green Army militants (including Cerkes Edhem) into official party and moved its press to Ankara, Kemal then dissolves the Green Army. A number of Edhem's irregulars integrated into the Kemalist army. Edhem tries to provoke resistance, which proves futile. Government issues an edict prohibiting the recruitment of irregular forces by anyone. Outflanked, Edhem's troops disbanded or were crushed as part of the general repression of early January 1921, and Edhem fled. The Kemalist government then integrated the publishing operations of the former Green Army into the official state press.

– October 1920: Mustafa Kemal attacks new clandestine Communist Party through 'official' Communist Party; expels Sharif Manatov. To avoid confu-sion of workers' and soldiers' soviets, Kemal orders Ali Fuad Pasha, Kemalist commander of Western front, to become member of the official CP's central committee.

– Fall 1920: Major sticking point between Turkey and the Soviet Union is Armenia, where Bolsheviks commit themselves to right of self-determina-tion; where Kemal Pasha wants three provinces for Turkey previously lost to Tsarist Russia. Kemalist forces push beyond pre-1914 Turkish borders with apparent goal of annexation. Chicherin (then in charge of Soviet for-eign policy) and Soviet government suspicious of secret agreement between Kemal and Allies enabling Britain to open new anti-Soviet front.

- November 1920: In speech in Baku, Stalin lauds Soviet-Turkish relationship.
- November 1920: Mustafa Suphi replies to Kemal's letter announcing that accredited CP mission was leaving for Ankara, pledges not to divide nationalist fighting forces.
- November 1920: Most militants of clandestine party refuse order to liquidate and join 'official' CP; launch counter-attack in November. Salih and others from core group fuse with some deputies of left-wing of the People's Party and found the Türkiye halk istirakiyyun firkasi. They issue circular announcing the creation of new party, while denouncing 'official' Communist Party in name of Third International and Bolshevism.
- November 1920: Collapse of Wrangel's White Army in the Crimea. Subsequent transfer of thousands of Red Army soldiers to the Caucusus. Kemalists calm down and focus on annexing parts of Armenia.
- December 1920: Statutes and programme of new Communist Party recognised by Ministry of the Interior at the end of December 1920; party briefly becomes legal.
- Late 1920: Sefik Hüsnü and Sadrettin Celal resume control of Turkish CP, applying the Comintern line under influence of Baku Congress of the Toilers of the East, and benefiting from the increasing debacle of the Turkish Socialist Party. In 1920–1, the Turkish Socialist Party, with real working-class base and affiliated with Second International, took militant turn in occupied Istanbul with threat of a general strike (January 1921). Another strike was threatened at the gas works in April, followed by May Day demonstration of unprecedented size.
- Early December 1920: Mustafa Suphi and twenty comrades leave Baku for Turkey, apparently convinced by Kemal's letter that they are welcome. In Kars, they receive an official welcome from Kazim Karabekir, Kemalist commander of the Eastern front. At this juncture, government has decided that the Communists should return to Russia. Kazim Karabekir orders the governor of Erzurum, Hamit bey, to whip up press campaign and 'appropriate demonstrations' against Mustafa Suphi and his comrades to dissuade them from remaining in Turkey.
- 8 January 1921: As part of wave of repression of December 1920 – January 1921, Kemal violently denounces Edhem and the 'propagators of communism' before the Grand National Assembly. CP paper banned after it reprints an article from Bulgarian communist newspaper attacking dictatorial nature of Kemalism and predicting civil war in Anatolia.
  Salih arrested on 11 January; shortly thereafter, Muslim clerics issue a fatwa calling on believers to avoid communist groups. CP nonetheless forges ahead, launches daily newspaper, *Emek* (*Labour*) in mid-January. Newspa-

per suppressed by the government in general crackdown on all left organisations; party, with no public presence, fades away.
- January 1921: Outflanked, Edhem's troops disbanded or crushed as part of
the general repression; Edhem flees. Kemalist government then integrates
publishing operations of former Green Army into official state press.
- 20 January 1921: New constitutional law affirms fidelity to the person of the
sultan-caliph, to Islam and to institutions of Ottoman monarchy.
- 22 January 1921: Angry crowd in Erzurum prevents Mustafa Suphi and his
comrades from leaving the train station, and they return toward the coast,
everywhere encountering crowds shouting anti-communist insults and hurling rocks.
- Late January 1921: Most CP party leaders arrested, charged with 'spying for
a foreign power', excepting three who had parliamentary immunity. Party
dissolved on 2 February. Leaders received lengthy prison sentences.
- 28 January 1921: Suphi and 14 CPers arrive in Trabzon where they immediately depart by boat. They are overtaken by another boat, murdered, and
thrown into the sea. (Yahya, the local ferryman who suggested the motorboat, was arrested for the murders. In detention, he threatened to 'talk', and
was murdered in turn. Theories abound on who was behind the killings.)
- January–Febrary 1921. Anti-communist repression in Turkey draws no comment in Moscow. Emphasis is on progress of Turko-Russian 'friendship'.
- February 1921: Dissolution of People's Communist Party.
- 17 February 1921: Turkish negotiators arrive in Moscow. Armenian question
still a central source of tension. Military confrontation also seems possible
in Georgia, where both Red Army and Turkish troops are present. Turkish
Minister of Foreign Affairs, Bekir Sami, makes anti-communist speeches in
capitals of Europe.
- March 1921: In the Soviet Union, Kronstadt rebellion, Anglo-Soviet trade
agreement, the implementation of the 'New Economic Policy' (NEP), in
Germany, defeat of the 'March Action', underscoring isolation of Russian
Revolution.
- 16 March 1921: In order to retain alliance with Kemalist regime, the Soviet
government signs a 'treaty of friendship and fraternity' with Turkey, same
day as Anglo-Soviet trade agreement signed in Moscow. The Kemalist government agrees to crack down on pan-Turanian agitation aimed at Russia,
and the Soviet government agrees not to promote anti-Kemalist agitation in
Turkey.
- April 1921: Communist parliamentary deputies stripped of immunity, convicted of attempting to overthrow government, sentenced to 15 years hard
labour. Less prominent figures receive shorter sentences.

- 1 May 1921: The mass demonstration organised by the TSP.
- May 1921: First mention of January murders of Mustafa Suphi et al. appear in the Soviet press.
- June–July 1921: Third Congress of the Comintern. One Turkish Communist calls for purging the party of all undesirable elements, including the 'provocateurs' working for the Ankara government, the followers of Enver Pasha and the pan-Turanists of the Green Army.
- In late July 1921, Greek victory over the Kemalists seems close at hand; Enver Pasha prepares invasion of Turkey with Soviet money and arms.
- September 1921: Kemal's victory at Sakarya turns tides against Greeks; Greek Communist anti-war agitation accounts for tens of thousands of Greek desertions. Enver Pasha breaks with Soviets and begins to organise anti-Soviet Basmachi rebellion.
- 29 September 1921: Grand National Assembly votes to amnesty the communists arrested the previous January, in a new rapprochement with the Soviet Union motivated by need for money and arms. At this juncture, Kemalist government decides to wipe slate clean on Soviet support for Enver Pasha, to provide aid to victims of the famine in Russia, and to sign, on 13 October, the Treaty of Kars which put an end to border disputes in the east. Kemalist regime pardons Communists convicted in early 1921 repression, including Salih Haciolglu, as part of rapprochement.
- December 1921 – January 1922: M.V. Frunze, commander-in-chief of Soviet forces in the Ukraine, makes extended visit to Ankara, a high-water mark in relations.
- January 1922: Important tramway strike in Istanbul.
- March 1922: Several released communists authorised to reconstitute the 'People's Communist Party of Turkey'.
- April 1922: the Cheka accuses the Turkish embassy in Moscow of espionage; Kemal Pasha recalls his ambassador. Kemal also refuses to condemn the Basmachi revolt led by Enver Pasha.
- Summer 1922: Communist Party militants manage to get a significant worker confederation off the ground in Cilicia, in southeastern Turkey.
- September 1922: Final crushing of the invading Greek troops; chill in Turko-Soviet relations becomes manifest.
- Late August–early September 1922: Communist Party congress in Ankara is banned, takes place in clandestinity.
- August 1922: Enver Pasha, leading Turkoman Basmachi guerrillas, killed in battle with Red Army.
- October 1922: Cilicia confederation's congress, attended by full Central Committee of the Communist Party and 40 proletarian delegates, calls for eight-

hour day, guaranteed minimum wage, paid vacations, collective bargaining contracts. Further repression of communist groups intensifies.

- 11 October 1922: The contending armies sign the Armistice of Mudanya ending the Turko-Greek war. In the midst of national celebrations of the military victory, PCTP dissolved by the government, which accuses it of treason and of espionage on behalf of the Soviet Union. Sixty-odd party militants, including a number of working-class sympathisers, arrested in Ankara on 20 October, and a few days later further arrests follow throughout Anatolia. The new Cilician confederation was also banned. All in all, 200 people are arrested. Once again, for the Soviet government and the Comintern, the importance of the relationship to the Kemalist government trumps solidarity with the political prisoners. The French Communist Party newspaper *l'Humanité* simply runs the headline 'Hands Off Turkey'. Izvestia and Pravda continue to hail Turko-Soviet friendship and fret about whether the Soviet Union will be included in the Lausanne Conference.

- 1 November 1922: Kemalist government abolishes the Ottoman sultanate.

- November 1922: Following the Anatolian crackdown of October, Sefik Husnü's Socialist Party of Workers and Farm Laborers is the only legal left-wing organisation in the new Turkey. But tensions between Allies and the Kemalist regime during the Lausanne negotiations provoke yet another shift in Turkish-Soviet relations. After the Fourth Congress of the Comintern, Hüsnü, with a base in Istanbul, and Salih Hacioglu, back from Russia and representing Anatolia, emerge as the two key figures of Turkish communism. Hüsnü's journal *Aydinlik* (with its 'Spartakist' origins) became the party's theoretical expression. Hüsnü and his followers apply new Third International tactic of 'conquering the masses' and seek a mass organisation to 'enter'. They are excluded from the only real worker-based organisation in Istanbul, the General Workers' Union of Sakir Rasim. Rasim and his militant followers have real success in a campaign against foreign enterprises, to the approval of the Kemalists and the Turkish employers, while leaving the *Aydinlik* group on the margins.

- 15 November 1922: Long articles on the repression in Turkey finally appear on the front pages of *Izvestia* and *Pravda*. In the interim two weeks, the Kemalists had continued various anti-communist harassments. The Soviet embassy in Ankara is forced to close its commercial outlet and a Soviet courier's diplomatic pouch is confiscated.

- Late November 1922: A new silence on the repression in the international communist press resumes. The Lausanne Conference opens on 20 November with Soviet participation, and the settlement of the status of the Straits looms large in the offing.

- 22 November 1922: A major article by Karl Radek in *Pravda* asserts that the Soviet Union will 'support the legitimate demands of Turkey' at Lausanne. The Fourth Congress of the Comintern dots the i's by reaffirming the decisions of the Third Congress, inviting communists of the colonial or semi-colonial world to collaborate with 'bourgeois democracy'. Communists, in contrast to what Lenin had said in 1920, might even collaborate with pan-Islamists. At Fourth Congress, Salih Hacioglu critiques wars of national liberation for TCP left; is defeated.

- December 1922: The communists get their chance to end isolation when the 'official' Communist Party announces nationwide economic congress in Smyrna, to convene in February 1923. The congress invites peasants and farm labourers, business people, workers, industrialists and artisans to propose economic reforms for the new regime. Sefik Hüsnü draws up a programme for a workers' commission calling for the eight-hour day, an absolute ban on child labour, three days' leave per month for women, sixteen weeks' maternity leave, a weekly rest period, abolition of all legal limits on the right to strike and to association, a health care system and 'factory committees' for communication between workers and bosses. A further text in *Aydinlik* calls for modernisation of Turkish agriculture and a series of measures improving the situation of the Anatolian peasantry. This document recognises the necessity, for the interim, of dealing with foreign capital. *Aydlinlik* is in effect calling for the creation of a state-sponsored creation of a Turkish capitalist class.

- Early 1923: Various communist groups at liberty to have public existence and publications. With the end of military hostilities and the reunification of the country, focus of communist activity shifts from Anatolia to Istanbul.

- November 1922 – July 1923: Negotiations for the Treaty of Lausanne which formally recognises the Kemalist victory in Turkey and scraps the punitive Treaty of Sèvres of 1920. Kemalist-Communist relations warm yet again. Soviet press blows hot and cold, praising the alliance with Turkey while attacking the Turkish rapprochement with the Allies.

- February 1923: National 10-day economic congress. Soviet ambassador arrives on the same train as Mustafa Kemal and causes sensation by his presence on congress's tribunal of honour. The authorities choose 'worker' delegates (187 total, many of them having no working-class credentials) with an eye to sidelining potential subversives. The more circumspect General Union of Workers from Istanbul presents a more moderate programme than Hüsnü's, oriented to petitioning the employers for benevolence. Despite hostility, worker delegation manages to get its programme forwarded to the government. Sefik Hüsnü congratulates the Turkish worker delegation on its maturity and its ability to make itself heard. Hüsnü and the Socialist Party of Workers and Farm Laborers, with the war over and a significant impact at the national conference, think their moment, after the chill of the fall arrests, has arrived.

– March 1923: Unfortunately for Hüsnü, a new pendulum swing of Turko-Soviet relations takes place. After their triumph at Lausanne, the Kemalists no longer need the Soviet alliance. Once the Allies concede control over the Straits to Kemal Pasha, the Kemalists unleash a police operation against communist militants in Istanbul. Kemalist 'health inspectors' raid the offices of Hüsnü's party and proceed to arrest Salih Hacioglu.

– 17 March 1923: Ad hoc tribunal launches trial of the militants arrested the previous October, as well as of Salih Hacioglu and a number of radical workers.

– March 1923: Sefik Hüsnü urges supporters to vote for the Kemalists in upcoming national elections, barring the way to 'reaction'.

– 21 April 1923: A new wave of harassment and then arrests of communists, this time netting Sefik Hüsnu and other party leaders. Aralov, the Soviet ambassador in Ankara, is asked to take a leave, and several employees of the Soviet consul in Istanbul are expelled from Turkey.

– May Day 1923: Renewed strikes, above all in Istanbul.

– May 1923: *Pravda* headlines 'White Terror in Turkey' about April arrests. But mere weeks later, those arrested are acquitted and released at the end of May. Those arrested in October 1922, charged under a law potentially prescribing the death penalty, are condemned to three months imprisonment plus a fine. Numbed by these experiences, Sefik Hüsnü and his militants are unable to throw themselves back into mass work when the climate between Russia and Turkey improves again, following their release.

– 24 July 1923: The signing of the Treaty of Lausanne is the signal for a strike wave that lasts until November. The opportunist, moderate General Union of Workers is able to take advantage. A wave of nationalism and even xenophobia, based on the long humiliations of the past, makes foreign companies targets of preference. Moslem workers demand the firing of Christian blue and white collar workers, and the expulsion of European managers. Greek and Armenian emigration intensifies. The intensity of anti-foreigner feeling among the strikers and the resulting militancy at foreign companies makes it possible for Kemalist officials to publicly sympathise.

– October 1923: A wave of measures enforce Turkish as the sole public language, not only in commerce and industry, but in everything from advertising to the sub-titles of films. Foreign companies are required to employ only Turkish Moslems. The General Union of Workers, which had earlier already tried its hand at nationalism and xenophobia, rides the wave, even as they cultivate ties with the British Labour Party and the Second International.

- 29 October 1923: Proclamation of the Turkish Republic. Sefik Hüsnü's group is again an isolated sect.
- 18 November 1923: Railway strike completely paralyses the railway network of European Turkey.
- 26 November 1923: During railway strike, Sakir Rasim and the General Union of Workers of Istanbul convoke a congress with 250 delegates representing 19,000 workers. Organisation renamed the General Union of the Workers of Turkey. Despite having an anti-communist figure close to the Kemalists as vice-president, the union is ordered to disband on 18 December 1923. Government suspicious of union's ties to Second International.
- January 1924: Well-placed friends of General Union of Workers of Turkey issue a counter-order to the order to dissolve. Push for a new labour law, as promised the previous year at the economic conference. Sakir Rasim makes public letter of 2 February from Kemal Pasha promising new labour law.
- 3 March 1924: The caliphate is abolished. Kemalists introduce economic reforms and completely secularise education.
- May Day 1924: Big worker demonstrations.
- May 1924: Hüsnü in *Aydinlik* expresses disappointment with Republic, characterised as 'bourgeois', but continues support for Kemal against the 'imperialists'. Hüsnü calls for statist policies. After mid-1924 suppression of the foreign tobacco monopoly, Hüsnü calls for state monopolies, statist measures in industry, foreign trade, communications, the tertiary sector, expropriation of large properties, free distribution of land to the poor peasants.
- Mid-May 1924: Court orders union to cease its activities. In response, summer 1924 sees spontaneous actions at foreign companies. Tramway strike in July. Police are called, several are wounded, 30 are arrested. Postal strike, lockout. Scabs break the strike. Agitation spreads to Anatolia. Railway strikes erupt, including in Eskisehir. Government brings in Christian strikebreakers (French, Greek, Bulgarian).
- June–July 1924: Fifth Congress of Comintern. Hüsnü's *Aydinlik* faction attacked polemically by Manuilsky for 'class collaboration'. Hüsnü argues in reply that Turkey is only at the beginning of national liberation. The critique pushes Hüsnü et al. to pay more attention to worker milieu.
- 24 September 1924: Union reborn under the name 'Association for Workers Improvement', with appearances of a Kemalist organisation. Socialists and Communists work together to infiltrate and control organisation. Resumption of agitation, but defeat follows defeat.

- January 1925: Secret Third Congress of CP. Salih Haciologu attends, freshly out of prison.
- February1925: Vast Kurdish revolt in eastern Turkey led by Chaikh Said. The revolt pushes the Kemalists back toward the Soviet Union. Turkey also faces possible military threat from Iran and tension arises with Britain over Mosoul. Turkey and the Soviet Union need each other again.
- 4 March 1925: Grand National Assembly votes full powers to government; state of emergency declared. Worker organisations retreat.
- Mid-May 1925: 40 Turkish CPers arrested. Hüsnü in Germany. Trials begin in mid-August. Hüsnü et al. get 15 years hard labour in absentia. From that time on, party must go clandestine. Party has 500–600 members at time of crackdown.
- 17 November 1925: Salih Hacioglu denounces *Aydinlik* faction of TCP before Comintern Eastern desk; threatens to oppose Comintern and USSR. Later expelled from TCP Central Committee (1926), from the party itself (1928) and finally sent to the camps in the Soviet Union (1929), where he died in 1934.

CHAPTER 3

The Spanish Revolution, Past and Future; Grandeur and Poverty of Anarchism; How the Working Class Takes Over (or Doesn't), Then and Now

Introduction: Why the Spanish Revolution Today?

... anarchism and revolutionary syndicalism in general lacked a vision of the problems of political orientation, without which the most powerful and most heroic revolutionary surge is condemned to failure.

HELMUT RÜDIGER, AIT, *Ensayo critico sobre la revolucion española* (1940)[1]

∵

For many years, I had held the classical left anti-Stalinist view that after the 'events' of May 1937 in Barcelona – the crushing of the left-centrist POUM[2] and the further marginalisation of the anarchists by the Stalinists and by forces in the sway of the Stalinists – the revolution begun in July 1936 was essentially over. My references were classic works such as Orwell's *Homage to Catalonia* and Bolloten's *The Spanish Revolution*.[3] And 'politically', this dating is correct. However, Robert Alexander's two-volume *The Anarchists in the Spanish Civil War* and Walther Bernecker's study of the industrial and agrarian collectives[4] show that the Spanish anarchists, who were the great majority of armed workers in Catalonia, who dominated considerable rural agrarian collectives in Aragon, and were also important in the Republican zones of the Levant, Extremadura and Andalucia, remained a social and military force to

---

1 Helmut Rüdiger was a German anarcho-syndicalist, associated with the AIT (Associacion International de Trabajadores), who was active in Spain from 1933 to 1939.

2 Partido Obrero de Unificacíon Marxista, denounced as 'Trotskyist' by the Stalinists and their fellow travellers, and denounced as 'traitors' by Trotsky and his tiny group of followers in Spain.

3 Orwell 1952 [1938]; Bolloten 1979.

4 Alexander 1999; Bernecker 1982 (from the 1978 German original; unfortunately no English translation available).

be reckoned with right up to the end of the Civil War in March 1939, even after losing out on the political terrain in May 1937. The eradication of the primarily anarchist social revolution occurring in July 1936, an eradication carried out by the Stalinists, Socialists, Left Republicans and Catalan nationalists, and finally completed by the fascists, was a work in progress right up until Franco's final victory.

The Spanish Revolution was, in light of this history, the richest and deepest social revolution of the twentieth century. I was rather startled to find Leon Trotsky, major figure of the Russian Revolution and no friend of anarchism, saying, in 1937: 'From the first day of the revolution, thanks to its specific weight in the economy of that country, and to its political and cultural level, [the Spanish proletariat] has been, not below, but above the level of the Russian proletariat at the beginning of 1917'.[5] Despite all the factors (international, political, military) working for their demise, the Spanish working class and parts of the peasantry in the Republican zones arrived at the closest approximation of a self-managed society, sustained in different forms over two and a half years, ever achieved in history. Catalonia in 1936 was more broadly industrial than Russia in 1917, and the Catalan, Aragonese and Levantine peasants who formed collectives in 1936 mostly supported the revolution wholeheartedly, in contrast to the grudging support of the Russian peasants for the Bolsheviks, as the little-loved but lesser evil to the Whites.

This experience and its implications have not been fully absorbed by the contemporary revolutionary left. Currents describing themselves as anarchist and anarcho-syndicalist have emerged in parts of Europe and the United States in the past few decades, while hardly with the numbers and depth of the 'historical' Spanish anarchists and anarcho-syndicalists from 1868 to 1939, nor above all with the same working-class and popular rootedness. For many of them, 'Spain' is an historical reference (more often symbolic than seriously studied and absorbed) in the way that 'Russia' has been such a reference for many Marxists. Spain was the supreme historical test for anarchism, which it failed, in the same way that Russia was, to date, the supreme test of, at least, Leninism, if not of Marxism itself.

---

5   Quoted from Trotsky's writings on Spain, in Iglesias 1977. Grandizo Munis, during the war a member of the very small (Trotskyist) Bolshevik-Leninist group, writing in 1948 when he was evolving away from Trotskyism, concurs: 'To a certain extent the case of the Spanish organs of power was even more demonstrative than that of the Russian Revolution ... the number of organs of working-class power was proportionally higher in Spain than in Russia during the first months of dual power'. Munis 1948, pp. 291–2.

But dealing critically with contemporary anarchism is hardly my main concern,[6] except by ricochet from the failures of anarchism in Spain. The real lessons for today of the Spanish Revolution of 1936–9 are at least twofold: first, the concrete takeover of an incipiently modern industrial region, Catalonia, by workers' factory collectives, which attempted, in very difficult circumstances and under attack from all sides, to move from the initial, spontaneous local level to regional and national coordination, and a simultaneous takeover of agriculture by peasant collectives with similar attempts at coordination beyond the local. Second, and closely related to the first, the political dimension of the 'military question', the defence and extension of the revolution against domestic and international counter-revolution. The revolution was lost both in the gradual destruction of the workers' and peasants' collectives and in the replacement of the initial armed militias and urban patrols by a traditional army and police forces. Some anarchist leaders were involved in both processes, and the eminently 'pragmatic' reasons for this will be one focus of my study. Further, left-wing military theorists such as the 'anarcho-Marxist' Abraham Guillén[7] have shown how politics was as much

---

6 Take the recent, generally very good book *Black Flame: The Revolutionary Class Politics of Anarchism and Syndicalism* (Schmidt and van der Walt 2009). The authors fall all over themselves not to discuss Spain in depth, preferring to 'de-centre' anarchism in order to talk about anarchist movements elsewhere, primarily in Latin America. Yet Spain was the only country where anarchism made a revolution, and was confronted with the problem of state power over a two-and-a-half year period. As the reader will see, the following text is anything but unsympathetic to the Spanish anarchist movement. But to write a book of 345 pages in which Spain gets only a few pages here and there, and in which preoccupation with its failures is referred to as 'Spanish exceptionalism' is, to put it mildly, a long exercise in changing the subject, something tantamount to a history of Marxist movements which would scant the Russian Revolution as 'Russian exceptionalism'.

The evasion in the Schmitt/van der Walt view is underscored by one of the best recent surveys – one among many – of anarchist theory, practice and history, by an anarcho-syndicalist militant exiled in Mexico, B. Cano Ruiz: 'It is obvious that in no other country in the world did anarchism have the rootedness and influence that it had in Spain ... In Spain anarchism was a mass movement integrated in diverse manifestations, from a workers' movement embodied in the CNT (Confederación Nacional de Trabajo), which reached a membership of two million ... the rationalist schools (of Francisco Ferrer) ... the libertarian ateneos, the Libertarian Youth, Mujeres Libres (Free Women) ... the FAI (Federación Anarchista Iberica), closely linked to the CNT ...' (Bano Ruiz 1985, p. 322).

7 Abraham 1980. Guillén as a young man fought in one of the anarchist columns in the Civil War, then spent much of the rest of his life in Latin America, where he became a theoretician of urban guerrilla warfare.

if not more important than firepower and sheer numbers in determining the outcome of different battles of the Civil War.

Finally, I am not writing about Spanish anarchism for historical edification or from some antiquarian impulse, but rather to pose the question, raised by Abad de Santillán[8] and generally ignored by most of the contemporary radical left, of how to prepare today, programmatically and practically, for a takeover of a modern capitalist economy where, in contrast to Spain in 1936, shutting down a large swath of socially useless and socially noxious activity will be a top priority from day one.

1   Part One: Theses

1. The history of the origins and development of the Spanish Revolution of 1936–9, and particularly of its anarchist majority, is as complex, if not more so, than that of the Russian Revolution. It is significantly less known globally because the Russian Revolution had a much greater global projection,[9] and because anarchism's defeat in Spain completed a decades-long eclipse of anarchism by the significantly more widespread impact of Soviet and other 'socialisms'.

Spain, as late as the final loss of its last colonies to the u.s. in 1898 and even in 1936, was still a predominantly agricultural country, with pockets of industrial development mainly in Catalonia and the Basque provinces, and mining in Asturias.

Nonetheless, Spain had its first general strike in 1855, and the working class was an active force in the ephemeral First Republic of 1873–4.[10] Spain was, in short, more directly influenced by developments in western Europe and

---

8   As de Santillán wrote in his *Porque perdimos la guerra* (*Why We Lost the War*): 'Even in our revolutionary ranks we worked much more intensely and with more inclination preparing the insurrection than in really preparing for what we would build afterwards' (de Santillán 1940).

9   In 1935, Spain accounted for only 1.4 percent of world imports and 1.0 percent of world exports.

10   The First Republic had already concretised the anarchist's 'localist' orientation. As Bernecker writes, 'The localist tradition of Andalucia, whose maximum expression was the "cantonalist" uprising of 1873, also in 1936–1937 prevented the linking up of committees and organs of local power which were operating without mutual coordination; the Andalucian anarchists obstinately refused to enter "legalized" municipal councils and to abandon their powerful position in spontaneously created committees' (Bernecker 1982, p. 384).

at an earlier stage than Russia. Spain had a socialist party from 1879 onward with a working-class base in Asturias and Madrid, but it entered the twentieth century, and indeed the revolutionary crisis of the 1930s, with a far larger anarchist and anarcho-syndicalist movement, dating from 1868, especially in Catalonia and Andalucia.

2. Understanding this 'anomaly' of a mass anarchist movement in both Spanish industry and agriculture in 1936, when anarchism had been largely superseded by socialism and then communism in most of western Europe (starting with nearby France and Italy), is a key, if not the key, to understanding the special contours of the Spanish Revolution.[11] Gerald Brenan's classic[12] emphasises the historical decentralisation of Spain, with multiple regions in constant centrifugal opposition to the artificial centralism of Madrid, as a major factor in the ongoing appeal of anti-statist anarchism, above all where prosperous peasant smallholders were absent or weak. Socialism, in the form of the PSOE,[13] was a pedestrian local copy of the more mature Second International French and German parties of northern Europe. If the historic split internationally between anarchism and Marxian socialism, in 1872, stemmed from the Marxian insistence on political activity and trade unionism, the lack of any sustained bourgeois democracy in Spain hardly provided conditions in which such reformist activity could take root. Spanish anarchism in its early decades was more propelled toward actions organised underground, such as innumerable local peasant uprisings in Andalucia, crushed in isolation, or lightning strikes against industrial firms where worker organisations had little sustained above-ground existence and few if any strike funds.

3. At the same time, anarchism and anarcho-syndicalism in Spain were quite impressive in their reach. ('Anarchism' refers to the earlier decades of Bakuninist local insurrectionism and then the demoralised individual terrorism of the early to mid-1890s, 'anarcho-syndicalism' refers to the later focus on mass

---

11   I give it a shot in my little book *Ubu Saved From Drowning*. See Goldner 2000, pp. 93–124; available online at: http://bthp23.com/Portugal-Spain.pdf. I also underscore uncanny echoes between Russia and Spain, the only countries in Europe where workers took power and held it for a few years.

12   *The Spanish Labyrinth*, available in multiple editions from 1943 to 1974, but see e.g. Brenan 1950. Elsewhere, in a memoir (Brenan 1974, p. 277) Brenan said of anarchism that 'Probably it is only feasible in Spain, for everywhere else in Europe the seeds of social life have been destroyed'.

13   Partido Socialist Obrero de España.

organisation when these earlier forms showed themselves to be dead ends.)
The movement placed great store in education, and had countless newspapers; it had 'rationalist' schools and 'ateneos', or cultural centres; it produced
numerous books and pamphlets, including translations of Bakunin, Malatesta,
Kropotkin and Reclus (among others). Brenan recounts peasants riding don-
keys on back roads, reading anarchist literature, and Diaz del Moral's classic[14]
describes illiterate peasants memorising their favourite articles to recite them
in front of enraptured audiences in remote villages. In 1918–20, the mere arrival
of the news of the Russian Revolution set off insurrections in some of these
places in Andalucia, the south.

4. A survey of anarchist ideology shows common traits that persisted up to
the revolution and civil war. Anarchism comes across as a rationalist theory,
an extreme left version of radical Enlightenment. In part because of the break
with 'authoritarian' Marxism, anarchist theory shows no engagement with the
post-Enlightenment development in German philosophy from Hegel through
Feuerbach to Marx.[15] Marxism, arguing for a transitional 'dictatorship of the
proletariat', was for the anarchists a 'statist' world view,[16] and was indeed centralist; anarchism was decentralist and federationist. It was radically atheist,
but lacked the *supersession* or *realisation* of religion,[17] the 'heart of a heart-
less world' one finds in Marx. It has no notion of historical development or
a strategy flowing from such development; the potential for a radical egalitarian society is always *now*, once the landowner, the priest, the police and the
notary public are removed, regardless of the 'development of the productive
forces' which exercise Marxists. Hence anarchism did not see much use for concrete analysis of specific conditions,[18] or for the critique of political economy
as developed by Marx in the *Grundrisse* and *Capital*. 'Anarchism has an ideal

---

14   *Historia de las agitaciónes campesinas andaluzas*: see e.g. del Moral 1969 [1929], though
      there are various other reprints.
15   Or rather, when Hegel was mentioned, it was assumed that Marx, as his 'successor', was
      also an admirer of the state.
16   Marx and Engels were distressed that the very statist drift of Lassallean Social Democracy
      in Germany was taken by anarchists to be 'Marxist', when in fact they criticised the early
      SPD as harshly as the anarchists, both in the 'Critique of the Gotha Program' (1875) and in
      their private correspondence.
17   'Mankind has long possessed a dream which it must first possess in consciousness in order
      to possess in reality'.
18   As one comprehensive study of the anarchist world view puts it, 'the analyses of the
      social question studied here are impoverished. Nowhere more than on this point is
      the anarchist affinity for abstract and moralizing reasoning so clear; one begins from

to realise', as Guy Debord put it. Marx, by contrast, says in the *Manifesto* that communism is 'not an ideal sprung from the head of some world reformer', but rather emphasises the immanence of the new society in this one, 'the real movement unfolding before our eyes'. Words such as 'the Idea',[19] 'our ideal' and 'justice' pervade anarchist ideology right through the Civil War. This echoes eighteenth-century Enlightenment theories of Man, abstracted from any historical development or specificity. Diaz del Moral reports Andalucian peasants asking the local latifundia owner when the day of equality for all will dawn. Anarchism in Spain also had much of the ideology of the 'patria chica', the excessive focus on the local that pervaded (and still pervades) much of Spanish life.[20] It was an easy step from rejection of the centralism of Madrid to rejection of the centralism of Marx. Anarchists inherited the federalism of Pi y Margall, briefly head of state in the First Republic, and disciple of Proudhon.

Many anarchists looked down on socialist strikes for mere economic improvement,[21] the 'school' of the working class in struggle, in Marx's view. Their vision of the new society was austere. Their social centres banned alcohol, tobacco, and gambling; where they could, anarchists shut down brothels, preaching instead free love and free unions outside marriage. In some cases they shut down cafés as sites of frivolity and idleness. The anarchist Mujeres Libres (Free Women), founded in 1934, fought for full equality between the sexes but attacked 'feminism' as an ideology of middle-class women. Brenan, who lived for long years in rural Andalucia and knew many anarchists, may have gone too far in characterising them as latter-day 'Lutherans', reacting against the luxury of Spanish Catholicism, but captured something of their austere rejection of the sensuous decadence of the dominant culture around them. They had an uncritical faith in science and technology which would strike most

---

metaphysical principles such as natural harmony and justice – so favored by Proudhon, and so definitively critiqued by Marx in *The Poverty of Philosophy* – or from social classes as supra-historical entities, and one never finds concrete studies of the Spanish situation as varied and changing' (in Junco 1976, p. 190). The author goes on to point out that the 'Marxists' of the day were no better.

19   Anselmo Lorenzo, the grand old man of nineteenth-century Spanish anarchism, in his memoir *El Proletariado Militante* (Lorenzo 1974 p. 97), wrote of the 'immense happiness, great hopes, the quasi-mystical veneration of the idea which animated us'.

20   As Brenan 1974, p. 303, writes: 'This was the normal pattern – every pueblo hated its neighbor, but had friendly feelings for the next pueblo but one'.

21   At the Fourth Congress of the First International (September 1869), the libertarian collectivists had opposed strikes (see Maitron, 1975, vol. 1, p. 50). Brenan wrote later: '... Anarchists are the only revolutionaries who do not promise a rise in the standard of living. They offer a moral gain – self-respect and freedom' (Brenan 1974, p. 277).

people today as overblown. Some practised nudism, vegetarianism or ate only uncooked fruit, and studied Esperanto as the universal language of the future.

5. Despite disclaimers, many of the divisions that have split the Marxist movement, such as reform vs. revolution, recurred in different guise within the anarchist movement. After a period of ebb during the 1880s, anarchism revived, and in 1888 a split took place between labour-oriented and insurrectionist currents. A long-term division existed between a Bakunin-influenced 'collectivist anarchism' and the Kropotkin-inspired 'anarchist communism'.[22] A new upturn in mass struggle in the 1909 'Tragic Week' in Barcelona led to the founding of the anarcho-syndicalist CNT (Confederación Nacional de Trabajo) in 1910, focused, like many syndicalist movements in Europe at the time (Italy, France, Britain, the American IWW) on the strategy of the general strike to usher in the new society.[23] The CNT's influence peaked initially (prior to 1936) in 1919, in the wave of general strikes following World War One, and it created the *sindicato unico* (single union) to deal with the antagonism between craft and industrial workers, much like the IWW.

The defeat of the general strike ('La Canadiense') in early 1919 began a downturn, and the following years of ebb were dominated by the 'pistolerismo' of hundreds of tit-for-tat assassinations between employers and prominent union militants, a period ended by the Primo de Rivera dictatorship (1923–30) and years of underground illegality and exile for the CNT. In response to this difficult situation, and also to keep the reformist wing of the movement in check, the FAI (Federacion Anarquista Iberica) was founded in 1927 by radical elements, sometimes called 'anarcho-Bolsheviks'. From 1917 until 1921–2, the Russian Bolsheviks had for their part courted anarcho-syndicalists in western Europe, but the experiences of the latter in the Soviet Union, and the repression of Kronstadt and of various Russian libertarians, alienated them definitively, reconfirming their suspicions of Marxist 'statism' and centralism.

Anarchist claims to 'apoliticism' and 'antipoliticism' were also belied by the electoral participation of the anarchist working-class base, when the CNT-FAI lifted the policy of abstentionism in the 1931 elections, providing the margin of victory for republican forces. Disappointed by the anti-worker and anti-peasant policies of the Republic, anarchists abstained in 1933, elections followed by the

---

22   On these divisions see Bookchin 1998, pp. 29–31, and elsewhere.

23   See Rosa Luxemburg's critique of the anarcho-syndicalist general strike strategy at the beginning of her pamphlet 'The Mass Strike' (Luxemburg 2008 [1906]). Between 1904 and 1911 there was a flood of translations of revolutionary syndicalists such as Pouget and Griffueles.

hard-right turn of the 'biennio negro' (two black years). As a result, the CNT-FAI again lifted the abstention policy for the February 1936 elections – even Durruti called for a vote for the Popular Front – and anarchists provided the margin of victory for the left parties, though claiming they voted only in hopes of freeing some 9000 anarchist political prisoners.[24] After the left won, the prisoners were freed by mass break-ins by crowds at the jails, which the Republican authorities did not dare repress.

6. Thus the stage was set for the crisis of the Second Republic (1931–9), culminating in revolution and civil war after 1936. Spain had been spared participation in World War One, which tore apart the large socialist parties of France, Italy, and Germany, giving rise after 1917 to mass Communist Parties there, and also posing a severe test for other anarchist and anarcho-syndicalist movements, where important sections and figures (Hervé in France, Kropotkin in Russia) rallied to the nationalist colours. By contrast, the Spanish Communist Party,[25] having no 'social patriot' majority to denounce, was a stillborn sect of a few thousand breaking away from the PSOE youth, then forced underground during the Primo de Rivera years and then with the return to legality from 1931 to 1934 practising the sterile Third Period 'social fascist' policy against the PSOE and the anarchists, thus being hardly larger or more rooted in the working class in 1936 than it had been at its founding.[26] The CNT, despite the expulsion of thirty moderate ('Treintista') union leaders, towered over both the PSOE, to say nothing of the PCE, in both numbers and rootedness in the Catalan working class and Andalucian peasantry.

7. General Francisco Franco's coup in July 1936 was aimed at ending the social chaos of the Second Republic in the form of strikes, land seizures by peasants, street battles between leftists and rightists, and parliamentary impotence. One should recall the European context of right-wing military governments throughout eastern Europe, the first fascist state, founded by Mussolini in 1922, Hitler's seizure of power in Germany in 1933, and Austrian dictator Dollfuss's

---

24   Ironically, the estimated 1.3 million CNT votes seem to have been mainly for the as yet insignificant Communist Party, helping the PCE go from one deputy to 14 in the parliament (the Cortes).

25   PCE, Partido Comunista de España. The communist party in Catalonia was known as the PSUC, Partido Socialista Unificado de Cataluña.

26   The PCE had 400 members when it returned to legality in 1931, and 5000 by May 1935, rising to 50,000 in June 1936. This in comparison with the anarchists' half-a-million to 1,000,000 members. See Rafael Cruz 1987.

bombardment of working-class housing in Vienna in 1934. The latter two especially emboldened the Spanish right and far-right, and strengthened the resolve
of the PSOE, PCE and CNT-FAI on the left. The Stalinist Third International's
1934–5 'anti-fascist' turn to alliances with social democrats (yesterday's 'social
fascists') and 'progressive bourgeois elements' led to the electoral victories of
the Popular Front in Spain in February 1936 and then in France in May, followed
in the latter by mass factory occupations in May–June.

8. Franco's coup was defeated by spontaneous, heavy street fighting over 3–4
days, above all in Barcelona and also in Madrid, and various forms of popular
resistance in about sixty percent of Spanish territory. In Barcelona, the CNT and
the FAI were the absolute masters of the situation, based on the armed working
class. Wherever the coup triumphed, in some cases almost without resistance,
as in leftist bastions such as Zaragoza – the most anarchist city in Spain – and
Seville (not to mention large parts of the anarchist Andalucian countryside)
mass executions of militants (20,000 in Seville) followed immediately.[27]

9. It is here that we arrive at the nub of this text. The Spanish anarchists had
made the revolution, beyond their wildest expectations, and did not know
what to do with it. On the night of the victory in Barcelona, top leaders of
the CNT-FAI, including Juan Garcia Oliver and Buenaventura Durruti, called on
Luis Companys, a Catalan nationalist and head of the Generalitat, the Catalan
regional government. The army had dissolved or gone over to Franco; the police
had also largely disintegrated, and were being replaced by armed anarchist
patrols; the bourgeois state in Catalonia at that moment was reduced to a few
buildings. Companys told the CNT-FAI leaders that the power was theirs, and
if they wished, he would resign and be a soldier in their army. The CNT-FAI
leaders decided to leave standing the skeleton of the bourgeois state and its
momentarily powerless head, Companys, and instead formed the Committee
of Anti-Fascist Militias, which became for all intents and purposes the effective
state power in the following months.[28]

---

27   The fascist uprising failed in Catalonia, the Levante, New Castile, the Basque region, Sant-
      ander, Asturias and half of Extremadura. It won control of most of Andalucia, southern
      Extremadura, Mallorca, Old Castille, Navarre and Aragon. The anarchists were key in Cata-
      lonia, the Levante, Santander, and much of Asturias.
28   As Bernecker puts it: 'It is difficult to overestimate the importance of this decision. It was
      the expression of a strong "revisionist" current within the CNT, determined for months
      the course of the war and revolution in Catalonia and, at the same time, underscored the
      anarcho-syndicalists' lack of strategic conceptions ... To the moral scruples about taking

The anarchists, as they put it in their own words, had to either impose a 'full totalitarian dictatorship' or leave the parties supporting the Popular Front intact. They chose the latter course, and through the door of the small, powerless edifice, which they did not dissolve, came, in the following months, under the cautious management of Companys, all the forces of the counter-revolution. Everything in the anarchists' history militated against 'taking power' as 'authoritarian', 'centralist' Marxist theory would dictate, and it hardly helped that 'Marxism' in Spain at that moment was the lumbering reformist PSOE (albeit with a leftward-moving faction), the left-centrist POUM,[29] and the small PCE,[30] barely recovered from its 15 years of sectarian marginality and not yet pumped up into a mass party of the frightened middle classes by Soviet money, weapons and NKVD 'advisors'.[31]

2   The Anarcho-Syndicalists after the Revolution: Political, Economic and Military Considerations

I begin this section with a thought experiment. What if the CNT-FAI, instead of leaving intact the Catalan state under Companys, had decided to 'go for broke' ('ir a por el todo' was the Spanish formulation, favoured by an important number of anarcho-syndicalists such as Juan Garcia Oliver) and replace the skeletal bourgeois state with full working-class power in some approximation of immediately revocable delegates in 'soviets' (class-wide institutions), as the

---

over all power, another consideration prompted the anarchist and union leaders to allow the government to subsist: up to that time, the radical refusal of the established (state) order had had as its consequence a total lack of preparation to intervening in its configuration and improving it, i.e. the revolutionaries lacked all practical knowledge in the affairs of government and public administration. Thus they preferred to leave government and therefore official responsibility to the Republicans and liberals, while controlling them through a new "revolutionary" organ of power' (Bernecker 1982, pp. 386–7).

29   Partido Obrero de Unificación Marxista, founded only in 1935, as a fusion of the Bloque Obrero-Campesino and the Izquierda Comunista. The POUM had a hard time of it, being denounced (as indicated in footnote 1) by the Communists as 'Trotskyist-fascists', and by the Trotskyists as 'traitors'. On the POUM, see Morrow 1938, pp. 43–4.

30   On this Soviet-sponsored turnaround in the fortunes of the PCE, see above all the classic account of Bolloten 1979.

31   To be fair one should not omit the 50-odd members of the Bolshevik-Leninist group, orthodox Trotskyists, which included the young Grandizo Munis, who in 1948 published one of the best books on what had happened: *Promesas de Victoria, Jalones de Derrota* (Munis 1948).

ultimate 'authority', since worker control of industry and peasant collectives were already widespread?

This is of course 'history as if'. We know with 20–20 hindsight what really happened, and tracing in detail the destruction of the revolution by the forces of the Popular Front, led by the Communist Party and the PSUC,[32] is less our focus than the anarchist blind spots which facilitated it. (The role of the Communist Party in the internal counter-revolution is relatively well known;[33] how the anarchists were 'taken', and taken in, less so.)

None other than Durruti told a Canadian radio interviewer in August 1936, commenting on the prospects in Spain outside Catalonia and in the rest of Europe: 'We are alone'. Grandizo Munis, on the other hand, without mentioning the debate within the CNT and the FAI, says that

> the working-class organs of power should have unified on a national level and formally proclaimed the dissolution of the government ... The situation ... was characterized by an incomplete atomization of political power in the hands of the workers and the peasants. I use the word 'atomization' because *duality* is insufficient to give a complete picture of the real distribution of powers. Duality indicates two rival, contending powers, with a capacity and will to struggle on both sides. The bourgeois state was only in this position three months after the July days ... In the meantime, the atomized power in the local government-committees was the only existing authority that was obeyed, limited solely by its lack of centralization and by the right-wing interference of the working-class bureaucracies ... This great experiment of the Spanish Revolution offered the world the paradox of anarchists and anarcho-syndicalists acting as the principle agent of the Marxist conception, and negating in fact the anarchist conception.[34]

The common slogan of the Popular Front was 'win the war first, then make the revolution', an argument still made by its apologists and its ideological heirs proposing similar strategies today.[35] But three objections to such a formulation

---

32   Once again, the name of the Communist party in Catalonia.

33   Again, the reader is referred to the books of Orwell 1952 [1938] and Bolloten [1979].

34   Munis 1948, pp. 294–5.

35   de Santillán 1940, p. 129, has an answer to such arguments: 'We knew it was not possible to triumph in the revolution if we did not triumph first in the war, and we sacrificed everything for the war. *We sacrificed the revolution itself, without realizing that this sacrifice also implied sacrificing the objectives of the war*' (my emphasis – LG).

immediately come to mind, recalling Rosa Luxemburg's remark that 'who posits different ends also posits different means'. First is the failure of the Republic to offer independence or even autonomy to Spanish Morocco (the Rif area in the north), which would have had the potential of undercutting Franco's rearguard, his base of operations, and, in the Moroccan legionaries, an important source of his best troops. Second was the failure of the Republic to conduct guerrilla warfare behind Franco's lines, appealing to the many workers and peasants who were by no means pro-fascist but who, in July 1936, happened to find themselves in the territory that fell to the coup.[36] The Moroccan question immediately illuminates the military limitations of a bourgeois republic which was not about to give up its Moroccan protectorate to save itself, especially since doing so would immediately alienate France, which controlled the larger part of Morocco,[37] and from which Republican leaders vainly hoped for material aid. (Juan Garcia Oliver proposed guerrilla activity behind Franco's lines in 1938, but nothing came of it.) Third is the strategy of the 'people in arms' as later theorised by Guillén, which had saved Madrid from Franco's forces (including German and Italian personnel and equipment) in November 1936, something considered little less than a military miracle. The navy was also initially almost entirely in anarchist hands, but by summer 1937 it had been taken over by the Communist Party. The Republic never used the navy throughout the war, in spite of its potential to control the Straits of Gibraltar, entrance to the Mediterranean.

The international situation, dominated by the lengthening shadows of fascism on the march, was not favourable to revolution. The bourgeois democracies, Britain and France, declared a policy of 'non-intervention' and blockaded Spanish ports, a policy which, especially since Nazi Germany and fascist Italy were actively supporting Franco with aircraft, weaponry and military personnel, was a mockery. In 1935, the Soviet Union under Stalin had made an alliance with France for mutual security after Hitler's seizure of power, increasing Stalin's interest in maintaining the European status quo, which was threatened

---

36   Different groups exiled in France were able, after all, to conduct guerrilla warfare in
       Franco's Spain until at least the early 1950s.

37   In fact, Juan Garcia Oliver of the CNT-FAI did organise feelers to Moroccan nationalists in
       autumn 1936, offering them independence. They did not want independence at that time,
       fearing absorption by either Nazi Germany or Mussolini's Italy; they asked for autonomy
       on the Catalan model. These efforts were squelched by the Socialist Largo Caballero,
       under pressure from Socialist Leon Blum, then head of state in France. Given widespread
       ferment and uprisings throughout North Africa at the time, as one commentator said, 'One
       push and the whole French empire in Africa could blow sky high'. See Paz 2000.

by revolution on France's borders. As inadequate as Soviet shipments of arms and supplies were (the common metaphor was an 'eyedropper', enough to prolong the war, not enough to win it) one can hardly imagine ongoing Soviet support for a full-blown revolution led by anarchists. On the other hand, some might argue, the French working class had just staged a major strike wave, with factory occupations, in May–June 1936, mere weeks before the war. That strike wave had been stopped in its tracks by the intervention of the French Communist Party, hewing to Soviet concern not to weaken its new ally. But the fact remains that during the ensuing two-and-a-half years of war, neither the French nor any other working class in the 'democracies' (Britain and the u.s. for starters) took any serious action to force governments to aid Spain, or even to lift the 'non-intervention' policy[38] which was blocking shipments of food and weapons at the French border.

Prior to July 1936, the Republic had alienated parts of the peasantry and the rural landless workers by its insipid efforts at land reform. In September 1932, an Agrarian Statute was passed, establishing the Institute of Agrarian Reform (IRA) which by July 1936 had distributed very little land.[39] The spread of land seizures in the last months before the coup and the establishment of agrarian communes on expropriated land afterwards reflected highly different landholding patterns: small proprietorship and fixed-terms tenancy in Galicia and the Basque provinces; sharecropping in most of Catalonia; a mixture in Aragon; small and medium property and sharecropping in the Levante; vast semi-feudal large landholdings, with millions of landless labourers, west and south of Madrid in Extremadura and in Andalucia. The CNT was strongest in Aragon, the Levant, Andalucia and Galicia.

3   Political, Military and Economic Situation

The CNT Congress of May 1936 was held in anticipation of the outbreak of mass action at any moment. The moderate 'Treintistas' were readmitted. The Congress sketched outlines for an anarchist military and drew up an agrarian programme. Diego Abad de Santillán and Joan Peiró, two anarchist economists, attempted to introduce concrete preparation for a revolutionary takeover. But

---

38   It is true that a vast propaganda campaign by all concerned, except for the anarchists, successfully concealed the social revolution which had taken place in July 1936, turning the international perception of the war into one of 'democracy versus fascism'. International anarchism was too weak to counter this barrage with the truth.

39   As of July 1936, only 110,000 peasants had received land.

one cannot consider the (idyllic programme) ... as a guideline for the encounter with the questions posed. In the course of the war, the word 'commune' almost completely disappeared and ... was replaced by the expression 'collective', but the structural organization of the units of self-management also differed considerably from the model elaborated in Zaragoza. The lack of a sense of reality shown in May 1936 seems connected ... above all to the lack of a well thought-out theory and to systematic projection on the macro-sociological and macroeconomic level of theories which possibly might be applicable to one isolated village.[40]

On 17 July, Franco flew from the Canary Islands to Spanish Morocco, and from there launched the coup on 19 July, moving (with German help) thousands of Moroccan legionaries to key points. Faced with this situation and workers in various major cities demanding weapons, the Madrid government, its back to the wall, reluctantly agreed on 20 July to arm the workers, whom it feared more than Franco. The rebellion failed in Catalonia, Madrid, the Levante, New Castile, the Basque region, Santander, Asturias and half of Extremadura. The rebels controlled most of Andalucia, southern Extremadura, Mallorca, Old Castile, Navarre and Aragon. The anarchists had been key in Catalonia, the Levante, Santander, and much of Asturias.

On 24 July, the first militia organised at the Paseo de Gracia in Barcelona, estimated at between 2000 and 5000 men. In next few days, 150,000 volunteered. The Durruti column left immediately, with the intention of liberating Zaragoza within the next ten days.

The most critical military question thrown up in the first year of the war, however, was that of transforming the militias into a professional army. This posed the political dimension of the war point blank. The strongest advocates of this professionalisation were the Communists, who immediately set about building their Fifth Regiment. By the fall of 1936, the CNT-FAI, after various reverses on the Aragon front and the failure to liberate Zaragoza, grudgingly came around to that view as well.

To understand the backdrop of these clashes, it is necessary to keep in mind the profound social and cultural revolution which, for the first few weeks after July 1936, swept Barcelona. Not only were most factories occupied and expropriated, and their owners shot or run off, with armed CNT militias replacing the army and the police, and churches burned, but on a cultural level as well, it seemed that all hierarchy in daily life had dissolved; even rich bourgeois

---

40   Bernecker 1982, p. 89.

disguised themselves in worker clothing, the formal 'usted' was replaced every-where by the informal 'tu', 'Señor' by 'compañero', and all the bowing and scraping and toadying of the old regime was replaced overnight by forthright waiters and shopkeepers and bootblacks looking clients in the eye. 'Everybody is friends with everybody in a minute', wrote Borkenau, who arrived in August. By September, he noted that 'revolutionary fever is withering away'. Visitors who had lived these weeks and returned mere months later already noticed a conservative change, and a few months after that, by early 1937, a further hardening.[41]

From July 1936 onward, when the CNT-FAI made its fateful decision to leave intact the Catalan Generalitat under Companys, all the parties of the Popu-lar Front in Catalonia, especially the PSUC (Communists), but also the PSOE (Socialists) and the Esquerra Catalan (Catalan Republicans, the party of Com-panys) began to move against it, slowly and stealthily at first, then more deliber-ately. Well before the CNT decided to join the national government in Madrid, it was already participating in regional and municipal state institutions; the decision to accept four ministerial portfolios in November 1936 was simply the culmination of a process.

Virtually at the same time as the departure of the first militias for Zaragoza, on 25 July the central government in Madrid decreed the creation of a state committee to intervene in industry to 'control' industrial companies and if necessary to 'direct them'.

In Barcelona, workers took over most large factories, all important services and transport, hotels, and large warehouses. They did not touch the banks because of long-standing anarchist contempt for money, but left them rather (and fatefully) in the hands of the socialist UGT,[42] which would soon be con-trolled by the Communists of the PSUC. In the port of Barcelona, longshore-men suppressed the hated middlemen who controlled access to jobs. In many places, where assemblies took over, technicians and sometimes even bosses, when willing, were integrated into them. All 745 bakeries in Barcelona were integrated into one socialised system. All of this resulted from a spontaneous popular wave, outside any organisation. 'Because of their contempt for the

41   Quotes are from Borkenau's book *The Spanish Cockpit* (Borkenau 1937, pp. 80, 83). When he returned to Barcelona in January 1937, he found that the 'multicolored Robin Hood style of the militia men had completely disappeared ... [there was a] definite attempt at uniformity ... most did not wear any political insignia ... petty bourgeois have made a strong impress on the general atmosphere' (p. 175).

42   Unión General de Trabajo, historically the trade union federation of the PSOE, with strong roots among Asturian miners and in Madrid; by 1937 controlled by the PCE and the PSUC.

political dimension of power, the anarchists paid little attention to the institutionalization of its functions ...'[43] From the beginning, on the other hand, the CP pushed for centralisation and single management.

The anarchist economist Diego Abad de Santillán, now confronted, mere weeks after the May CNT Congress in Zaragoza, with a real revolution, based his organisational project on the individual enterprise. Communes, in his view, should be federated. 'What was really new in Abad de Santillán's project was the proposal for a Federal Economic Council with economic and administrative functions of coordination. [His] fundamental purpose was to overcome, as anachronistic, the economic conception based on local-communalist principles and to reach "the highest grade of coordination of all productive factors" ... He felt that the anarchist conception of the economy could not be immediately put into practice, and envisioned a period of economic transition in which "all social movements" would have the right for "free experiments". But he envisioned no transition period in the political sphere and argued for the immediate suppression of the state'.[44]

On 31 July, the Catalan government issued an order recognising rights for factory committees created spontaneously, and to assure salaries for workers. This was followed on 2 August with a decree on state control of all industries abandoned by their owners. The anarcho-syndicalists viewed the economic policy of the Republic in Madrid as conservative and harmful to the revolution.[45] The Catalan government, on the other hand, given the CNT's overwhelming preponderance there, was obliged to sanction much more radical legislation.

On 7 August, a collective of 800 firms for conversion to war production (non-existent in Catalonia at the time) was created. Some months later, even bourgeois politicians such as Companys underscored the extraordinary role of the industrial workers in the spontaneous construction of a previously non-existent armaments industry. The Communists, on the other hand, pushed for control from Madrid, leading to political appointments and a proliferation of bureaucrats. In the first months in industry generally, workers' new sense of responsibility often led to increased productivity.[46] The initial anarchist error,

43   Bernecker 1982, p. 286.
44   Ibid. p. 293.
45   Diego Abad de Santillán's book *Porque Perdimos la Guerra* recounts in excruciating detail how Madrid again and again overrode anarchist requests for material aid and foreign currency with which to acquire it, directly affecting the outcome of specific battles, such as the fall of Irun (de Santillán 1940).
46   Foreign military specialists said that Catalan workers and technicians in the new war

however, was neglect of a general overview of the economy and a tolerance, for too long, of blind 'enterprise egoism'. Out of this tension, and many other 'exogenous' factors, by late 1937 planning and centralised direction in the form of national firms had taken over.

In this accelerated flow of developments, virtually from day to day, it is virtually impossible to separate the political, military and economic spheres which gradually crushed the initial euphoria of July; clearly, political and economic decisions influenced military strategy, as has already been seen in the questions of Morocco, guerrilla warfare behind Franco's lines, and 'professionalisation' of the original militias. In early September 1936, Largo Caballero, the socialist politician and 'the Spanish Lenin', became prime minister and minister of defence of the Republic, and moved to create a centralised military command. In this context, the Communist Party extended its influence in the war ministry. The Stalinist commander 'El Campesino', after his break with the CP, said years later that the Russians had especially equipped his Fifth Regiment, which was a virtually independent force, and which attracted pro-Republican officers with its greater efficiency. On 6 September, the anarchists in Asturias accepted militarisation, as did Ricardo Sanz, Durruti's successor. Militarisation meant the return of hierarchy of rank, uniforms, saluting, and the end of democratic assemblies to elect commanders and to decide on strategy. Militarisation began on 29 September, and the first Soviet aid arrived in early October, further strengthening the PCE and the PSUC, which were growing rapidly, based on recruitment of frightened middle-class elements and land-owning peasants who feared for their property. As if to focus attention, in September 1936 Franco's forces captured Irun and San Sebastian in the north.

In September 1936 as well, the CNT, the PSUC, and the POUM entered the Catalan Generalitat, and the CNT accepted the voluntary dissolution of Central Committee of Militias, which had been the de facto government of Catalonia since the revolution.

Shortly afterwards, the CNT demanded socialisation of the banks, Church property, large agrarian property, large commercial and transport companies, workers' control in industry and private commerce, and the management of the means of production and exchange by the unions.

From 25 September to 17 December, Joan Fabregas, another CNT economist and proto-technocrat, accepted the post of 'consejero de la Economia' for Catalonia, and during his tenure issued 25 decrees for regulation of the economy

---

industries had achieved more conversion in two months than France had achieved in two years during World War One. See de Santillán 1940, p. 134.

and 86 related orders. In his conception, production was to be coordinated through industrial councils constituted by the unions, and these in turn would be under a higher system of coordination, the Consejo de Economia, which not only 'oriented' the economy but 'regulated it' by different technical bodies. When Fabregas took over, the Catalan economy was in 'disorder and chaos'. On 2 October, he called on Catalan workers to halt takeovers until there were homogeneous guidelines for economic transformation, but this call was not heeded. Tension quickly arose in the Consejo de Economia between the left Republicans, the PSUC and the UGT on one hand, and the POUM, the CNT and the FAI on the other, over the collectivisations.

Reflecting the growing influence of the conservative forces, the Republic on 7 October issued a land decree tilted toward landowners, and designed to control the collectives and slow their further diffusion. By spring 1937, Communist-controlled police and military units would begin attacks on collectives. Already in October 1936, in the Aragonese *comarca* (county) of Monzon, the CNT and the increasingly crypto-Communist UGT had faced off in a skirmish in which thirty people were killed.

Further, on 23 October, the Catalan CNT and the UGT signed an action programme which made no mention of socialisation. In signing, the CNT was hoping (in vain) to obtain weapons for its unarmed militias on the Aragon front, to end the Stalinist campaign of calumny against it, and finally to calm the petty bourgeoisie, as well as the peasant middle classes, which were leaving the CNT for the more moderate UGT.

The next day, CNT leader Juan Garcia Oliver, who had been head of military affairs for the Comité Central de Milicias, pushed for creation of an officer training school. Abad de Santillán, on the other hand, was a strong opponent of militarisation.[47] Camillo Berneri, an important Italian anarchist fighting in Spain, was also opposed. Militarisation meant not only (as previously indicated) uniforms, ranks, and saluting, but also the appointment of political commissars.

The Catalan decree on collectivisations had been seen by the anarcho-syndicalists of the CNT as a way to control them. For the moment, in the Consejo de Economia, there were anarchists, POUMistas, socialists and left Republicans. The UGT and the CNT had three delegates each; the PSUC, the POUM and the FAI two each; with one each for several other organisations. Its programme was improvised in the onrush of events. For the CNT and the FAI, entry into the Consejo de Economia was yet one further step away from its 'apolitical' stance.

---

47   See Alexander 1999, vol. 1, p. 267.

The Consejo announced the creation of the Caixa de Credit Industrial e Comercial (CCIC), designed to supply credit to the collectives. The Caixa grew out of the experience of the first collectivisations. In these early months, a firm-centred egoism ('egoismo de empresa') had already become manifest. The Caixa was also created to circumvent the crypto-Communist UGT majority among bank employees and the dependence of most banks on their headquarters in Madrid. With a one-year delay in its creation, the CCIC was not formally opened until 10 November 1937, by which time anarchist influence generally was in serious decline, despite their large numbers. Matters were greatly complicated by the steady fall of Catalonian industrial production from July 1936 onward.

In these deliberations, the CNT had seen its initial error and wanted to avoid workers thinking of themselves as the new owners of their individual factories instead of being motivated by solidarity with other sectors of the economy. On 31 October 1936, Fabregas issued orders developing the decree of 24 October to limit spontaneous actions of workers and to control production to the extent possible. Workers' control in a firm henceforth required many documents, giving the state fuller control.

Throughout these efforts at the coordination of the Catalan economy, the long-standing anarchist 'ascetic' concept of a new order was present. We have already mentioned the anarchists' contempt for money and their lack of interest in collectivising the banks because of this. Federica Montseny, a major CNT figure, said on the other hand that the old dream of the immediate abolition of money was 'infantile revolutionism'. The CNT replaced the word 'salario' (wage) with 'asignación', but in reality this often amounted to little more than semantics.

In the rural anarchism of Andalucia, the principle of 'take what you need' from the collective store gave way to a differentiated family salary based on specific needs. Ration cards were supplemented by 'pocket money' for personal 'vices' (wine, cigarettes) and trips outside the village. In the Catalan collectives, money was rarely suppressed. In many 'anarcho-communist' collectives, individualism reimposed itself; the exit of a few small property owners led on occasion to the blow-up of the collective. 'Libretas de consumo', or consumption booklets, became the common practice. Milicianos at the front sent savings to their collective, not to their families. All in all, a general lack of accounting makes a judgment on the functioning of agrarian collectives difficult.

Franco's offensive against Madrid was imminent. At the beginning of November, after highly charged internal debate, Juan Garcia Oliver and three other members of the CNT accepted ministerial portfolios in Largo Caballero's cabinet in the central government of Madrid. This followed, as indicated, prior anarchist participation in municipal and regional governments. Garcia Oliver became Minister of Justice;[48] Juan Peiró, the 'Treintista' economist, became Minister of Industry; Juan Lopez Sanchez, another Treintista, became Minister of Commerce, and Federica Montseny Minister of Health.

The four CNTistas were surprised, at their first cabinet meeting, to find the top order of business the move of the capital from besieged Madrid to Valencia. They felt, in fact, that they had been invited into the government precisely to give their cover to this obvious retreat, which they opposed. Franco expected to be attending mass in Madrid within a week, but that mass was postponed for two and a half years. During the ensuing battle, however, the Largo Caballero government moved its capital to Valencia.

The Battle of Madrid began on 6 November. Terror bombing by the Franco forces, far from cowing the population, actually brought them into the streets in the 'people in arms' strategy later theorised by Guillén. The International Brigades arrived on 10 November and played an important role, as did the anarchists of the Durruti Column. On 19 November, however, Durruti was killed, probably by a fascist sniper. He, more than any other single figure, was 'the' symbol of the libertarian revolution in Spain. A few days later, a million people marched at his commemoration in Barcelona. The battle for Madrid continued into January 1937, before stalling in a standoff, one which would be broken only in March 1939.

The statist institutionalisation of the revolution proceeded apace. In December 1936, the Catalan Generalitat was reorganised with the CNT taking over the councillorship of defence. Soviet aid also peaked at that time, most of it going to its political and military supporters. The Soviet ambassador, Marcel Rosenberg, met with Largo Caballero daily, often for hours. In early 1937, the government decreed that regular municipal councils, which had been replaced by revolutionary committees, be reestablished. A plenum criticised the deficiencies of the collectives to date for poor organisation, lack of technical management, extravagant economic ideas and little experience. New efforts at unity between the CNT and the UGT were broached. By the middle of January, the anarcho-syndicalists were calling for a centrally-planned economy, and on 30 January 1937, a statute aimed at concentration of all collectivised firms was passed. A further blow was the fall on 8 February of Malaga, whose anarchist commander

---

48   Garcia Oliver's contortions about joining the central government are described in his
      memoir, written in exile, *El Eco de los Pasos* (Oliver 1978, pp. 291–3).

was condemned to death under pressure from the Communist Party; he was later pardoned after an inquiry revealed the equal culpability of the CP in the debacle.

This growing tension between the PCE-PSUC and forces to its left, the POUM and the CNT-FAI, came to a head in Barcelona in May 1937.[49] For months, the Stalinist media had been inundating the Republic and the world with denunciations of the 'Trotskyist-fascist' POUM; with the anarchists, on the other hand, they were forced to remain more circumspect, correctly assessing that they might well lose a direct military confrontation. May Day celebrations had been cancelled for fear of an outbreak of fighting between the CNT and the UGT. The telephone exchange in downtown Barcelona was dominated by the CNT since July 1936. The Communist police chief of Barcelona arrived there with the intention of taking over the building. The situation escalated, with the CNT, the POUM, the Friends of Durruti,[50] and the Anarchist Youth building their barricades, facing off against the barricades of the PSUC and the UGT. (The Stalinists were also intent on the ouster of Largo Caballero as prime minister, with all his prestige, still intact, in the Spanish working class. Largo Caballero, having tired of PCE-PSUC and Soviet pressure on his government, had issued a decree on 21 April requiring his personal approval of all Commissars, and for the few further months until his orchestrated ouster, he moved closer to the CNT.) The POUM and the POUM Youth had been rapidly moving to the left and were working with the Friends of Durruti. The standoff continued on 4 May, and from Valencia, Juan Garcia Oliver and Federica Montseny broadcast radio appeals to their comrades to lay down arms and return to work. The CNT daily *Solidaridad Obrera* echoed their appeal. Anarchist columns at the front, prepared to march on both Barcelona and Madrid, stopped in their tracks.[51] The Italian anarchist Camillo Berneri was murdered by the Stalinists on 5 May. British destroyers appeared just off the bay, rumoured to be preparing to intervene. Fighting spread to the Barcelona suburbs and other towns along the coast. It was put down by 4000 Republican Guardias de Asalto, the elite police force, arriving from Valencia. At dawn on 7 May the CNT issued another radio appeal for 'normality'. By 8 May, the city was finally quiet, with hundreds killed

---

49   For a close account of events leading up to the showdown and the actual street fighting in Barcelona between 3 May and 7 May, I refer the reader once again to the accounts of Orwell 1952 [1938] and Bolloten 1979.

50   A radical left anarchist current calling for a 'new revolution' against the sellout of the CNT leaders in the Barcelona and Madrid governments.

51   A Stalinist commander threatened to bomb the anarchist Ascaso Column if it marched on Madrid. Many of these details are taken from Thomas 1965, pp. 545–50.

and thousands wounded. The gap between the anarchists in the streets and the CNT ministers in Valencia had become unbridgeable.

Politically, the revolution begun in July 1936 was dead. There remained, however, the tasks of grinding down the industrial and agrarian collectives and dealing with the still considerable CNT-FAI regiments at the front, however professionalised they may have become.[52]

The four CNT-FAI ministers left the Republican government in the wake of the events in Barcelona, and Largo Caballero resigned shortly thereafter. The anarchists were under no illusions about the trail of errors they left in their wake, as reported to the workers in a balance sheet of their activity. The ex-Minister of Commerce Juan Lopez had been blocked in his projects because of the opposition of Largo Caballero and all defenders of the status quo: 'We have to recognize the uselessness of our governmental participation in the economic sphere'. The CNT made a new unity overture to the UGT but it came to nothing. On 25 May 1937, the government issued a decree requiring collectivised firms to join a commercial register; they thus became legal 'judicial personalities' continuous with the old firms they had replaced. 'The legalization of collectivization led, through state control, to the undoing of the revolution; the final steps of this policy, which had been successfully pushed by the Communists, energetically supported and passively tolerated by the anarchists were openly visible after the crisis of May 1937 ...'[53] On 18 June, the government required registration of all radio stations and two months later prohibited all criticism of the Soviet Union.

In late June, the CNT was also expelled from the Generalitat, and there was a temporary ban on its daily *Solidaridad Obrera*. In August, the Stalinist General Lister began his attacks on the rural collectives in Aragon, and the POUM was pushed out of the Catalan Consejo de Economia.

The Stalinist offensive in all institutions of the Republic continued unabated. In fall 1937 at the UGT Congress, the Catalan Stalinist Ruiz Ponseti, member of the PSUC, proposed the elimination of trade union delegates in all firms, attacking the 'excess of the intervention of the democratic principle in the constitution of the enterprise councils'. Events were pushing the libertarians in the same direction; in September 1937, the Congress of the CNT, the FAI, and the Libertarian Youth demanded the immediate nationalisation of all war industries, foreign commerce, mines and banking, as well as the municipalisation of

---

52   'Even after the days of May 1937 – a defeat within the triumph – some elements of dual
       power were still resisting and often bases from which to reconquer the lost ground' (Munis
       1948, p. 292).

53   Bernecker 1982, p. 339.

housing, public services, health and social assistance. They conceded the need for private enterprises in light industry, retail commerce and in small agrarian property. This was a real departure from the Zaragoza programme and the 'pure' anarchist line. As in the May events in Barcelona, the congress showed the emerging divorce between the base and the leaders of the CNT, a clear process of 'oligarquization'.[54] The plenum declared: 'The CNT has understood that there cannot be a prosperous economy, speaking collectively, without centralized control and coordination in its administrative aspects'.

On 20 November 1937, the Generalitat issued the 'decree of special interventions' giving the government an override of worker-elected factory inspectors. In response to this and other developments, the anarchists attacked in particular the 'multiplication of the army of parasites' and the impenetrability of the countless commissions. On 1 December, Ruiz Ponseti, in the Consejo de Economia, said that directors named by workers lacked the necessary technical formation and were thus unfit to assume management positions.

A further CNT Plenum met in January 1938. 'The tendency to centralization and concentration of forces in the leadership of the union was patent at this plenum ...'[55] It dispensed with the previous assembly format and had instead a prepared agenda. In unprecedented fashion, the national committee intervened directly in all debates. 'With the creation of labor inspectors, union committees of control, administrative and technical councils, people in charge of distributing work (in many cases with the power to lay off workers), and directors given full powers ... the CNT was converted into a bureaucratic-centralist organization which gave up the principles of rank-and-file autonomy and responsible self-decision for a total hierarchical restructuring and economic planning. The process of centralization imposed by the war in every area did not stop at the doors of the union organization itself'. Vernon Richards, English anarchist, said these decisions meant the end of 'the CNT as a revolutionary organization controlled by its members'. Bernecker concurred: 'The abandonment ... of the original anarchist economic program must be attributed on one hand to their interpretive weaknesses and a simplified conception of the economic process, which was not understood in the slightest, and on the other hand, because of the war, the unavoidable economic centralization and global planning advocated from the beginning by the Communists ... the process which led from the "libertarian" economic configuration to the dirigist interventionism of the state, from the programmatic declaration of September 1936

54   Ibid. p. 298.
55   Ibid. pp. 300–1.

to the Expanded Economic Plenum (1938), showed the adoption of "authorit-arian" schemes of organization in industry and in the internal structure of the CNT'.

This process was opposed by the Friends of Durruti. 'The Friends of Durruti had an intransigent position close to the Trotskyist wing of the POUM. They called for struggle not only against the Communists of the PCE and the PSUC, against the bourgeois parties, the state, the government, etc., but also fought against the moderate line of the committees of the CNT and the FAI. They called for a new revolution'.[56]

4   Agrarian Collectives

Nearly a year passed before the CNT created a competent agrarian organisation for all Republican territory (the Federación Nacional de Campesinos). Its prin-ciples, by summer 1937, were in open contradiction with certain basic anarchist postulates. Mandatory decisions taken on a national level were incompatible with decisions coming 'from below'. As Bernecker puts it, 'after an initial period of sacrificial solidarity, mutual aid and aid given freely with nothing in return, the unions – as also occurred in industry – in many prosperous agrarian collect-ives had to fight against the "neocapitalism" of the latter which did not want to help other collectives in deficit ...'[57]

a   *Catalonia*
In Catalonia, initially, there had been only informal criteria for entry into rural collectives; the CNT repeatedly stated that small proprietors did not need fear for their property. Rent, electricity, water, medicine, hospices for elderly and infirm were free. But already in August 1936, the Catalan government created mandatory membership for independent peasants in the Catalan peasants' union, a measure aimed at creating a counterweight to CNT influence in the industrial collectives. Tenant farmers were attracted to the PSUC (once again, the CP in Catalonia) for its propaganda aimed at small peasant landowners. By January 1937, the Catalan government was trying to sabotage rural collect-ives. A CNT regional plenum of peasants, however, placed collectives under the control of the CNT, the UGT and the rural growers union. It recognised the use of money for the foreseeable future. There were perhaps 200 rural col-

---

56   Ibid.
57   Ibid. pp. 131–3.

lectives in Catalonia, but they were not as important there as were private farms. In July 1937, the Generalitat expropriated, without indemnity, rural *fincas* belonging to persons who supported fascist uprising. In August 1937, following the events of May 1937, the Catalan government issued a decree providing for regulation and recognition of rural collectives, extending state control over them.

b   *Aragon*

Much of Aragon had initially fallen to Franco's coup. Many collectives were established there as militia columns clawed back lost territory on the way to liberate Zaragoza. The Durruti column spread collectivisation, with about 450 collectives overall.[58]

In mid-February 1937, the Federacion de Colectividades de Aragon was established to 'coordinate the economic potential of the region'. The federation drew up a standardised family rationing card, and made plans to create experimental farms, nurseries, and rural technical colleges. Comarcal (county) federations were set up to deal with radio, post, telegraphs, telephones, and means of transport. Weapons were distributed to collective members. Another federation established central warehouses. Electricity was spread to villages, and hospitals were built. One collective in April 1937 allowed individuals to abstain if they wished, as had occurred in the Levant. The collectives implemented mandatory work for those between 18 and 60, except for pregnant women or women with child care responsibilities. There were night classes in literacy. Plenary assemblies elected an executive committee, which was immediately revocable. Elections were held on the basis of one vote, one member, no matter how large or small the individual's initial contribution of land, tools and animals to the collective.

The CNT-FAI had in fact never spoken of 'agrarian collectives' before the war. In Aragon, the CNT improvised new methods for exchange of goods without 'money'. These forms often varied from village to village and were often

---

58   Casanova 1985 provides a more nuanced view of the Aragonese collectives. In his view, in Aragon as a whole, the respective weight of the CNT and the UGT was about equal (p. 31). He concurs with Bernecker 1982, p. 315, that the May 1936 Zaragoza congress arrived at its agrarian resolution 'without clarifying the most elementary economic concepts'. Where they later were in control, 'the anarchists did not implant a model of collectivization which would resolve the problems of production and exchange' (Casanova 1985, p. 318). 'Those defending the "eternal aspiration to equality" ignore numerous examples ... of the marginalization of social groups (women, unaffiliated peasants) and ignore the real conditions'.

incompatible. Borkenau emphasised the ethical dimension in anarchist collectives and in the suppression of money.

In August 1937, Stalinist general Enrique Lister, as part of the Communist Party's appeal to small landowners, attacked the majority of Aragon collectives. (Communist propaganda portrayed the collectives as created by violent compulsion (!) and inefficient.) Hundreds of anarchists were arrested, members of the CNT were excluded from participation in municipal assemblies, many collectives were destroyed, and their land was re-privatised. Granaries were opened and looted for military exactions. Some collectives, however, were later reconstituted. The Communist Party later backed off from its anti-collectivisation campaign; it had frightened collective members who stopped work and returned to cultivating small parcels of their own, threatening the fall harvest.

c   *The Levante*

On 18–20 September 1936, the Regional Federation of Levantine Peasants (Spanish initials FRCL) met in Valencia. At that point, 13.2 percent of the land in the Levant had been seized, and one-third organised into collectives. In some of them, there had been total collectivisation and the abolition of money.[59] All collectives had their own schools by 1938. The FRCL was the top of a pyramid of organisations, beginning with local *sindicatos* and collectives, moving up to the federation of each *comarca* (county), and thereafter to provincial federations. The FRCL had a sizeable number of accountants to coordinate efforts at a higher level. The congress also decided not to interfere with private plots if their owners did not interfere with the collectives.

On 7 October, however, there was a land decree tilted toward landowners, designed to control collectives and to slow their further diffusion. By the spring of 1937, the police and military would begin their attacks on collectives. Nonetheless, in 1938, there were 500 to 900 collectives in the Levante, involving 40 percent of the population.

Separate from the Levantine collectives, in October 1936, the CNT and UGT created the CLUEA, a regional cooperative for orange exports, a major Levantine crop. The CLUEA was designed to eliminate middlemen and also raise foreign currency for the Republic. It nonetheless met with hostility from the central government. Borkenau also reported a battle between the CNT and the CP, with the latter defending rich peasants.[60]

---

59   Alexander 1999, vol. 1, pp. 394–402.
60   Borkenau 1937, p. 198.

d   *Elsewhere*

Also in July 1937, there were armed confrontations between anarchists and communists in rural Castile. This was one clear-cut case, among many, where apparently 'economic' policy was inseparable from military strategy; Daniel Guerin, in his book *Anarchism*, argues that ambivalence on collectives of the government in Valencia contributed to the defeat of the Republic; poor peasants did not see the point of fighting for it.

e   *National Coordination*

In June 1937, when the tide had turned against it in the wake of May 1937, CNT rural groups created a national organisation, and held a National Plenum of Regional Peasant Organizations. The Law for Temporary Legalization of Agrarian Collectives was passed in the same month, designed to ensure harvests over the coming year before peasants bolted from them under government pressure. In 1936–7, the Institute for Agrarian Reform gave 50 million pesetas to those collectives accepting state intervention, thus cutting out the CNT. Many people who had been expropriated in the summer of 1936 were trying to get their land back. According to Bernecker, as of August 1938 there were 2213 legalised collectives, but Robert Alexander places the number much higher.[61] All in all, three million people of an agrarian population of 17 million were involved in the collectivised rural economy. Malefakis[62] estimates that two-thirds of all cultivated land was taken over by collectives. There were, however, no collectives in the Basque Provinces, Santander and Asturias. According to Bolloten, a large part of the rural population resisted collectivisation. Different collectives also had different rules. In general, however, they established schools, built many libraries and *ateneos* (social centres), some hospitals and senior homes. They set a formal retirement age and closed brothels.

In July 1937 the FAI held a peninsular plenum in Valencia. It marked the end of 'classical' Spanish anarchism. The plenum voted to give up the lax internal structure of 'affinity groups' and replaced them with 'territorial groupings'.

5   More on Politics and Military Developments

We have to some extent bracketed the military developments that were simultaneous to the political and economic events described above, in order to

---

61   Ibid. p. 325.
62   Malefakis 1970.

underscore the steady process of anarchist accommodation to the institutions of the Popular Front. We now attempt to round out this picture from the military standpoint, after the decisive political turn of May 1937.

In December 1937, Republican forces attacked Teruel and occupied it; it was unfortunately the coldest city in Spain, in the dead of winter, and, with tens of thousands of casualties on both sides, many from inadequate food and clothing in sub-zero temperatures, the fascists recaptured it in February 1938. It was, again, a clear case of military strategy inseparable from politics. The ex-Communist commander El Campesino wrote many years later that anarchist troops had been purposely sacrificed to discredit them and to oust PSOE member Indalecio Prieto as Minister of Defence.[63] Also in February 1938, all collectives in Aragon were occupied by Franco's troops, completing the work of demolition begun by General Enrique Lister the previous August.

On 18 March 1938, prompted by the collapse of the Aragon front, the CNT and the UGT signed a common programme. It was described at the time as 'Bakunin and Marx embrace in a big hug'. The programme was widely touted by the PCE and the PSUC as a major step forward for trade-union unity; it called for nationalisation (as opposed to the earlier collectivisations) and underscored respect for individualist peasants. The real goal of the PCE-PSUC, however, was to exclude unions from the government, since the CNT was still the largest union. Further concessions by the CNT included the end of the federated system of 'free municipalities' and the creation of more stratified entities. The pact was 'the major abandonment of previous principles and ideals in the ideological evolution of Spanish anarcho-syndicalism'.[64] Shortly after the signing, the CNT and UGT did enter the cabinet of Juan Negrin.[65] But with ongoing military

---

63   Indalecio Prieto was the most important leader of the right wing of the PSOE, and the long-time opponent of Largo Caballero. He was hardly sympathetic to the anarchists, but was also considered insufficiently docile by the Stalinists. Using military defeat and setbacks, sometimes created intentionally to discredit those in charge, was a typical PCE-PSUC strategem for replacing unwanted figures, socialist or anarchist, with more pliable people. A POUM commander, Mika Etchebehere, in her book *Ma guerre d'Espagne a moi*, describes similar episodes, such as when a POUM batallion was left in a hopeless position, without relief, during the defence of Madrid (Etchebehere 1976).

64   Bernecker 1982, p. 311. Borkenau 1937, p. 210, wrote that the 'only difference with Russia is that the ruling bureaucracy belongs to three or four parties instead of one ...'

65   Negrin had taken over in May 1937 after the 'events' of that month. He was also a right-wing Socialist, supported by the CP for lack of another candidate acceptable to others, but ultimately proved to be an independent figure.

developments, the realisation of the anarchist-socialist programme passed to a very secondary plane. The CNT, the anarchist union with more than a million members, wound up affirming traditional national patriotism.

On 5 April 1938, Franco's troops drove to the Mediterranean, cutting the Republic in half. On 30 April, the CNT, whistling in the dark, tried somehow to deduce a confirmation of its own agrarian policy from the Negrin government's 'thirteen points' of its war aims (apparently modelled on Woodrow Wilson's Fourteen Points).[66] In reality, despite having more than a million members, the CNT had been eliminated from all important centres of power.[67] It had been compelled to renounce all demands for the 'communalisation' or 'socialisation' of land. Both the CP and the POUM had been for mere nationalisation. The agreement reflected the Communist appeals to small and medium landholders, who had been 31 percent of all CP members in February 1937. Nonetheless, in May 1938, the anarchist press was still claiming that 2000 firms had adopted terms of the collectivisation decree.

As Thomas puts it, '... before the spring [of 1938], Anarchist leaders had justified their acquiescence to so many humiliations before the Communists because they felt they would be able to come to terms after the war; but the disasters in Aragon had clearly suggested that the war might be lost. The crisis in the movement therefore grumbled on all the summer, even more intensely felt because members of the CNT still held positions in the government, from the Cabinet downwards'.[68] (In fact, some Republican politicians favoured dragging out the losing war in the belief that the impending outbreak of World War Two would oblige the Allies to intervene of the side of the Republic. Stalin, meanwhile, was losing interest in Spain as he prepared overtures to Germany, resulting in the Stalin-Hitler Pact of August 1939.)

As if to drive home the new balance of forces, in May 1938 5500 of 7000 promotions in the army were Communist Party members. In July 1938, the

---

66   The thirteen points included absolute independence for Spain; expulsion of all foreign military forces; universal suffrage; no reprisals; respect for regional liberties; encouragement of capitalist properties without large trusts; agricultural reform; the rights of workers guaranteed; the 'cultural, physical and moral development of the race'; the army outside politics; renunciation of war; cooperation with the League of Nations; an amnesty for all enemies. The CNT-UGT committee of collaboration approved the programme, but the FAI denounced it as a return to the pre-July 1936 status quo (Thomas 1965, pp. 674–5).

67   Bernecker 1982, p. 140.

68   Thomas 1965, p. 675. Segundo Blanco of the CNT became Minister of Education and Health in March 1938.

last major Republican offensive of the war began when its armies crossed the Ebro river in Aragon. 60 percent of the troops on the front were from the CNT. Since virtually the entire offensive was carried out under Communist commanders, anarchist units were left on the front for long periods without rest, while CP units were rested. (Meanwhile, behind the lines, well-armed and well-fed Assault Guards and *carabineros* were not sent to the front until final phase of Franco's attack on Catalonia.) On 15 November 1938, admitting defeat, Republican troops were withdrawn back over the Ebro. It was the beginning of the end.

The final months of the war, up to Franco's final victory on 31 March 1939, involved an endgame of Republican attempts to salvage a negotiated peace settlement, attempts which were contemptuously dismissed by Franco. These months were, however, marked by one curious episode, the Casado coup a-gainst Negrin, backed militarily by Cipriano Mera, the anarchist commander of the IVth Army Group.

Colonel Segismundo Casado was commander of the Army of the Centre in Madrid. He was hardly an unambiguous figure, but was opposed to Negrin's ostensible plan to fight to the bitter end, even as many people in his cabinet were already getting passports and preparing to leave for France. Casado argued with Negrin for surrender, pointing to the desperate material conditions in Madrid and in what was left of the Republican army. His real wrath was aimed at the Communists, also calling for a fight to the end, whom he had seen again and again meddle in military matters for their own advantage. On 28 Febru-ary, Britain and France had recognised Franco. Casado lined up support among top non-Communist military leaders, insisting that he could get a better peace from Franco than Negrin. CNT commander Cipriano Mera moved his troops to Casado's headquarters in Madrid on 4 March, and a manifesto announcing the coup was broadcast that night, arguing again for a negotiated peace. On the fol-lowing day, Communist commanders moved on Madrid and by 7 March, most of Madrid was under their control. Heavy fighting took place on 8 March. Mera's troops captured the CP positions on the 9th. Casado's cabinet, again whistling in the dark, drew up peace terms for further negotations with Franco. These included no reprisals, respect shown for fighting forces, including officers, and twenty-five days to leave Spain for all who wished to do so. A truce was negoti-ated with both sides in the Casado coup returning to their positions of 2 March. An estimated 5000 Republican troops on both sides had died in the melee. In the view of many anarchists, it was a case of something that should have happened in May 1937.

Casado, now in charge of negotiating surrender with Franco, tried to gain time to allow people to flee. 'Franco expressed his pleasure that he was being saved "the trouble of crushing the Communists".[69] Casado had achieved no more concessions than Negrin, and had only won time for the Republican elite, but not ordinary people, to leave Spain. On 31 March 1939, the civil war was over.

6   How the Working Class Takes Over Today

There slowly formed a magnificent unity of people from all classes and all parties who understood, like us, that the revolution is something different from the struggle in the streets and that, in a real revolution, those who have the spirit and will to contribute their manual, intellectual, administrative or technical help to the common project, have nothing to lose.

DIEGO ABAD DE SANTILLÁN, *Porque Perdimos la Guerra* (1940)

∙ ∙
∙

Our main purpose here has been to explore the consequences of the decades long 'apolitical' and 'antipolitical' stance of the Spanish anarchist movement. We know what resulted from their decision to first allow the bourgeois state to remain standing[70] and then to join it; we cannot know what would have resulted if they had 'gone for broke' instead.

Clearly the Spanish Revolution suffered even more than the Russian Revolution from its international isolation. In 1917–21, not only were there mass radical movements in thirty countries, but the main capitalist powers themselves were weakened and discredited by four years of meaningless mutual slaughter. Without the readily offered counter-revolutionary services of Social Democracy in key countries, above all Germany, the capitalists would have been lost.

We can, today, no more anticipate the concrete situation of a working-class takeover – a revolution – than did the Spanish anarchists at their somewhat idyllic May 1936 congress. Thanks, however, to the far greater interconnectedness produced by globalisation, we can safely assume that such a development will not be limited to one country, at least not for long. Nonetheless, we can

---

69   Ibid. p. 751. A full account of the Casado coup is in Thomas 1965, pp. 734–55.

70   Speaking of the example of the judiciary, Abad de Santillán notes a CNT proposal to abolish lawyers. Why, he asks, was the Palace of Justice reopened? Old judges reappeared and 'we put an instrument at the service of the counter-revolution which we ourselves had revalorized' (de Santillán 1949, pp. 80–1).

agree that for the moment (2013) the international radical left hardly pays more attention to Abad de Santillán's call to think more concretely about what to do in the immediate aftermath of a successful revolutionary takeover than did its counterparts more than 75 years ago.

Like the anarchists and anarcho-syndicalists of that time, today, no important militant current, Marxist or anarcho-syndicalist, has devoted serious energy to outlining a concrete transition out of capitalism. There is always the next meeting, the next street action, the next strike, the next riot, the next prison hunger strike, the next episode of police run amok, and these are of course real concerns. But such a typical conception of activism actually reproduces in different guise the old formulation of ill-famed reformist Edward Bernstein, in his debate with Rosa Luxemburg, that 'the movement is everything, the goal is nothing'. The trick is to locate the 'goal' within the daily life of the movement, but this requires a rethink of priorities.

There have been very good reasons for this avoidance of a long-term vision, going back to Marx's critique of the detailed schemes drawn up by the utopian socialists, Owen, Fourier, or the St-Simonians. (We have seen the link between this early nineteenth century kind of abstract utopian thinking and classical anarchism in Thesis 4 of Part One above.) In the Hegel-Marx tradition of an evolving self-acting totality, the answer is already implicit in the question, and the *Manifesto* warns against (again, as previously quoted) any 'idea sprung from the head of a world reformer', counterposing to it the 'real movement unfolding before our eyes'. And this insistence on the 'immanence' of solutions, against any artificial standard imposed from outside the world historical process, is exactly correct.

Our method is therefore different.[71] We begin precisely from an immanent 'inventory' of world material production and above all the material reproduction of those who are engaged in it. We include in this the reproduction of nature, such as climate change, the solution to which, like the distribution of world resources, necessarily and obviously points beyond any 'localist' solutions,[72] such as those which often held back the industrial and agrarian collectives in Spain. *This* is the concrete totality of the Hegel-Marx method, 'acting

---

71   Elaborated in 'The Historical Moment that Produced Us' (Insurgent Notes 2010), available online at: http://insurgentnotes.com/2010/06/historical_moment/. See the final section of 16 proposed points for global reconstruction, which are merely suggestions, and hardly definitive.

72   For example, the oil workers in the Gulf will not, by themselves, decide where to ship the oil, while having as much control over their conditions of work as is possible within a global coordination.

upon itself' in the reproduction of the world, starting with the reproduction of labour power. We look at the concrete struggles of this 'labour power in contradiction with itself' that *is* capital, from the Marikana miners in South Africa to the 120,000 'incidents' (strikes, riots, confrontations over land confiscation) a year in China, to the gas and water wars against privatisation in Bolivia, to the strikes and riots in Greece against European Union austerity, to the militant attempts of Egyptian workers to find a path independent of both the Islamists and the military, to the mobilisation of public employees in Wisconsin, Ohio or Indiana against assaults on their wages and benefits. Most of these upsurges, often quite impressive, are actions of the class 'in itself', however militant, on the way to becoming a class 'for itself', namely ready to pose an alternative social order, based on a (self-) recognition that their protagonists, once aware of their tasks, *are* the incipient alternative. We seek in them clues to the future convergence of a class-for-itself, as for example in the growing recognition among transport workers of their special power in shutting down 'choke points', one Achilles heel of 'globalization'.

Spain in 1936 was a society in which the great majority of workers and peasants lived very close to the bone, and, as in the upsurges of the 1960s and 1970s (May-June 1968 in France, the wildcats in Britain from 1955 to 1972, the American wildcats c. 1970 in auto, the Teamsters, the phone company, the post office, albeit recognising a much transformed standard of living) democratic self-management of the existing means of production was the obvious programmatic next step.

That obviously remains central today, but the galloping decay and proliferation of socially useless and socially noxious activities (already quite in evidence in 1970) has reached a level where as many workers would be voting to abolish their own jobs as would be placing them under workers' control, in an overall strategy, with all the labour power thus freed, to radically shorten the working day. This is a fundamental point which a developing revolutionary movement must communicate to broader layers of society today. Those who labour in state and corporate bureaucracies, or the FIRE (finance-insurance-real estate) sector, or as cashiers and toll takers, or homeland security personnel, for starters, are in their ample majority wage-labour proletarians, like those who produce material commodities such as cars, bread, steel, or houses but also nuclear submarines or weapons of mass destruction (e.g., drone bombers). While it is obvious that a society after the abolition of commodity production will no longer produce the latter, the important point is that, for the wage-labour work force as a whole, there is no bedrock 'real' collection of use values separate from the forms currently imposed by capital, and all will be judged, and transformed, based on global needs once true production for use value, centred on the reproduction of the ultimate use value, labour power, is possible. The millions of cars and trucks produced annually may appear empirically as 'use values' today, but we must consider their reality relative to the existing potential of mass transportation, both within cities and between them, to determine their true 'use value' in the totality. Truth, as Hegel showed two hundred years ago, is in the whole, and the revolutionary movement has to start communicating the above realities to broader layers, above and beyond next week's demo.

The potential productivity of masses of workers, once embarked on the construction of a new world, is incredible. To return briefly to Spain: in 1936 in Catalonia, there was no war industry whatsoever. Following the July defeat of Franco's coup, 800 factories in Barcelona, transformed into industrial collectives, pooled their resources to create one, under the pressing needs of the war. According to foreign military observers, the Catalan workers in two months achieved a greater transformation of factories for war production than France had achieved in the first two years of World War One.

Hopefully our revolution will not be burdened by the same urgent needs of civil war (though that is not to be precluded). The point is rather that tremendous energies are bottled up in capitalist social relations today that can, in the right circumstances, totally transform what are perceived as 'use values', once ordinary working people see the 'beach' under the 'pavement', as one slogan in France in May 1968 put it.

A revolutionary organisation today, to conclude, must apply this 'Hegel-Marx' sense of the totality to itself. This means first of all a modest appreciation of its own true stature, in the broader global development of the 'class-for-itself'. It must recognise the primacy of the 'real movement' and see its main goal as its own abolition as a separate grouping, once its tasks are accomplished. It must attempt to create within itself the closest possible approximation of the relations of a liberated humanity within its own internal life, which means the deepest possible involvement, above and beyond the indispensable daily tasks of militancy, with analysis of the world productive forces, and first of all of the world work force, to see the maturation of the methods of struggle. It must prioritise 'internal education', starting with the history and theory of the revolutionary movement. It must attempt to embrace everything valid in contemporary culture, science and technology, and appeal to those cultural and technical strata who see the need to link their fate to that of the communist revolution. It must acquaint itself with military strategy, in the different traditions of Engels, Trotsky, Makhno, or the Cipriano Meras (a former construction worker). It must prepare, in a word, the groundwork for the takeover of production and reproduction. The better prepared in advance the movement is, the smoother and less violent that takeover will be.

Anti-Capitalism or Anti-Imperialism? Interwar Authoritarian and Fascist Sources of a Reactionary Ideology: The Case of the Bolivian MNR

The following text is a history and analysis of the fascist and proto-fascist ideologies which shaped the pre-history and early history of the Bolivian MNR (Movimiento Nacional Revolucionario) from 1936 to its seizure of power in 1952.

Friends and comrades who know of my brief (two week) visit to Bolivia in fall 2010 have generally been expecting the text to be a critique of the contemporary government of Evo Morales and the MAS (Movimiento al Socialismo). That was in fact part of my intention in going there, but the enormity of the task, the brevity of my visit and my experiences there began to alter that plan after I returned to the U.S. My momentum in writing about the present was also undercut by the discovery of the excellent articles of Jeffery Webber on Morales's neo-liberal economic policies since coming to power, based on much more in-depth research and a much longer involvement in Bolivia itself than mine, saying more or less exactly what I intended to say, and more.[1] Finally, in past writing about different countries (e.g., Portugal, Spain, Korea) an indispensable aid has always been finding 'my crowd' in such places, and while I met many excellent people who gave freely of their time and knowledge, this did not occur in Bolivia.

But the impulse behind the direction the article finally took lies deeper. Long ago I was deeply influenced by the book of Jean-Pierre Faye, *Langages totalitaires* (published in France in 1972, and still outrageously not translated into English) which describes the 'oscillation' between the elements of the far left and the far right in Germany between 1890 and 1933 (personified in the figure of Karl Radek), the 'red-brown' crossover between nationalism and

---

1 These articles appear in three parts in *Historical Materialism*, beginning with No. 16, 2008. See Webber 2008a, 2008b, 2008c. They are followed by more recent updates on the situation in Bolivia, available online; above all http://www.isreview.org/issues/73/feat-bolivia.shtml. As good as these articles are on Morales's and the MAS's domestic agenda since 2005, I of course reject Webber's situating of the Morales government in a 'counter-hegemonic bloc' led by Cuba and Venezuela, with the implication that such a bloc is 'progressive' and 'anti-imperialist'.

socialism that ultimately produced National Socialism and its more radical spinoff, the National Bolsheviks. These various 'Trotskyists of Nazism' (such as those most famously associated with the 'red' wing of the Nazi Party led by the likes of Ernst Roehm and Gregor Strasser) were massacred by Hitler's SS along with hundreds of others on the 'Night of the Long Knives' in 1934. (Faye hints briefly in an afterword at a 'National Bolshevik' moment in Bolivia, though in the 1970s, not in the period leading up to the MNR revolution of 1952.) There was the further enticing hint of the very same Ernst Roehm's two-year presence in the Bolivian Army High Command in the late 1920s, which in fact turned out to confirm my early working hypothesis in spades. Finally, I noticed that even the best treatments of the early MNR founders gave short shrift to their fascist moment.

Lacking access to 'my crowd' in Bolivia (if it in fact exists), I had to fall back on books and whatever discussions came up. Almost immediately I encountered what would be a main, and troubling, theme of the trip: the apparently wide-spread belief that Marxism, class, capitalism and socialism were 'Eurocentric' concepts, to which the 'plurinational', 'pachakuti'[2] higher synthesis of 'Europe-an' and 'Andean-Amazonian' cultures – essentially the ideology of the regime – was the real alternative. It seemed on further inquiry to be a local variant of the identity politics that had overwhelmed much of the Western left after the defeat of the upsurge of the 1960s and 1970s.

While this is indeed the ideology of the Morales regime and is articulated by staffers, foreign and local, of the swarm of NGOs from which the regime seems to have drawn many of its personnel, I first heard it from the intellectually-inclined manager of a La Paz bookstore, where I was buying volumes of the Trotskyist Guillermo Lora's highly useful (if politically not fully reliable) his-tory of the Bolivian working class. What was particularly troubling about this 'discourse' (to use a loathsome word from contemporary faddish jargon) was the utter caricature of the West to which the indigenous side of the synthesis was counterposed. It was as if, in these people's experience, 1950s Soviet-type Zhdanovian 'Marxism' was all they had ever encountered. Marxism was 'lin-ear', 'developmentalist' and hardly different epistemologically from Newton and Descartes.[3]

---

2   'Pachakuti' is a term taken from the Quechua 'pacha', meaning time and space or the world, and 'kuti', meaning upheaval or revolution.

3   One strange sub-text of the anti-Eurocentric posture, which I encountered two or three times in person and also in books, is the recourse to quantum physics to buttress this perspective. Bell's Theorem posits the possibility of one atomic particle being in two places at the same time, across galaxies, and nonetheless in communication. This is supposed to be a scientific

Octavio Paz once described Latin America as the 'suburbs of history', trapped for geopolitical reasons in something of a backwater. I would not want to exaggerate this, particularly since, in the law of combined and uneven development, today's apparent backwater can be tomorrow's cutting edge. But in conversations with militants in Bolivia and then Peru (where I also spent a week in fall 2010) it emerged that almost no one had ever heard of Marx's *Ethnographic Notebooks*, Rosa Luxemburg's extensive writings on pre-capitalist societies (in her *Introduction to Political Economy*),[4] the *Grundrisse* (though it was translated into Spanish in 1972), Ernst Bloch, Korsch, Lukács, the Hegel Renaissance in Marxism generally, I.I. Rubin, Bordiga, German-Dutch council communism, the Socialism or Barbarism group, Guy Debord, Camatte, Dauvé, C.L.R. James or many other figures one could mention from the ferment in the West since the 1950s. Rosa Luxemburg seemed little known, and even Trotskyism (the major current of the Bolivian working class from the 1940s to the 1980s) seemed to have been largely eclipsed by the perspective of 'social movements' and pluri-nationality. (In Peru, the left is dominated by Stalinism and Maoism, with Trotskyism a poor third; the Shining Path movement is making a comeback with guerrilla action in the countryside and a significant urban base of supporters.)

Much could be said about this, and since I was little more (where Andean South America is concerned) than a better-informed-than-average tourist, I hesitate to press very far. In addition to the Aymara and Quechua majority, there are approximately 35 identified 'ethnicities' in Bolivia, such as the Guarani in the Amazonian region. One Aymara woman in Cochabamba told me 'yes, I was an anarcho-Marxist militant for a number of years, but then I realised that these were Eurocentric ideas'. When I countered, hoping to draw her out, that a large number of the Trotskyist miner militants from the 1940s to the 1980s had been Quechua or Aymara, she replied that, 'yes, that was true, but up until recently the left never talked about it. For the left, they were just workers'.

---

grounding of the *parakuti* synthesis, as elaborated for example in the ex-Trotskyist Filemon Escobar's 2008 book *De la revolucion al Pachakuti: El aprendrizaje del Respeto Reciproco entre blancos y indios*. Escobar at least comes to his 'revolution of the coca leaf' from more than 40 years of worker militancy, but an even more elaborate counterposition of this indigenist synthesis to a vulgar Marxist straw man is by an academic, Blithz Lozada (Lozada 2008). Escobar and Lozada both see Marx as expressing a world view not qualitatively different from that of Newton and Descartes.

4   Long unavailable in English, except for a translation published in Ceylon in the late 1950s, there is an excerpt from Luxemburg's 1912 *Einführung in die politische Ökonomie* in Luxemburg 2004.

Clearly the turning point in modern Bolivian history and the backdrop to this ideological turn was the gutting of the mines under the mid-1980s neo-liberal regime, in which 80 percent of Bolivia's miners were laid off and dispersed around the country.[5] It was a rollback as great as Thatcher's defeat of the British miners' strike, at exactly the same time. Many of these miners did manage to re-establish themselves somewhat, particularly in the huge hard-scrabble exurb of El Alto, just above La Paz, where the 2005 gas war was centred and which was definitely strengthened by their earlier militant experience of mass struggle.[6]

One sad reality of the trip, however, was the absence from Bolivia, while I was there, of Oscar Olivera, by all accounts a central self-effacing rank-and-file leader of both (2000 and 2003) water wars. Prior to 2000, he had been a militant in a shoe factory. His book *Cochabamba!*[7] contains his riveting account of the uprisings, which amounted to the constitution of a virtual soviet taking over the city and stopping the privatisation of the local water works, a 'social movement' that pulled in what seemed at times like almost the whole population. The savagery of the privatisation law was such that, in addition to price increases sometimes amounting to 20 percent of family incomes, people with wells on their property were required to cap them, and it was illegal to trap rain water in a barrel.

Oscar Oliveira also made a scathing critique of the Morales government in August 2010,[8] having been declared an 'enemy' by Morales two years earlier. In summer 2010, he decided to withdraw from political activity, apparently deeply demoralised. At the time, he was the head of the *Federación de Trabajadores Fabriles de Cochabamba*, an association of one hundred workplaces in the city. When he submitted his resignation for personal reasons, it was overwhelmingly rejected by the membership. At that point, Morales intervened, trying to get the MAS supporters in the organisation to oust him. They refused, and instead the membership put Oliveira on a kind of leave of absence, welcome to return at any time. (He was apparently taking a personal trip to Europe.) Oliveira had refused Morales's offer of a ministerial position and all other perquisites, preferring (unlike many key figures of the 2000–5 struggles) to stay with the base.

---

5   An account of Jeffrey Sachs's 1985 'shock therapy' in Bolivia, under the very same Victor Paz Estenssoro who figures in the following narrative of the 1940s and 1950s, is in Klein 2007.

6   This continuity with the past, following the dispersion of the Trotskyist-oriented Bolivian miners after 1985, is recounted in Sándor John 2009.

7   Published by the problematic South End Press as Olivera 2004.

8   See Olivera's statement, available at: http://mywordismyweapon.blogspot.com/2010/08/oscar -olivera-opposition-in-times-of.html.

Though I missed the chance to meet Oliveira, Cochabamba was nonetheless where I had one of the outstanding encounters of the trip. I was in a local bookstore with a cultural anthropologist I had met, and she pointed to a big book: 'You should read this. It's by a guy who broke with Morales even before he came to power'. This turned out to be the above-cited book of Filemon Escobar, who from the 1950s onward was, with Guillermo Lora, the leading Trotskyist miner militant in Bolivia, where, as indicated, and unlike in all but a handful of other countries (Vietnam in the 1930s and 1940s, Ceylon – now Sri Lanka – up to the 1960s) Trotskyism was the dominant current of the mass workers' movement and Stalinism a miserable sect on the margins.[9] (Stalinism in Vietnam, of course, was unfortunately not a marginal sect.)

I was fortunate enough to meet Escobar shortly thereafter. I had read a good deal of his book, and my aim was above all to hear from someone with such a rich experience as a Marxist militant in the Bolivian workers' movement, over decades, how he had come to reject 'Eurocentric' Marxism and embrace the 'pachakuti'. Escobar did me the great favour of showing me all the 'underground' books on the indigenous question written over the past century, to which the radical left had been deaf and indifferent, and a fair number of which I read upon returning to New York. There is in fact a lineage of indigenous writers going back 200 years to Pazos Kanki, an Aymara who translated Thomas Paine c. 1810. Another key figure is Pablo Zarate Willka, who led an indigenous insurrection of considerable proportions in 1899, in the middle of a civil war between two factions of the white elite, which ended in defeat for the indigenous forces and Zarate's execution (Willka is an Incan word meaning a kind of chief). Given my bent for uncovering German romantic populists and folklorists at the origins of authoritarian movements in developing countries,[10] Escobar did me the further favour of putting me on to the foremost Bolivian ideo-

---

9   For a good overview of this Bolivian exception, see Sándor John 2009. A hilarious episode took place when a Soviet delegation came to Bolivia in the 1960s to deliver some technology to one of the big state mines. The staid and suited bureaucrats were greeting by a mass of workers holding up pictures of Lenin and Trotsky, and at the end of the ceremonial speeches held up four fingers (the Fourth International), to which the bureaucrats responded with three fingers, for the Third. Things were capped off by a reporter from *Life* magazine writing that the Bolivian workers were so backward they didn't even know that Trotsky had fallen from power 40 years earlier, thereby revealing his own profound ignorance.

10   See the role of Ziya Gökalp (1875–1924), who imbibed the Prussian nationalist Treitschke through Emile Durkheim and who was effectively the ideologue of Kemalist Turkey, influential long after his death, in Chapter Two.

logue of such a sensibility, Franz Tamayo (1878–1956), an unabashed admirer of Fichte with years of experience in Wilhelmine Germany. The discovery of Tamayo, and from such a source, was the true beginning of the text that follows.

One key part of the *pachakuti* ideology, in Escobar's book and in the general movement, is the idea of 'reciprocity', apparently the key to the Aymara and Quechua communities. Explained in simple language, it seems to mean (as Escobar put it) that you eat before I eat, and in reciprocity you make sure that I eat. Somehow, it didn't sound so different from the ethos of the primitive Christian communities. Similarly, shortly before his execution, Zarate Willka (in a quote highlighted at the beginning of Escobar's book) had said: 'With great feeling I order all Indians to respect the whites ... and in the same way the whites must respect the Indians'. Hard to disagree with, but a sentiment that one could have heard in any speech in the early civil rights movement in the U.S.

Closely tied to reciprocity in the indigenist ideology is the centrality of the *ayllu*, the pre-Columbian community that some have even elevated to assert that Incan society prior to the arrival of the Spanish was 'communist'. Decades of debate raged in the past over this question, which seems to have ebbed away in the grudging recognition that the Incan empire, which barely established itself one century before the arrival of Pizarro, had in fact been expansionist, and had crushed and enslaved populations of previous dominant groups in the Andean region from what is now Ecuador to Chile.

The cultural anthropologist who put me onto Escobar had this to say about the survival of the *ayllu*:

> The structure of the *ayllu* with its traditional authorities still persists, but within a much smaller territorial space than was the case in pre-Columbian times, in some areas of the highland regions of Bolivia, mostly in the *altiplano*, northern and southern Potosi, the western highlands of Cochabamba and a few places in Chuquisaca. In some cases, the *ayllu* has been reconstituted in areas where it had ceased to exist after the law of popular participation of 1994.

> The main problem with Filemon's (and others) idea of using the *ayllu* as the building block to develop an Andean version of socialism is that it highly romanticises social relations within the *ayllu* and/or community as if these were horizontal and equal, denying the social differentiation that exists within them since pre-Columbian times. This differentiation may be minimal within very poor regions.

In short, I found, somewhere among the identity politics against which I had polemicised for some time, a Bolivian variant of the Russian peasant commune which fascinated Marx and Bordiga, and the 'new Marx' emerging from previously unpublished (or unread) writings on cultures and movements on the margins of capitalism.[11]

My problematic, however, was populism as an anti-working class ideology and political reality. From the era (1930s to 1950s) of Peron in Argentina, Vargas in Brazil, or Cardenas in Mexico, nationalist populism as a statist, top-down movement, backed by the military, has turned a page. (The Bolivian MNR, in less developed circumstances where the military temporarily collapsed, presents a somewhat different dynamic.) The more recent Latin American populism of Lula, Chavez or Morales is a 'social movement' populism, much as, in Europe in the 1960s and 1970s, 'worker self-management' replaced the older hierarchical unions as a form of working-class containment.[12]

One thread in the following text is the German ideological influence in Bolivia, from the Fichtean Tamayo, who first posed the 'indigenous question' in 1910, to the Spenglerian Carlos Montenegro, the foremost theoretician of the MNR's 'national revolution' against 'foreign' influences, including Marxism. The shift from Latin America's authoritarian populism and corporatism, as it existed into the 1950s, to the more supple 'social movement' populism of today, calls to mind a parallel shift before and after 1945 in two German theorists of the so-called 'Conservative Revolution' with complicated relations to Nazism, Ernst Jünger and Martin Heidegger. Jünger's soldier-worker, the 'storms of steel' on the Western front in the First World War, and technicist 'total mobilisation' of reality gave way after 1945 to mythical musings about astrology as expressing 'the need for metaphysical standards' and about 'a revolt of the earth with the help of man'. The hardened 1920's 'decisionism' of Heidegger which led him into his involvement with the Nazi Party was replaced after World War Two with poetic *Gelassenheit*, or 'letting Being be'[13] and studies in the 'history of Being'.

---

11   On identity politics, see the essays in *Vanguard of Retrogression: Post-Modern Fictions in the Era of Fictitious Capital* (Goldner 2001), also available on the Break Their Haughty Power website: http://home.earthlink.net/~lrgoldner; on Bordiga and the Russian commune, the article 'Communism is the Material Human Community: Amadeo Bordiga Today' (Goldner 1991); and finally Anderson's Marx at the Margins (Anderson 2010), reviewed in issue no. 2 of *Insurgent Notes* at http://insurgentnotes.com/2010/10/review-marx-at-the -margins/; see also Franklin Rosemont, 'Karl Marx and the Iroquois', available at: http:// libcom.org/library/karl-marx-iroquois-franklin-rosemont.

12   See Petras and Veltmeyer 2005.

13   On Jünger's and Heidegger's post-1945 transformation of the elitist, 'hard' Conservative

This text, then, limits itself to the earlier, 'Conservative Revolution' phase of Bolivian populist ideology, as it evolved from Franz Tamayo to Carlos Montenegro, and must necessarily leave the flowering of the *Pacha Mama* (Mother Earth)/indigenist cover for the Morales-MAS neo-liberalism to others.

LG, New York, February 2011

Introduction

Few people on the U.S. and European left today remember the Bolivian Revolution of 1952. Fewer still are aware of its history, and above all of the early (1930s, 1940s) fascist origins of the MNR (*Movimiento Nacional Revolucionario*)[14] which it brought to power. The radical phase of the revolution was short enough, and its memory has faded, having been eclipsed for contemporaries by more recent developments in such countries as Cuba, Chile or Nicaragua. The rise and decline of the MNR, nonetheless, ranks with developments in Mexico (1910–40) and Cuba (1958–) as one of the most important Latin American revolutions of the twentieth century.

Of all of these Latin American revolutionary movements, however, the Bolivian MNR stands out as a prime example of the recycling of proto-fascist and fascist ideologies of the interwar period in 'progressive', 'anti-imperialist' form after 1945.[15]

Revolution of the 1920s into a preoccupation with myth (Jünger) and 'poetizing thought' (Heidegger), still replete with distance from and condescension toward concrete social reality and the masses of ordinary people, see Morat 2007. This shift involved a 'turn to a proto-ecological thought critical of technology ... Ecological thought, since the 1970s, found its political home on the left, even if in this political repositioning many of the traditional anti-modern aspects drawn from *Kulturkritik* were hidden from the ecology movement ... In this philosophically exaggerated avoidance of guilt motivated by collective peer group biography, the intellectual contributions of Heidegger and the Jünger brothers amounted to the quiet rehabilitation of the German "Tätergesellschaft" [in effect, the legacy of the 1920s Conservative Revolution – LG]'.

14 The abbreviation 'MNR' will be used throughout.

15 The reactionary anti-imperialist and populist movements in interwar (1919–39) Latin America had their parallel in the 'Third World' status of parts of central and eastern Europe in the same period. The first theoretician to use the concepts of 'core' and 'periphery' was the complex but ultimately proto-fascist German sociologist Werner Sombart. For a remarkable account of the migration of these concepts, first to Rumanian corporatism and its theoretician Mihail Manoilescu, and from there to Latin America in the 1950s and

1   The Setting

Bolivia was and is, in the Americas, second only to Haiti in poverty. But much
more than Haiti, it has been weighed down by the contrast between its rich
endowment in raw materials (tin, oil, natural gas and, most recently, lithium)
and the overall impoverishment of the country by foreign investment in those
materials. Along with Peru, Bolivia inherits the complex and ongoing legacy
of the pre-colonial Andean civilisations, present in its large Quechua and
Aymara-speaking populations, as well as the thirty-odd smaller ethnicities in
the Amazonian east of the country.

Remote, poor and landlocked as modern Bolivia may have been, its political
and social evolution nonetheless fits the global pattern of the impact of German
romantic populist nationalism in the process whereby conservative and fascist
ideologies, initially spawned in Europe between 1870 and 1945, migrated to the
semi-colonial and colonial world and were then re-imported by the Western
left in suitably 'anti-imperialist' guise.

Bolivia's history, in the eighty years preceding the MNR revolution, was a rude
awakening to the world market dominated by Anglo-American imperialism. Its
political system, like most political systems in Latin America between the 1870s
and the 1929 world depression, was a restricted affair of two political currents,
Republican and Liberal, both representing factions of the small elite which
had wrested independence from Spain in 1825, and which was periodically
elected, after 1880, by the narrow enfranchised sliver (two percent) of the
population. This elite in turn dominated the much larger *mestizo* and above
all indigenous, overwhelmingly rural population which periodically expressed
itself in local and occasionally national revolts, the fear of which shaped the
elite's unabashed racism.[16]

One such failed nationwide indigenous revolt, associated with the name of
Pablo Zarate (*El Temible*; The Dreaded) Willka, took place in 1899, in the midst
of a civil war (1898–9) in which the Liberals ended two decades of Republican
domination and won control of the political system until 1920.

Republican or Liberal, the Bolivian elite hardly excelled in protecting national interests. Between 1879 and 1935, Bolivia lost a significant part of its national
territory and its entire coastline in successive wars and conflicts with Chile

---

1960s work of Fernando Enrique Cardoso and Celso Furtado, see Love 1996. Love's book
lacks only an account of the further migration of these ideas to the Western left through
the 'dependency school' and such outlets as Monthly Review Press and its international
resonance.

16   Dunkerley 2006, p. 102.

(1879), Brazil (1903)[17] and finally with Paraguay in the infamous Chaco War (1932–5), the bloodiest engagement ever fought in Latin America in modern times and the real beginning of the ferment leading to the MNR revolution in 1952.

2   German Romantic Populism Comes to Bolivia

It is little appreciated today to what extent Germany, from the Kaiserreich to Nazism, influenced developments throughout the semi-colonial and colonial world, including Bolivia, prior to 1945. After its long-delayed national unification in 1870, and its stunning defeat of France (previously considered the dominant continental army) in the Franco-Prussian war of the same year, Germany began the long process of contesting Anglo-French and later American dominance in the world economy. Being itself, as a latecomer, largely excluded from the imperialist land grab of the 1870s and 1880s, and having been compelled, in its own struggle to unify, to shake up the European balance of power built on the fragmentation of the Germanic lands since 1648, Germany up to 1945 could plausibly present itself in many parts of the world, to nations and nationalist movements under the heel of the dominant imperialist powers, as a supporter of 'national liberation'. Germany was, in that very real sense, the first successful 'developing country'; its (initially) highly successful economic and military emergence made it a 'model' for would-be developing countries everywhere, much in the same way that Japan (itself a star pupil of Germany) became such a model for Asia a bit later, and above all after World War Two. But along with economic and military prowess, Germany increasingly attracted the attention of the semi-colonial and colonial elites with its stellar culture, a culture developed precisely in opposition to the dominant Anglo-French liberal paradigm from the Enlightenment onward. From Japan, Korea and China to the African Negritude movement, via the origins of Turkish and Arab nationalism, to the German immigrants and military advisors in Latin America, there is scarcely a part of the pre-1945 developing world that was untouched by attempts to imitate the 'German model' in all its various dimensions.

In Bolivia, the 1880s saw the founding of the first commercial houses for German immigrants. German-Bolivian trade took off in that period with the

---

17   Unlike in the Pacific War with Chile and the Chaco War with Paraguay, Bolivia ceded territory to Brazil not from military defeat but simply because it lacked the resources to develop it.

sale of German heavy machinery and locomotives in exchange for Bolivian rubber. While British finance capital, funding above all railway construction, was still dominant over Germany in Bolivia, the Krupp and Mauser arms producers were already selling weaponry to most Latin American armies, including Bolivia's. Overall, from 1880 to 1920, Bolivia's foreign trade was expanding greatly. German trade there surpassed France's by 1900.[18] By the 1890s, tin had replaced silver as Bolivia's main export, and by the 1930's the three largest 'tin barons', known popularly as *La Rosca* and quite detached from the real life of the Bolivian masses, were the core of the dominant oligarchy.[19] In 1910, Bolivia was the world's second producer of tin.

By 1900, German (mainly Prussian) military officers were training armies throughout Latin America, and with the well-known role of military elites in nation-building in the developing world, were often, along with trade and immigrants,[20] the conduit through which broader German influence entered a specific country. Between the Franco-Prussian War and the outbreak of World War One, these officers repeatedly displaced French officers in training new armies, from Japan to the Ottoman Empire to Argentina, Chile and finally (after 1911) Bolivia. Some German-trained officers of the latter countries in turn trained armies in Peru and Ecuador. 1908 also saw the German-Bolivian Treaty of Friendship and Commerce.

Undoubtedly the most notorious German military adviser to the Bolivian Army, over a twenty-five-year period, was General Hans Kundt, the commander of a number of German officers with colonial experience in such settings as Cameroon or the suppression of the 1900 Boxer Rebellion in China. In 1914, Kundt returned to Germany to play an undistinguished role in the First World War, after which he participated in the proto-fascist *Freikorps* and then in the failed 1920 Kapp Putsch against the newly-founded Weimar Republic, whereupon he had to leave Germany and returned to Bolivia.

Despite these German ties, Bolivia sided with the Western allies in the war, breaking relations with Germany in 1917, under the pressure of the U.S. and Britain, the major investors in Bolivian tin and also the major market for it. Kundt returned to La Paz in 1920 and became Minister of War, and would continue to deeply influence the Bolivian army until the debacle of

---

18   Bieber 1984 on these general trends.

19   By the time of the systemic crisis of the 1930s, tin baron Simon Patiño was one of the wealthiest men in the world. See Peñaloza Cordero 1987, vol. 7. See pp. 129–55 for the holdings of the Patiño empire alone.

20   Brazil, Argentina, Chile, Paraguay, and Bolivia all experienced significant German immigration by 1914.

the Chaco War. During his tenure there, Bolivia's *Revista Militar*, the leading journal of strategy for the officer corps, was not accidentally dominated by Germanophiles.

3   A Bolivian Fichte: Franz Tamayo and the pre-MNR Tradition of Paternalistic Indigenism

German influence, in Bolivia as elsewhere, was hardly limited to the economic and military spheres. The first intellectual of the 'cosmopolitan', i.e., Anglo-French-oriented Bolivian elite to pose the question of the indigenous majority, as least as a cultural programme imbued with German romanticism, was Franz Tamayo. He was undoubtedly the foremost Bolivian intellectual and cultural figure of the pre-MNR generation. In his 1910 book *Creacion de una Pedagogia Nacional* (first serialised in fifty-five articles in a newspaper), one of the most arresting formulations was: 'What does the state do for the Indian? Nothing. What does the state take from the Indian? Everything'.[21] Tamayo asserted that 90 percent of the energy of the Bolivian nation came from the indigenous majority and that instead of slavishly copying European models, Bolivia should put the Indian at the centre of its culture and education.

Franz Tamayo (1878–1956), played in Bolivia a role somewhat similar to that, somewhat later, of Jose Carlos Mariategui in Peru (see below), although, in contrast to Mariategui, totally outside of any Marxist or leftist problematic. Tamayo was born into the latifundia class; his father, Isaac Tamayo, had published a sociological novel in 1914, *Habla Melgarejo*, which by some estimations contains all of his son's later affirmations about the centrality of the Indian in Bolivian history and culture, and the elder Tamayo is considered by some to be the 'true father of *indigenismo* in Bolivia'.

Franz Tamayo was a major literary, intellectual and occasionally political figure in Bolivia from the early twentieth century until his death. Like many men from the Latin American elite, he had spent years prior to World War One in England, France and above all Germany on the mandatory tour of the continent. (Unlike most such Bolivian men, however, his mother was Aymara, and Tamayo grew up bilingual in both Spanish and Aymara.) In Paris, he married a Parisian beauty of *la belle époque* and brought her back to live, incongruously, on his remote Bolivian estate. His major intellectual influences were Goethe,

---

21   See the reprint of *Creacion de una Pedagogia Nacional* in Tamayo 1979. When Spanish-language sources are cited, all English translations are mine.

Nietzsche, the geopolitician Rätzel and, above all, Fichte. Like many similar figures from underdeveloped countries, he (like his father) pointed repeatedly to
Japan as a model for such countries to follow, because it had (in his estima-
tion) totally internalised what the West had to offer, while preserving its own
culture.

Tamayo's work consists more of poetry and other literary forms than political
writings. The work *Creacion de la Pedagogia Nacional*,[22] his main venture into
social analysis, is a call for Bolivia to emerge as an indigenous nation, and
was profoundly influenced by Fichte's *Speeches to the German Nation*. From
Fichte, Tamayo took the idea of 'national will'; he denounced the Europe-
addled 'Bovaryism'[23] of the Bolivian elite, with its pale imitations of Europe,
saying rather that Bolivian education needed to prepare the youth for struggle,
because 'life is struggle, the struggle of interests, struggle on every terrain and
of every kind'. Bolivia, in Tamayo's view, 'had to eliminate the European and
mestizo elements and make itself into a single indigenous nation'.[24] The work
is shot through with nineteenth-century Teutonic terms such as 'life', 'force' and
'race'. 'National energy' required 'fighters, not literati'. Tamayo saw Nietzsche as
the philosophical negation of, in his words, 'the poisonous books' of Rousseau.
Fascinated as well by Schopenhauer, Tamayo similarly had no use for the world
historical progress informing the outlook of Hegel.

Tamayo, for all his desire to escape from 'Europe', was totally a prisoner of
late nineteenth-century European race theory, in which biology was destiny; a
race for him was

> a group from people possessing the same biological inheritance, identifi-
> able by external physical characteristics, which have a definite relation in
> types of behaviour and which give rise to cultural differences.[25]

Tamayo had no more use for any universalist outlook than today's theorists of
identity politics, who might at least blush at the biologist foundation of such a
predecessor:

---

22   Tamayo is celebrated in the pamphlet published as Terán 2007; a work which mades
     virtually no mention of Tamayo's sometimes reactionary politics.
23   Bovaryism was a late nineteenth-century concept taken from Flaubert's novel, referring
     to a dreamy, ultimately impotent relation to reality.
24   Andrade 2008, p. 81.
25   From *Creacion de una Pedagogia Nacional*, quoted in the extended commentary in Valdez
     1996, p. 45.

> The ideal of humanity! That is an unreality which never existed, except as a false and artificial product of French romanticism which nations have never practiced!

And:

> The human ideal, if it exists, is a preparation for the forces of the nation, not for an impossible Saturnalia of peace and universal concord, but in a recognition that everything is a struggle without truce, a struggle of interests, a struggle on every terrain and of every kind, in markets as on the battlefield.[26]

In Tamayo's paternalistic view, of course, the indigenous masses of Bolivia are not to be the protagonists of any struggle to throw off the weight of European culture:

> Who is to carry out this movement (for the overthrow of Spanish culture) …? It is not the Indian directly, but rather us, the thinkers, the leaders, the rulers, who are beginning to become conscious of our integral life and our real history.[27]

Given his central role and his controversial views, there were obviously many reactions to Tamayo. In the view of one critic, Juan Albarracin Millan,[28] 'Tamayo's irrationalism, basically racist, posits "Bolivian man" as the "new man"'. 'With its insistence on the mystique of blood, race and soil', in Albarracin's view, 'Tamayo's orientation was not called irrationalism, voluntarism, vitalism or mysticism, but, quite the contrary, "indianista"'. Tamayo was, in this view, 'anti-liberal, anti-democrat, anti-socialist and anti-masses'. Eduardo Diez de Medina, a writer and diplomat, cursed Tamayo for 'his puerile adoration of Fichte, Nietzsche, Max Stirner, the Kaiser and Hitler', and said that 'only Adler, Jung, Scheler … or Freud could have understood Tamayo's writings'.[29] Augusto Cespedes, a

---

26   Ibid. pp. 47–8. The identity theorists might also bridle at seeing their anti-universalism expressed in such an unabashed association of Prussian militarism and Social Darwinism.

27   Ibid. p. 73. The racism of Bolivian society was such that, until the eve of the MNR Revolution in 1952, the indigenous population was expected to stay off of main streets and out of sight. Lehman 1999, p. 101.

28   Millán 1981, pp. 78–85.

29   Arnade 2008, p. 92.

major MNR intellectual and generally an apologist for the MNR's early anti-Semitism and proto-fascism,[30] said of Tamayo that 'his mind admitted only an abstract national pedagogy suitable for an empty utopia ... his condition [was that of] a latifundist, landowner and master of serfs'.[31] Guillermo Lora, the leading Trotskyist in Bolivia over decades, contrasted Tamayo to another figure of the elite, Bautista Saavedra (Bolivian president 1920–5), saying that if the latter had not left his study and gone to seek the masses in the outlying neighborhoods, 'he would have remained in the same position as Franz Tamayo, the poet, essayist and owner of haciendas and houses, forgotten in the midst of a flood of intellectual memories and dusty books'.[32]

Tamayo does not fare better in the critique of a major theoretician of *indianismo*,[33] Fausto Reinaga.[34] In Reinaga's view, Tamayo soared in thought, 'but always had his feet planted on the side of feudal exploitation'. After the 1952 MNR revolution, according to Reinaga, the 'youth turned to Tamayo', and the latter responded: 'No revolution'. With his 'black class hatred', Tamayo opposed agrarian reform. He joined the 'Rosca', the oligarchy deposed in 1952, in calling the MNR 'communist'. His work had been hailed in the publications of the *Falange Socialista Boliviano* (FSB), the authentically fascist current after World War Two. After 1952, Tamayo had written 'I had always considered communism to be the most terrible retrogression ...'[35] He had been, in Reinaga's view, 'the greatest enemy and detractor of the working class in Bolivia'; the working class for him was *la canalla*. In a speech to parliament in 1931, Tamayo had already said 'We know that communism is an immoral doctrine, destructive of all principles, it is a human pestilence'.[36] In the estimate of his most serious intellectual biographer,[37] Tamayo's reactionary outlook was closest to those of Burke and Maistre. Charles W. Arnade, whose book *Historiografía Colonial y Moderna de Bolivia* surveys the gradual discovery of indigenous reality in Bolivia's long tra-

---

30   In the view of Abecia López 1997, p. 57, 'Cespedes, as a writer, journalist and politician, was the most representative intellectual of the National Revolution by his literary, political and historical works'. For more on Montenegro, see below.

31   Abecia López 1997, p. 63.

32   Lora 1994–2012, vol. 19, p. 66.

33   In Bolivia, 'indigenismo' refers to attempts to deal socially, economically and practically with the situation of the indigenous majority; 'indianismo' is more of a literary 'appreciation' of the indigenous, written from the 'outside'.

34   Reinaga 1970.

35   Ibid. p. 111.

36   Ibid. p. 162.

37   Gumocio, 1978, pp. 328–9.

dition of Eurocentric historiography, considered that Tamayo had pushed the 'the racial themes to absurd extremes'.[38]

The assessment of Marcos Dumich,[39] albeit theoretician of the Bolivian Communist Party, is no less harsh. He sees Tamayo as a healthy reaction to the early twentieth-century reactionary and cultural pessimist Alcides Arguedes, author of the 1909 book *Pueblo Enfermo* (A Sick People), but who then falls into talk of the 'indigenous race'. In Dumich's view, Tamayo opposed humanism, liberalism, scientism, and intellectualism, for which he substituted voluntarism and authoritarianism.[40] Politically, Tamayo's contempt for bourgeois democracy and his 'heroic authoritarianism and grandiloquent nationalism' puts him on the ideological terrain of pre-fascism. In a 1934 speech, Tamayo denounced the Russian Revolution and called for a 'strong hand against its Turano-Mongol nihilism'. 'Tamayo', for Dumich, 'contributed to creating that emotional tone so hard and so necessary for the fascist currents'.

Tamayo, in fact, did not limit himself to theory and literary works. He intermittently intervened in politics throughout the period under consideration here. He founded the Radical Party in 1912, falling on the Liberal side of the intra-elite battle between Liberals and Republicans. Tamayo played a leadership role, becoming chancellor, in the disastrous Chaco War with Paraguay (1932–5), and was then elected president in 1934 but prevented from taking office by the coup of 1935, while both his house in La Paz and his rural estate were burned to the ground. He had run at the urging of the proto-fascist, later pro-Axis secret military lodge *Razon de Patria* (RADEPA), and then had become the president of the Constituent Assembly in 1943 in the government of Villaroel, also a RADEPA member. Tamayo (who left political office in 1945) remained notably silent during the mini-civil war of August 1949, preparatory for the MNR revolution three years later, as well as on the 1950 massacre of workers in the Villa Victoria district of La Paz. The MNR seriously considered him for their presidential candidate in the decisive 1951 elections, which began the immediate crisis prior to the 1952 revolution, but he was passed over for Victor Paz Estenssoro.

Tamayo's Fichtean nationalism, then, based as it was on a racial affirmation of the 'true' Bolivia rooted in the *indio*, was the kernel of what would become, in a more cultural but still highly Germanic form, the ideology of the 'national revolution' against the 'foreign' elite elaborated by Carlos Montenegro.

---

38   Arnade 2008, p. 3.
39   Ruiz 1978.
40   Ibid. p. 38.

Charles Andrade's study, reputed to be the first which brushed aside the white elite-centred historiography and unearthed the indigenous tradition, also places Franz Tamayo in perspective, while revealing the racism of much of the treatment of the indigenous question, for and against. Rene Moreno, the most important Bolivian historian of the nineteenth century, was a declared racist. Nineteenth-century historians generally were 'a mixture of narrow provincialism and French intellectualism ... they failed to understand the great social problems of their nation'.[41] The above-mentioned Alcydes Arguedes (1879–1946), another Francophile historian of the period, was influenced by reactionaries such as Le Bon, Gobineau, and Vacher de Lapouge, but was nonetheless 'one of the fathers of Bolivian indigenism'.[42] (He also was funded by the Patiño tin empire to write a tendentious multi-volume history of Bolivia.) Jaime Mendoza (1874–1939) was, for Andrade, 'the first aristocrat who, without vacillation, demagogic intensions or pat phrases, proclaimed the potential equality of the Indians ... he opposed changing the mode of life of the Indians, in the sense of subjecting them to Europeanization'.[43] Mendoza's book *Factor geografico* (1925) emphasised the Indians' 'love of the land' and thus, in Andrade's view, 'the cult of *Pachamama* was born'.[44]

Such, then, were some of the contending currents with which the Bolivian elite entered the global crisis ushered in by World War One and its aftermath, prior to the appearance, after 1928, of the future MNR generation.

4   Prelude to the Crisis of the Chaco War, 1918–32

The period 1914–45 was a period of violent reorganisation of world capitalism, of the demise of the British world hegemon and the struggle for succession to world hegemony between the emerging contenders, Germany and the United States, a struggle which played itself out quite explicitly in Bolivia. It was also a period of transition, on a world scale (to use Marx's language) from the phase of 'formal'/extensive to the 'real'/intensive domination of capital.[45]

---

41   Ibid. p. 61.

42   Arguedes later pronounced eulogies for the German regime and received the Rome Prize from Mussolini.

43   Ibid. p. 69.

44   Ibid. 'Pachamama', or Mother Earth, became one of the by-words of the current Morales regime in Bolivia.

45   A full elaboration of this transition cannot concern us here. See my 'Remaking of the American Working Class: Restructuring of Global Capital, Recomposition of Class Ter-

After the First World War, Bolivia's economy was hard hit by the 1920–1 world depression. With the end of war demand, the world tin price, and hence Bolivia's tin exports, collapsed. It was at the same time a period of heavy foreign investment in the country's public utilities and government securities. In 1920–1, Standard Oil of Bolivia was created, and Spruille Braden, a dominant figure in U.S. business and diplomacy in Latin America over the subsequent decades,[46] negotiated the very advantageous sale of four million hectares of Bolivian soil to Standard Oil, a sale which would later inflame Bolivian nationalism before and during the Chaco War. With recovery after 1921, something of a new educated middle class emerged. German investment returned, carving out a spot behind U.S. and British interests in transportation and communication. In 1923, Wall Street banks floated the so-called Nicolas loan of $33 million, which refunded Bolivia's state debt, taking 45 percent of government income for repayment.[47] This was followed in 1927 with a $14 million loan from Dillon, Read. In the same year, Walter Kemmerer, a Princeton economist, spent three months in Bolivia as a consultant, ultimately outlining the 'Kemmerer reform', which proposed the U.S. Federal Reserve System as a model for the Bolivian Central Bank. Kemmerer also recommended tax reforms and a return to the gold standard. Kemmerer's intervention was followed in 1928 by a new Dillon, Reed loan of $23 million. In 1929, Bolivian tin production peaked at an all-time record, a level never attained again and, given the country's then-total dependence on tin exports, a serious problem over subsequent decades, as Bolivia was eclipsed by tin production in Malaya, Indonesia and Nigeria. On the eve of the world collapse in 1929, foreign debt was still taking 37 percent of the state budget, and government finance remained in deep crisis over the following decade.

Bolivia was, in short, a classic semi-colonial country, totally beholden to competing imperialist powers for finance and technology, and whose immense natural resources benefitted primarily those foreign investors.

---

rain' (Goldner 1981), available at: http://breaktheirhaughtypower.org/the-remaking-of-the -american-working-class-the-restructuring-of-global-capital-and-the-recomposition-of -class-terrain/. The title notwithstanding, the text offers a world perspective on the transition.

46   Braden tells his story of business deals and bullying diplomacy in a memoir, *Diplomats and Demagogues* (Braden 1971). Whereas he seemed like an earlier version of John Bolton of the Bush (Jr.) era, the U.S. was attempting in the interwar period, with its 'Good Neighbor Policy', to overcome some of the excesses of the earlier gunboat diplomacy with which Braden seemed more comfortable.

47   Not only did Bolivia pledge its customs receipts as income for the loan, but accepted surveillance by a three-member fiscal commission, two members of which were chosen by U.S. banks. See Lehman 1999, p. 66.

The Bolivian working class emerged in its modern form amidst all this economic turmoil, after an earlier period of the Proudhon-inspired mutualism widespread throughout Latin America prior to 1914. As happened in so many countries immediately after the war, a strike wave swept Bolivia in 1920, led by the railway workers, who called a general strike in January 1921. Tin miners had struck at the Catavi mines in August 1920, but their strike was crushed. Another general strike in La Paz in 1922 forced the government to concede, but the Uncia mining massacre of 1923 marked a pause in labor unrest.

Along with strike activity, as well as peasant ferment, a flurry of new left-wing organisations emerged. A (non-Marxist) Socialist Workers' Party was founded in the fall of 1920, and a Socialist Party, with ties to the more developed Chilean workers' movement, was founded in 1921. Later in the decade, the newly-created Third International began activity in Bolivia, from its continental headquarters in Buenos Aires.[48] In 1927, Tristan Marof (1898–1979),[49] an important left-wing figure over subsequent decades, helped found a Labour Party (*Partido Laborista*), the first self-identified Marxist party in the country. (For his troubles, Marof was exiled from the country for a decade.) In the same year, an indigenous revolt of 100,000 peasants in the Bolivian south was crushed, a revolt caused by a rise in the price of land due to railroad construction and land seizures by landholders. Agitation spread for the eight-hour day, which was adopted in some sectors.

All this economic turmoil, worker and peasant ferment, and the proliferation of socialist and labour organisations (many ill-defined) had to have ideological repercussions, and by the late 1920s a tumultuous mix including Marxism, nationalism and indigenism all reached the educated middle class, a ferment which would bear its ambiguous fruits after the Chaco War. In August 1928,

---

48   A detailed chronology of the Bolivian workers' movement throughout this period is in Lora 1994–2012, vols. 19, 20, and 21. Lora (1922–2009) was perhaps the dominant figure on the Bolivian radical left over subsequent decades, being a miner, a leader of the Bolivian Trotskyist movement, and a prolific writers (his complete works come to 69 volumes).

In June 1929, the Comintern organized the Conference of Latin American Communist Parties in Buenos Aires under a Moscow flunky named Vitterio Codavilla. As this was the 'Third Period' of 'class against class', the conference issued a call for the Stalinist version of a 'worker-peasant government' (see Lora 1994–2012, vol. 20, pp. 230–1). Jose A. Arce, later the leader of the ill-fated pro-Moscow PIR (Partido de la Izquierda Revolucionaria) was among the Bolivian representatives.

49   A full portrait of Marof (the pseudonym of Gustavo Navarro) is in Lora 1994–2012, vol. 20, pp. 277–301. His 1934 book *La tragedia del altiplano* launched what became a key slogan over the next two decades: 'Mines to the state, land to the Indian' (Marof 1934).

the first convention of the Bolivian University Federation (FUB) took place,[50] where particularly the Cochabamba intelligentsia was swept up in discussions of the Mexican and Russian Revolutions, as well as the ideas of Peruvian Marxist Jose Carlos Mariategui.[51] This agitation was also significant in that virtually all the major figures of post-Chaco radical politics came of age politically in these years. The deepening world depression after 1929 and looming Chaco War would provide the context for their emergence. The late 1920s, in short, was the period in which Marxism of different varieties swept educated strata in Bolivia.

5   Mariategui and Marof Pose the Indigenous Question for the Left

Peruvian Marxist Jose Carlos Mariategui (1894–1930), was the first Latin American Marxist to underscore the problematic of the Andean indigenous population for socialism, and had a major impact in Bolivia as well as early as the late 1920s. Mariategui, in a short life, wrote hundreds of journalistic articles. His major work is a collection entitled *Seven Essays for the Interpretation of Peruvian Reality*. Mariategui was denounced by the Comintern in the Third Period as a 'populist', and denounced by the populists (of Haya de la Torre's APRA party) as a Marxist.

Mariategui was initially formed by the leading Peruvian anarchist of the preceding (pre-World War One) generation, Manuel Gonzalez Prado, whose prominence was based on the early mutualist (Proudhon-inspired) phase of the Peruvian and Latin American workers' movement (which was more or less

---

50   Arze Cuadros 2002 dates the ideological origins of the MNR from the programme adopted at this 1928 congress. It highlighted 'selective immigration', the emancipation of the Indian, the 'moralisation of the lower mestizo', progressive socialisation, nationalisation of the mines and oil, and land to the Indians. It went on to call for a 'complete regulation of labor and credit', the latter aimed at avoiding exploitation by bank capital, progressive statification, a reduction of the military budget, the separation of church and state, lay education, the abolition of the monasteries, and finally 'war on war'. We shall see below how important elements of this programme later mixed with fascist elements during 'military socialism' (1936–40) and the Villaroel period (1943–6).

The 1928 convention followed up on a 1921 international congress of students in Mexico City, where first-hand acquaintance with the Mexican Revolution was to be had (Gallego 1991).

51   In the view of Dunkerley 2006, p. 175, this radical ferment was unprecedented in Bolivian history.

superseded by the global impact of the Russian Revolution). Mariategui travelled to Europe after the war and was in Italy during the factory occupations
of 1920. It was in Italy that he most directly experienced the realities of the
European workers' movement. He is a tangle of influences, including Georges
Sorel[52] and surrealism. He founded the highly original journal *Amauta* (1926–
30), which propagated his theses at a time when the Peruvian elite was totally
Europe-oriented, and both disdainful and fearful of the seemingly mute indigenous majority. He helped to found the Peruvian Socialist Party in 1928, so
named precisely to demarcate it from Third International Communism as well
as Haya De la Torre's APRA.

In addition to Mariategui, a second figure on the Andean left who raised
the indigenous question to prominence was the (above-mentioned) Bolivian
Tristan Marof,[53] the *nom de guerre* of Gustavo Adolfo Navarro. Marof was
an aristocrat who served as a diplomat in Europe from 1920 to 1926. He was
expelled from Bolivia, as indicated, for pacifism during the Chaco War, and
upon his return attempted to found a real Marxist party there. Marof, in Andrade's view, wrote an unprecedented history of Bolivia, albeit with an 'exaggerated interest in the Inca empire', which Marof saw as superior to the present.
For Marof as for Tamayo, the 'Bolivian people were the Indians, and they were
not sick but merely sad at the loss of their "great past"'.[54] Marof figured prom-
inently in a debate within Andean Marxism about the possible 'communist'
character of Incan society, a viewpoint that has faded away.

---

52   One thorough study of Mariategui's ambiguous involvement with Sorel (and Mussolini) is
      Salvattecci 1979.
53   From yet another viewpoint, Roberto Prudencio, who began as a nationalist and indigen-
      ist and wound up as a founder of the Bolivian Falange and had been an early admirer
      of German fascism, said that 'Mariategui and Tamayo were the fathers of the new Amer-
      ica' (Arnade 2008, p. 119). The Stalinist intellectual and leader Jose Antonio Arce accused
      Tamayo of being a traitor to his own writings because, since 1917, he had typified 'one of
      the most reactionary hatreds of feudal ideology' (ibid. pp. 138–9). Ultimately, according to
      Andrade, 'many writers who followed Tamayo were passionate leftists or fanatic nation-
      alists' (ibid. p. 155).
54   Ibid. p. 77. In Grindle and Domingo 2003, pp. 130–1: 'The Andrean socialist tradition of
      Marof ... was the overriding tendency that could imagine a past and a future at least
      partially in terms of Indian community struggle and political autonomy. Yet this was a
      marginal tradition on the left by mid-century, and the national revolution, with the peas-
      antizing project and corporatist unionism, would make it difficult for any such tendency
      to grow'.

6   Bolivia and the South American Revolutions of 1930

In 1930, under the impact of the world depression, revolts and revolutions overturned the governments of Bolivia, Brazil, Argentina, Uruguay and Chile.[55] These developments were the South American moment of the worldwide collapse of classical nineteenth-century liberalism in the depression decade, and in Bolivia, as in the other Latin American countries, this meant the impending defeat of the old oligarchic elite parties based on restricted suffrage, and the entry of the masses into politics.[56] In the Bolivian case, with the return to power of the Liberals, this collapse and reshaping of the political, social and economic system stretched over more than two decades, as the Bolivian moment of the world transition to forms of social organisation appropriate to the new 'intensive' form of accumulation.

During these developments, the German military presence had continued apace. Over the course of the 1920s, General Kundt had imposed more and more discipline on the military. Faced with instability and revolt, the Republican Hernan Silas government (1926–30) became more and more dependent on the army, and hence on Kundt. In 1926, Ernst Roehm, the founder of Hitler's stormtroopers, was invited to Bolivia as a military adviser and arrived there in 1928, along with a number of other far-right military personnel from Danzig, who had been demobilised by the Treaty of Versailles. The Liberal overthrow of the Bolivian government in June 1930 was a revolt from the right, placing in power Daniel Salamanca, after which Roehm briefly joined the Bolivian General Staff, though Hitler recalled him to Germany months later. In the upheaval, Kundt's house was attacked by a mob because of his association with Silas. Other German officers supported the rebels.

In January 1931, the Liberals consolidated their mandate in a landslide electoral victory (once again within the restricted suffrage). In the same year, Bolivia became the first Latin American country to suspend payments on its foreign debt during the depression decade. In March 1931, Salamanca took office as president. The Trotskyist[57] militant and intellectual Lora commented on this

---

55   Dunkerley 2006, p. 193, points out that the 1930 turnover in Bolivia cannot be compared to the simultaneous developments in the more modern and developed countries of Latin America, above all Argentina and Chile; be that as it may, it was part of the regional collapse of nineteenth-century elite arrangements in differing contexts.

56   At the time of the 1930 revolution, only two percent of Bolivia's population of two million were eligible to vote.

57   In this text the term 'Trotskyist' will be used throughout for those who designated themselves as such; see the brief appendix attempting to explain what Trotskyism means.

development: 'Our greatest liberals may have had a few democratic ideas in their heads, but their very existence was based on the servile labour of the peasants'.[58] Almost immediately, in April 1931, Salamanca was confronted with a general strike, centred in the postal and telephone workers, and managed to suppress it.

7   The Chaco War and the End of the 'Old Regime' of Elite Politics

For years, Bolivia and Paraguay had fought minor skirmishes on their vague shared border in the Chaco, a huge and very sparsely populated area of jungle, desert and shrub land in Bolivia's east. Disputes have continued ever since the Chaco War about the ultimate reasons for the conflict, which cannot be settled here. During and after the war, the great majority of Bolivians believed it was provoked by Standard Oil, backed by Argentina and/or Brazil, for reasons such as the desire for an outlet to the sea. Serious historians such as Herbert Klein dispute this.[59] Whatever the case, Chaco War fever initially helped Salamanca to divert domestic passions away from his abysmal failure to deal with the economic crisis. In May 1931, he pushed for military penetration of the Chaco just as he was unleashing massive repression of May Day demonstrations around the country. In early 1932, the Bolivian Parliament debated a 'Law of Social Defense' allowing it to exercise 'legal dictatorship', also denying the right to unionise and to demonstrate. A government roundup of leftist intellectuals ensued. Nonetheless, at the same time, there was growing anti-war sentiment in the labour

---

58   Lora 1994–2012, vol. 20, p. 255.
59   Klein 2003, Ch. 7. In 1932, Standard Oil of New Jersey had purchased a new petroleum concession in southeastern Bolivia, but oil could not be exported because Argentina and Paraguay refused transit rights. It was widely believed in Bolivia that U.S. and British corporations were supporting Paraguay through Argentina, and that both Standard Oil and Royal Dutch Shell were behind the Chaco War. The Bolivian mining elite was definitely pro-war. Wealthy Argentine and foreign investors had lucrative stakes in the dispute. The U.S., Brazil and Argentina all opposed intervention by the League of Nations, and the Argentine press was the first to suggest that Standard Oil was to blame. The Wall Street representative Spruille Braden, who had previously negotiated highly favorable deals for Standard Oil, strongly opposed Bolivian interests at the Chaco peace conference. On the other hand, Dunkerley 2006, p. 216, thinks that neither Standard Oil nor Royal Dutch Shell were backing either side in the conflict. The Louisiana populist Huey Long, on the other hand, denounced their role in the U.S. Senate. In October 1935, the Bolivian government did take action against Standard Oil over an illegal pipeline to Argentina.

movement, culminating perhaps in a major demonstration in Cochabamba on 19 May, but, according to Lora, many leftists also capitulated to war hysteria.[60]

Salamanca pushed for war in the Chaco, confident of victory. Bolivia had twice Paraguay's population,[61] and superior armed forces. What the Bolivian elite did not reckon with was the huge incompetence revealed by the general staff, the extremely hostile terrain (many more troops died of thirst and disease than from combat) and the rapid demoralisation of the front line troops, who were in their overwhelming majority indigenous draftees pulled from remote villages without the slightest idea of what the war was about.

In 1932, General Kundt, having fled after the overthrow of the Silas government in 1930, returned to Bolivia with full powers as commander-in-chief in the Chaco War, after Bolivia's initial defeat at Boqueron provoked a clamour for his reinstatement. Kundt's popularity was heightened by a growing fascist influence on middle-class youth, a number of whom had studied in Germany during the rise of Nazism. In addition to economic ties to Germany, cultural clubs and *colegios* (high schools) spread the growing appeal of authoritarianism and fascism in Europe.[62] Be this as it may, Kundt, who was seemingly committed to a cumbersome strategy of position, was definitively ousted after another defeat at Campo Via.

All in all, Bolivia lost 60,000 men in the Chaco War, and Paraguay lost 40,000, by the time Bolivia agreed to an armistice in 1935.[63] Deserters had

---

60   Lora 1994–2012, vol. 20, p. 257. Perhaps just as important as this ferment in the cities, the Tupac Amaru group was formed, expressing the 'twentieth-century indigenista agrarian radical ideology of Indo-American left'. Considered in 1932 'the ravings of an extremist and ineffectual minority of embittered and exiled intellectuals [it] would have profound impact on the postwar world' (Klein 2003, p. 144).

61   In 1935, the estimated population of Bolivia was made up of 1.6 million indios, 850,000 mestizos, 400,000 whites, 6000 blacks, and 300,000 unidentified. In Latin America, there were one million German speakers, of whom 180,000 were Reichsdeutsche.

62   Nazi Germany apparently built about 1,400 schools throughout Latin America. According to Mariano Baptista Gumucio (in Baptista Gumucio 2002, p. 10), the German *colegios* in La Paz and Oruro were 'active foci for the diffusion of Nazi ideology. Luis Ramiro Beltham remembers as a child in Oruro being in military parades with Hitler portraits'. A Bolivian, Federico Nielsen Reyes, was the Spanish translator of Hitler's book *Mein Kampf*, and the far-right militant Roberto Hinojosa, who would be the Chief of Information in the Villaroel government after 1943, wrote the sole Spanish-language biography of Hitler.

63   For an overview of the war, see http://worldatwar.net/chandelle/v1/v1n3/chaco.html. Foreign officers and technicians were present on both sides; White Russian veterans

been shot in droves, and leftists protesting the war were intentionally sent to the front lines to be killed there. Thousands of Bolivian troops perished from thirst when logistic lines were interrupted by incompetence and neglect. The peace negotiations, overseen by representatives from the u.s., Argentina, Chile and Brazil, dragged on until 1938, and ultimately awarded Paraguay territory that doubled its size. The economy was reeling under accelerating inflation.[64] By 1935, the traditional Bolivian Liberal and Republican parties of the tin barons had been totally discredited, never to recover in their old form. The social ferment unleashed by the Chaco debacle turned Bolivian society upside down. In that ferment, fascist, corporatist and socialist ideologies battled for dominance in a chaotic and highly fluid postwar situation.

8   Intermezzo on Corporatism in Latin America

The collapse of elite liberal and republican parties in southern South America, under the impact of the post-1929 world depression, as well as the rise of increasingly radicalised workers' movements, as often more anarchist than socialist, required the ruling classes of Argentina, Brazil, Uruguay and Chile to fundamentally remake their political systems if they were to retain power. This transformation was the Latin American moment of the worldwide proliferation of statist regimes of different types in the global restructuring of capitalism then underway. Earlier immigration to southern South America from Spain, Italy and Germany made crisis responses in Europe significantly present, to different degrees, in the debates over how to accomplish this. The Primo de Rivera dictatorship in Spain (1923–30) with its definite corporatist overtones, fascism in Mussolini's Italy, and, a few years later, Nazism in Germany all came into play as references for the new era of mass politics. These forces were received somewhat differently in the less urban, less industrial countries of the Andes such as Bolivia and Peru, with their large indigenous populations. Yet, in Bolivia, perhaps in the long run the model most studied was the Mexican Revolution (1910–40), particularly its left-corporatist phase under Cardenas after 1934. But this came later, after the Bolivian *movimientistas* were compelled, by the Allied defeat of the Axis in World War Two, to shed their infatuation with the Italian and German examples.

---

were commanders on the Paraguayan side, Chileans and Germans were advisers on the Bolivian side.

64   Gallego 1991, p. 82. There had been 80 million bolivianos in circulation at the end of 1932, and there were 388 million in circulation at the end of 1935.

Let us look, then, at some of the 1930s developments in neighbouring countries, confronting the dilemma, for the capitalist class, of organising top-down statist forms of working-class containment, or of facing the prospect of a bottom-up working-class revolt that could not be contained:

> ... In the Brazil of 1930, for instance, it was clear that the 'social question' could no longer be left entirely to the police to deal with ... the proletariat was a significant presence in the cities. Not only was it a proletariat; it was in a very disturbing sense an *organized* proletariat with an impressive history of protest, strikes, demonstrations ... one of the possible 'courses of action' of the new regime in relation to the urban proletariat was to give them some crumbs, so as to get their souls in exchange. The 'welfare state' was about to be born in Brazil: its midwife was the Ministry of Labor, which was set up in 1930.[65]

And:

> ... the basic finding of such an analysis (is): the fundamental effect of the labor laws has been ... to make it extremely difficult for the working class to organize effectively and autonomously for political action ... The very fact that the government changed its approach toward the working class (from repression to inducements plus repression) contributed to partially annihilate the ability of the working class to answer the renewed waves of repression with corresponding countermeasures such as strikes and public demonstrations.[66]

In his section on 'Corporatist Control of the Working Class' the author sums up:

> The legal framework of labor relations established by Vargas, and left practically intact up to present-day Brazil, is based on three structures: the syndicates, the labor courts, and the social insurance system.[67]

A few years later, a similar dynamic brought forth the same responses in Mexico, in the culminating (Cardenist) phase of its revolution:

---

65   Gomes 1986, pp. 155, 152–3.
66   Ibid. pp. 154, 160.
67   Ibid. p. 161.

What was decisive in this change in the conception of revolutionary polit-ics was not merely recognizing the working masses as its central element, but especially being disposed to convert them once again into an active element in the service of the revolution, of course, in the best imaginable way: by *organizing them*, and organizing them for something close to their hearts: *their demands* ... There is no doubt that the revolutionaries [here the author refers to the *Cardenistas* – LG] had rediscovered the master key to mass politics: *organization*.[68]

Finally, in Argentina from 1943 to 1950, the same drama was played out again, in the emergence of Peronism:

> ... At the very moment in which the masses were mobilized politically ... they were being co-opted into a corporatist project led by a national-ist sector of the armed forces ... Peron's overall labor strategy was now becoming clearer, as were his words in 1944 when trying to reassure Argentina's employers: ... "It is a grave error to think that workers' uni-ons are detrimental to the boss ... On the contrary, it is the best way to avoid the boss having to fight with his worker ... It is the means to reach an agreement, not a struggle. Thus strikes and stoppages are suppressed, though, undoubtedly, the working masses obtain the right to discuss their own interests at the same level as the employers' organizations ... That is why we are promoting trade unions, but a truly professional trade uni-onism. We do not want unions which are divided in political fractions, because the dangerous thing is, incidentally, a political trade unionism". Peron never deviated from this essentially corporatist vision of social affairs and his "revolutionary" image in a later period ... was never reflec-ted in practice'.[69]

9   The Post-Chaco Crisis in Bolivia: Corporatism, Fascism and Socialism in Contention

With this general framework as it developed in other parts of Latin America, we now turn to the complex process of ferment unfolding in Bolivia, in reaction to the Chaco debacle.

---

68   Cordova 1974, pp. 48–9.
69   Munck, Falcón, and Galitelli 1987, pp. 129, 132.

As early as 1933, the Legion of National Socialist Veterans (LEC) was founded, though it defined itself as a political party only in 1936. Its programme called for 'national socialist action'.[70] Some German immigrants had organised a National Socialist party after Hitler's triumph in Germany in 1933. Elections in 1934 put an end to Salamanca's bankrupt presidency, but a coup led by Jose Luis Tejado Sorzano prevented Franz Tamayo from taking office and set the stage for military government.

On the left, 1934 saw the formation of the POR (*Partido Obrero Revolucionario*), the Trotskyist group which would play a highly influential role from the late 1940s onward.[71] Also formed immediately after the war was the *Confederacion Sindical de Trabajo Boliviano* (CSTB). One intellectual influenced by Trotskyism, but more accurately described as a centrist for his career of overtures to bourgeois parties,[72] was (the abovementioned) Tristan Marof, whose book *La Tragedia del Altiplano* had made the case that the Chaco War had been fought to obtain an oil port for Standard Oil and to defend Standard Oil's four million hectares against Dutch Royal. Throughout the country, innumerable 'socialist' clubs were formed. War-weary youth were reading the post-World War One anti-war classics of Remarque and Barbusse. A *Partido Republicano Socialista* identified with 'evolutionary socialism' and flirted with the Italian fascist idea of corporatism.[73] In 1935, the South American Bureau of the Comintern established the Provisional Secretariat for the Communist Groups in Bolivia, with the aim of unifying disparate groups into a Communist Party. The Bureau denounced the peace negotiations then underway in Buenos Aires and called for a peace without annexations and without conquest, and for the abolition of Bolivia's external debt. It further called for the formation of Quechua and Aymara republics, and, in keeping with the Comintern's new global line, for a Popular Front.

---

70   In January 1938, under the German Busch government, Humberto Vasquez Rodrigues called for the organisation of the legions 'in a totalitarian form'. The reader will hopefully indulge the proliferation of party names and initials, and above all note their slight relationship to the real politics of various ephemeral groups.

71   Hereafter referred to as the POR. One key founder of the party, the brilliant revolutionary intellectual Jose Aguirre Gainsborg, died in October 1938 in an absurd self-inflicted accident, falling off a ferris wheel after undoing the safety bar in an act of bravado. An extensive portrait of Aguirre Gainsborg, 'one of the great revolutionary figures of the postwar period', is in Lora 1994–2012, vol. 21, pp. 103–24. (Here 'postwar' means post-Chaco war.)

72   And then some: by 1950, at the height of anti-MNR terror shortly before the revolution, Marof was the personal secretary of the reactionary, repressive President Urriologoitia.

73   Klein 1969, p. 205. Klein describes a 'fascination with corporatism' at the time.

Other veterans were sympathetic to the nationalism of Carlos Montenegro, one of the core future pro-fascist founders of the MNR. Perhaps most important of all for the subsequent decade, a group of Chaco junior officers, many of whom had been trained in Germany and in Mussolini's Italy, and who had then spent serious time in Paraguayan POW camps, founded the secret military 'lodge' called *Razon de Patria* (RADEPA), centred in the *Escuela Superior de Guerra* in Cochabamba,[74] clearly committed to fascist ideas. Its subsequent influence, up to 1946, would be second only to that of the MNR which, in 1936, existed only in embryonic potential in the overall ferment.

10   **'Military Socialism', 1936–40: The First Dress Rehearsal for the MNR Revolution**

On 17 May 1936, Tejada Sorzano, who had ousted Salamanca two years earlier, was himself overthrown in a coup by two Chaco war heroes, Colonels David Toro and German Busch, initiating the ten-year period (1936–46) in which European, and above all Italian and German fascist influence in Bolivia would contest hegemony with the 'sellout democracy' (*democracia entreguista*, selling the country out to foreigners) oriented to the U.S., Britain and, of course, the Bolivian oligarchy itself.[75] (During the war, Busch had risen to prominence by leading the 'great defence of the Camiri oil fields'.) The Toro-Busch coup began a four-year experiment they called 'military socialism', which, along with the further military government of Gualberto Villaroel (1943–6), would have an important impact on the development of the MNR (itself founded in 1942). Because of its secret character, it is not always possible to identify the influence of the RADEPA junior officers in the successive regimes, but there is no question that they were a serious presence.

Adolf Hitler had assumed power in Germany in January 1933, to the general enthusiasm of most of the German-speaking immigrants in Bolivia. Through-out the ensuing twelve years, until the defeat of the Third Reich, Germany's main thrust into Latin America would be economic and, secondarily, through espionage, although the propaganda wars on both sides often exaggerated the

---

74   Through the late 1930s and into the war years, the Italian OVRA (secret police) had a
       military mission in Bolivia, at the Escuela de Guerra in Cochabamba.

75   This was of course a South American phenomenon, hardly restricted to Bolivia. In 1935,
       there were one million German speakers on the continent, and 180,000 Reichsdeutsche.
       This ten-year battle for influence between pro-fascist and pro-Anglo-American (later
       Allied) forces is told in detail in Bieber 2004.

real German presence. Hitler's Finance Minister Hjalmar Schacht in August 1934 imposed strict barter on Germany's foreign trade, on a bilateral basis,[76] and a German trade delegation went to South America later that year. While the delegation did not go to Bolivia, it was definitely interested in Bolivia's extraordinary mineral wealth. The Reich's Foreign Ministry, on the other hand, wanted 'no political ties' to Bolivia.

The Toro-Busch period was the first real political expression of the post-Chaco attempt to remake the bankrupt Bolivian political and social system, in general revulsion at the traditional parties controlled by the tin magnates, echoing the parallel regime crises in Brazil, Mexico and Argentina mentioned above. As Herbert Klein put it:[77] 'Thus after fifty years of struggle, the civilian party system was overturned by a reawakened military establishment'. In this development, the ideology of 'anti-imperialism' was at its peak. Neither Toro nor especially Busch were sophisticated political figures, and the whole period evidenced serious eclecticism, generally of a corporatist kind. Mussolini's Italy was, for purposes of reorganisation, more of a model than Nazi Germany, if only because it was older and more formed. (Toro's ambassador to Germany did express admiration for German National Socialism, and Oscar Moscoso, the Defence Minister, was also a Nazi sympathiser.) Toro announced his regime as 'state socialism', and for the first time, in keeping with world trends, a 'right of the State' (in contrast to the old liberal constitutionalism theoretically founded on the individual) was articulated. On other occasions, the Toro regime called itself a 'syndicalist state'.[78] Carlos Montenegro, whose later book *Nacion y coloniaje* (1953) would be the quintessential statement of MNR nationalism (see below), had been a co-conspirator in the coup.[79] The government was also

---

76　In the context of world depression, and a vast state management of the domestic economy, Schacht created a multi-tiered system of different types of Reichsmarks for international purposes. These different types of marks were paid to trading partners and could only be used in purchasing German goods, and only certain specified goods; moreover, their value could be administratively manipulated, to the detriment of Germany's trading partners. In December 1934, Schacht created the so-called ASKI accounts (Spezial-Ausländer Sonderkonto für Inlandszahlungen, ASKI) as a commercial clearing mechanism. There were high hopes for using ASKI-marks for purchases from Bolivia, but in reality very little trade was financed in this way.

77　Klein 1969, p. 227.

78　For a portrait of the Italian original, see Roberts 1979. In the classic of Gaetano Salvemini, *Under the Axe of Fascism* (Salvemini 1936), corporatism under Mussolini was characterised as little more than a sham and spectacle thinly covering iron regimentation of workers.

79　According to Klein 1969, p. 188, Montenegro and Augusto Cespedes, both future MNR ideologues, most clearly articulated the 'national socialist' ideology. During the years

supported by labour and by the Legion of Chaco War Veterans (LEC). The LEC formed the *Frente Unico Socialista* and called for 'authoritarian nationalism'. Toro created state-controlled 'functional syndicates'; these had the official support of the Socialist Party, which wanted them to be anti-communist.[80] When the syndicates proved a failure, Toro tried to fashion a 'state socialist party'. The new regime saw the meteoric rise of young officers, among them members of RADEPA. This 'military socialism' never took up questions of latifundismo or of the indigenous masses, and its main base of support was the urban middle class. From Italian fascism, 'military socialism' took over mandatory unionisation, a corporate type of regime in parliament, mandatory worker savings plans, a social security system, and state-subsidised food stores. It established the first Ministry of Labour with the first worker minister, as well as the first Ministry of Indian Affairs in Bolivian history. The Ministry of Labour in particular was attacked for 'creeping radicalism'; it became notorious for hiring (self-designated) Marxists. The ministers of Foreign Affairs and of Hacienda were from the Socialist Party and were pro-corporatist.[81] On 25 May 1936, the Toro government announced its 'fifty-two points of action', including compulsory unionisation. The Toro and Busch regimes, with all their pro-worker rhetoric, were confronted with a number of general strikes in the 1936–9 period, led by the miners and railroad workers.

11 The MNR in Embryo

The true nucleus of the future MNR was the daily newspaper *La Calle*, founded in 1936 by a group around Victor Paz Estenssoro (1907–2001), who dominated MNR politics into the 1980s, and all the major 'movimientista' intellectuals such as Augusto Cespedes (1904–97), Carlos Montenegro (1903–53), and Jose Cuadros Quiroga (1908–75) (82). *La Calle* became an organ for German fascist propaganda and virulent anti-Semitism (83), and as of 1938, used only German news services; Augusto Cespedes himself called it the 'megaphone' of the MNR, and decades later said *La Calle* was 'almost fascist' in the years after the Chaco War. Jose Cuadros Quiroga, the most outspoken anti-Semite in the group, excelled in

---

of 'military socialism', German business also expanded in commerce and commercial aviation, and German instructors in the army made programmatic headway with the fascist-inclined junior officers.

80 'The SP was more worried about the presence of "demagogues" in the worker federations than by the latter's depoliticization' (Gallego 1991, p. 117).

81 Bieber 2004, p. 49: 'Toro wanted to implement state socialism using the left-wing parties'.

writing catchy, sarcastic headlines that made *La Calle* a popular broadsheet, in contrast to the staid press controlled by the tin barons. According to Guillermo Bedregal Gutierrez, (Quiroga's) 'philofascist and anti-Semitic streak was a "fashion" of the time. There was great German influence in Bolivia and Quiroga felt that "it was important to be anti-Semitic as an element of popular agitation"'. (84) (This takes on particular significance because it was Quiroga who, in 1942, wrote the founding programme of the MNR, in which these fascist echoes were still present). *La Calle* was pro-Republic in the Spanish Civil War which erupted in July 1936, but the *La Calle* team was 'awed' by early German and Italian successes in World War Two (85). Quiroga apparently wrote most of the anti-Semitic articles (86). For the group around *La Calle*, German Busch loomed as a saviour of Bolivia. Paz Estenssoro, who proved to be the greatest political survivor of all the founders, never wrote for *La Calle*, but did write for the weekly named (appropriately) *Busch*, edited by Montenegro, which was founded during a brief period when *La Calle* was suppressed (87). It was an elite group, condensing the ferment of the period. The 14 founders included three future presidents, and ranged ideologically from socialism and Marxism to totalitarian tendencies such as those of Cuadros and Roberto Prudencio (88).

La Calle was eloquent about its political options, on the subject of early Trotskyist influence in Bolivia, with headlines such as 'Trotzkyite (sic) Loud-Mouths Bring Anarchy to the FOT', and 'Will We Be Governed by Deserters?' Another article 'called for an "iron fist" to "purge the country" of the "red extremism" of "adherents of the Third and Fourth Internationals"'.[82]

Echoing the developments in Brazil, Argentina and Mexico described earlier, *La Calle* supported 'the renovation of union structures'. But this renovation could not be limited to such structures but must rather 'make concrete the institutionalisation of the regime in a Corporative State' and give special significance to the 'disciplinary function of syndicalism extended as a factor of social cohesion more than as an instrument for the defence of class objectives' (90).[83]

12   Crossover of Fascist Rhetoric and Left-Corporatist Policy Measures in 'Military Socialism'

The 1936–40 period of 'military socialism' was a maelstrom of ideological, foreign policy and organisational ferment which might be considered the first

---

82   John 2009, p. 59.
83   Gallego 1991, p. 117.

blush of the future MNR forces' attempt to position themselves in response to a whirlwind of both domestic and international pressures, not the least of them German Nazism. It is necessary to follow them in some detail, to navigate the flood of ideologically-motivated propaganda coming from all sides.

In January–February 1936, Montenegro (who was very close to Busch) and Augusto Cespedes had founded the Partido Socialista, which in Herbert Klein's view best articulated the 'national socialist' perspective.[84] The 'national socialists' in 1936 had been influential enough, as indicated, to get Toro to propose the corporate model and forced unionisation under state control. For Klein,[85] Toro articulated 'in essence and in its most articulated form' the 'philosophy which the small group of politically conscious and advanced young officers proposed for the regeneration of national life ... some of whom had received some type of training in Italy in the late 1920s and early 1930s'. Toro in fact issued a harsh anti-communist decree to appease the oligarchy, but it was stopped by Waldo Alvarez, the Minister of Labour. The radicals at the Labour Ministry were adamantly against the corporatist proposals and demanded worker independence. Their opposition in fact ultimately ended these plans.

In late June 1936, Toro and Busch created an all-military regime. Elias Belmonte Pabon, a founder of RADEPA (whose Nazi sympathies were, in Guillermo Lora's view, 'beyond question'),[86] was Minister of the Interior in the new cabinet. Belmonte had worked with Ernst Roehm during the latter's stay in Bolivia, and Busch sent him to Germany as a diplomat.[87] Other RADEPA members were sent to Italy. Militants from another far-right group, the Estrella de Hierro (Star of Steel) were also in the Busch government.[88]

---

84   Klein 2003, p. 188.

85   Klein 1969, pp. 245–6.

86   Lora 1994–2012, vol. 21, p. 357. Also Gallego 1991, p. 116.

87   Belmonte, according to Bieber 2004, p. 126, actually stayed in Germany until 1951, studying geopolitics there after the war. By his own account, he had graduated from the Colegio Miltar in 1923 and was a pilot during the Chaco War. From 1938 to 1945 he served as the Bolivian military attaché to Germany. After his return to Bolivia, he was a Professor of Geopolitics under the Ballavian government. Belmonte Pabón tells his story in the book *RADEPA: Sombras y Refulgencias del Pasado* (Belmonte Pabón 1994).

88   Another authoritarian nationalist group active in Bolivia in the late 1930s was the Asociacion Mariscal Santa Cruz. According to Lorini 2006, Pedro Silveti Arce in his *Bajo el signo de la Barbarie* (1946) argued that the Mariscal Santa Cruz had ties to the Chilean GOS (Grupo de Oficiales Selectos), the Argentine GOU (generally known as the Grupo de Oficiales Unidos), and the Paraguayan Ferente de Hierro, in a general *mouvance* of the South American extreme-right of the period.

The broader social context was increasingly tense. A strike wave began in early 1936 and by May it had evolved into the 'greatest strike movement that Bolivia had ever experienced'. There was intense discussion of the proposed mandatory syndicalisation in the labour movement. Some parts of the left saw Toro's labour policy as more fascist than socialist.[89] In early July, the radicals in the Ministry of Labour formed the ANPOS (Asemblea Nacional Permanente de Organizaciones Sindicales).[90] In Guillermo Lora's estimate, the ANPOS was 'one of the most important creations of the leftists connected to the Ministry of Labour', who 'wanted to transform society from above'; it ultimately had an ephemeral existence. This conception, in which 'worker associations recognised by the Ministry sent their delegates to the meetings', with the authority of the state 'recognising' different organisations of society, reflects the essence of corporatism.

The Busch-Toro regime in its first weeks pushed ahead with its plans for 'military socialism'. On 6 July, it issued a decree on mandatory work by all. Chaco veterans were to be reincorporated into their previous jobs within twenty days. Henceforth, anyone without employment papers (*carnet de trabajo*) would be declared 'unemployed' and liable to be enrolled in state labour brigades. Companies were called upon to make their labour needs known to the state. Lora[91] saw this as forced labour expressing a 'totalitarian, i.e., fascist-oriented' mentality, apparently inspired by Mussolini. Mass demonstrations took place in support of the Ministry of Labour and compulsory unionisation. Toro in a speech in late July declared himself 'in favour of a corporative state' and for a 'regime of trade-union association identified with the organs of power and political representation'.[92] As in Brazil, or Mexico, or later Argentina,

---

89   Gallego 1991, p. 115.

90   Lora 1994–2012, vol. 21, pp. 52–3. Lora writes: 'The ANPOS ... had some influence in the worker organizations. Its stated goal was to coordinate and orient the actions of the worker minister, but in reality it tended to set itself up as the supreme command over the unions and even of the left-wing forces. Some Marxists were sure they could convert the Ministry of Labor into their own citadel, from which they would be able to mold the masses and decide the fate of the government's policies. [in addition to well-known leaders,] second and third-tier leftists practically invaded the Ministry of Labor, which at the time was operating in the National Senate. Leftist leaders fell into complacency from being able to meet weekly in the hall of the high chamber ... At the beginning, they were all united in the hope of being able to transform society from above, almost painlessly, thanks to the backing which the military had handed over to men so capable of theorizing about the advantages of socialism'.

91   Ibid. pp. 55–6.

92   Gallego 1991, p. 115.

> ... the National State, as the definitive successor to the oligarchic State prior to the Chaco War, would replace class conflicts by a division of productive functions, in which contradictions would give way to integration within a development project directed by the State.[93]

On the day after the mandatory labour decree, Toro issued a *Ley Organica de Petroleos* to curb speculation and concessions to the foreign exploitation of Bolivia's oil. Two weeks later, on 24 July, this was followed by a decree creating the Banco Minero. On August the decree on mandatory unionisation was issued.[94] According to the decree, unions would henceforth 'be under the "permanent protection and control" of the socialist government and were "incorporated into the state mechanism"'. Employers and workers, following the Italian syndicalist model, would be in the same union. According to Lora, 'In practice ... it fell to the Ministry of Labour to organise the unions and to administer them in all times and circumstances'.[95] This fit into a broader plan of the government 'to mobilise the entire active population for an intensive programme of production'.[96]

In November 1936, the First National Congress of Workers took place, and debated the creation of a Confederacion Sindical de Trabajadores de Bolivia (CSTB) oriented to the left parties. By this time, however, Toro had moved to the right and appointed a leading lawyer for the Hochschild mining interests[97] to the Ministry of Labour, while the radicals were removed from the Ministry. As Klein put it, 'A mixed syndicalist-corporatist state grafted on to the old political party system was contemplated'.[98]

Further steps along such lines followed on 21 December 1936, with the creation of the Yacimientos Petrofileros Fiscales Bolivianos (YPFB – Bolivian State Oil Deposits), a preliminary step to Toro's historic nationalisation of Standard Oil in May 1937. This expropriation of a major U.S. firm was unprecedented in Latin America, a full year prior to the better-known nationalisation of oil by the Cardenas regime in Mexico. Further, the government regulation of the tin industry, initially a temporary measure during the Chaco War, was made per-

---

93   Ibid. p. 119.

94   Lora 1994–2012, vol. 21, p. 50.

95   Ibid. p. 51.

96   Ibid. p. 54.

97   Mauricio Hochschild, once again, was the Jewish tin baron in the 'big three' of 'La Rosca' and a major target of the populist anti-Semitism promoted by La Calle and the far right. His holdings are detailed in Peñaloza Cordero 1987, Ch. 7.

98   Klein 1969, p. 259.

manent.[99] In the wake of this rapid flurry of decrees and state takeovers, the Toro-Busch government came under fire from the right from the tin interests and from the left from various Marxists. Bolivia's statist measures were followed by similar steps in Argentina, Brazil, Chile, and Uruguay. In 'military socialism', of course, the Bolivian Army continued to account for 37 percent of the government budget.

On 13 July 1937, German Busch unseated Toro as sole military ruler. Busch viewed himself as champion of the May 1936 general strike. Toro had never lost labour support or persecuted the radical left, but he had lost the support of fascist[100] and reformist-minded junior officers around Busch. In some of his immediate measures, Busch closed state-subsidised food stores and rolled back some other controls of the previous year. (He also allowed Tristan Marof to return to Bolivia after ten years in exile.)

Once consolidated in sole power, Busch in November 1937 recommended an expansion of the earlier Labour Code (*Codigo de Trabajo*), itself (by some estimates) influenced by the Italian *Carta di Lavoro* and the Nazi *Arbeitsfront*.[101] In reality, however, mandatory syndicalisation never took hold. Klein summarised the period as follows: 'In the four years of military socialism the basis of the old parties had definitely rotted away ... in the end, the left emerged as the dominant factor in political life'.[102] In March 1939, in recognition of this shifting ground, a *Concordancia* of the three traditional political parties was formed,[103] in which the pre-1930 parties were forced to recognize the end of the old system and become (in Klein's estimate) 'class-conscious representatives of oligarchy'.

---

99   By the 1950s, state corporations in Bolivia would account for half of GDP.

100   In further developments on the far right, the Bolivian Socialist Falange (Falange Socialista Boliviana, or FSB) was founded, on the model of its Spanish counterpart, among student exiles in Chile. Pro-Catholic and nationalist, it was based on conservative and privileged high school students, especially from Cochabamba and the eastern part of the country; it remained a fringe group throughout. In 1952, it considered participating in the MNR revolt, but backed out at the last moment. After the MNR revolution, the tin barons turned to the FSB as the only viable party capable of advancing their interests. The Falange later evolved in a more Christian Democratic direction.

101   Augustín Barcelli, in a 1957 book (*Medio siglo de luchas sindicales revolucionarias en Bolivia*), argued for the influence of the Carta di Lavoro and German Arbeitsfront on the Toro government (see Bieber 2004, pp. 57–8). However, Nazi experts in the German embassy in La Paz apparently did not think the Toro-Busch government was very different from the previous one.

102   Klein 1969, p. 276.

103   Ibid. p. 305.

13   Influence of the Mexican Revolution

A further important development during the period of Busch rule was the March 1938 constitutional convention. The proceedings reflected the impact, among others, of the Mexican Revolution,[104] just then reaching its left-wing limits under Cardenas. The new constitution demarcated itself from its liberal predecessors, with their orientation to the individual and to private property, by a corporatist emphasis on state-recognised professional or occupational organisations, and anticipated further elaboration after 1952. It was accompanied by a new property law pushing social ownership. It proposed agrarian reform, legalisation of the *ayallu* (once again, the pre-Hispanic rural commune, still in existence in some regions), and the nationalisation of the mines (though this was ultimately rejected). It forced a regroupment of traditional parties from the pre-Chaco period. The regime decreed (in principle) free universal education and the creation of rural education centres for the highland indigenous population.[105]

March 1938 also saw the complete triumph of the Frente Unico Socialista in elections. Carried along on this momentum, the (in Klein's view) 'extremely radical' constitutional convention of 1938 amounted to 'a vital turning point in Bolivian history'.[106] It repealed the 1880 liberal constitution, and developed 'social constitutionalism' (a concept first elaborated for Latin American purposes by the Mexican Revolution). Property, previously conceived in individual terms, was redefined as a function of the state. (This re-centring of constitutionality on the state, and its legal recognition – and enforcement by compulsion of such recognition – of different bodies, from property owners to professional associations to labour unions, is the essence of corporatism.) The convention was also influenced by European radicalism and socialism as well as by twentieth-century indigenism, articulated by figures like Mariategui and Tamayo. It approved worker participation in profits, and proclaimed the function of the state as the provision of social welfare.

A few months later, again showing the continental projection of the Cardenas phase of the Mexican Revolution, the Confederacion de Trabajadores de America Latina (CTAL) was founded in Mexico City. According to Lora, 'it had a huge influence on the Bolivian trade union movement' and had a practical

---

104   Ibid. p. 191. Lehman 1999, p. 72, sees the 1938 constitution as specifically based on the 1917 Mexican charter.

105   The indigenous educational experiment in Warisata became known through the hemisphere.

106   Klein 1969, p. 278.

influence in shaping the character of the (Stalinist) Confederacion Sindical del Trabajo Boliviano (CSTB).[107] Later, during World War Two, the CTAL was controlled by the Stalinists, headed by the notorious Mexican Stalinist and trade union bureaucrat Lombardo Toledano.[108]

14   Attempted Implementation of a Schachtian System of Currency Controls and Managed Trade; Labour Regimentation

The intensifying geopolitical struggle between Germany and the U.S. was hardly absent from Bolivian developments in the late 1930s, as this social radicalisation was deepening. By 1938, Germany accounted for 17 percent of Bolivia's foreign trade. The German foreign trade boards, for their part, wanted to exchange railroad equipment for Bolivian raw materials under Schacht's new system of managed trade. Standard Oil was waging a major campaign for compensation for the Toro nationalisation of its Bolivian assets, and Busch told the Germans he 'didn't want much to do with Americans' given this standoff. The United States was making efforts through the Pan-American Union (which it dominated) to counter German influence.

In April 1939, German Busch proclaimed himself dictator. While the Bolivian ambassador in Washington declared that the Bolivian government and Bolivian people felt no sympathy for Nazi or Fascist ideology, Busch moved closer to the Third Reich.[109]

One anomaly in the last two years of 'military socialism' (1938–40) was Bolivia's unique policy, for the world at that time, of open admission of European Jewish refugees. The result was the arrival of between five and ten thousand Jews, mainly from Germany and the German-speaking areas of Central Europe. The purpose of the policy was to promote agricultural development of Bolivia's remote and nearly-empty eastern hinterlands, for which the largely middle-class professional population of Jewish immigrants were exceptionally unsuited. By the end of World War Two, most of these immigrants moved on to other countries, but their presence, and difficulties of assimilation in a

---

107   Lora 1994–2012, vol. 21, p. 250. John L. Lewis of the American United Mine Workers was present at the 1938 conference. By 1946, the CTAL was following U.S. State Department politics.

108   In November 1942, Lombardo Toledano actually visited La Paz, sponsored by the Stalinists of the PIR and and by the CSTB. The CTAL was seen as serving imperialism and La Rosca because of the Stalinist line.

109   Bieber 2004, p. 72.

country where they could neither speak Spanish well nor use their professional skills, also fed the anti-Semitism of *La Calle,* which found its way into the first programme of the MNR in 1942 (see below 4.16).[110]

In May 1939, however, the Busch regime issued a new Labour Code providing for greatly improved working conditions, effectively the most lasting change of his years in power.[111] The Code's first article excluded agricultural labourers, i.e., the masses of peasants. It was protectionist, setting a maximum of 15 percent of foreign workers in any given workplace. It provided for worker-employer unions, and granted the right to strike under government control, and also the employers' right to lock-out and imposed mandatory arbitration.

Guillermo Lora elaborates further:[112]

> (the decree) ... in reality was a document worked out during the presidency of Colonel Toro, when Waldo Alvarez was Minister of Labour and organised discussions in commissions created for that purpose. Organised workers participated in those discussions. This reality deflates the legend that Busch imposed the Labour Code from one day to the next on a working class that had done nothing to deserve it. There is a visible international, and particularly Mexican, influence on the Bolivian law ... The approval of the Labour Code had enormous political repercussions. It confirmed the workerist (*obrerista*) character of the new government and Busch was automatically transformed into the knight errant of the popular movements. This enthusiastic support allowed the regime to acquire an unexpected political stability. The Chaco hero, even though he had issued no equivalent measure for the nationalisation of oil, was identified by friend and foe as a caudillo of the left. The Labour Law and other measures adopted by the government even propelled a considerable number

---

110   The full story is told in Bieber 2010.

111   Lora 1994–2012, vol. 20, p. 357, elaborates: 'The Busch Labor Code of 1939, originally promulgated in the form of a decree and turned into law in December 1942, was a synthesis of most of the measures taken earlier, plus some new additions. The Code required firms employing more than 500 or more people (i.e. the most important mining companies and a few other firms) to provide hospitalisation and free medical care, and to maintain hospitals. It similarly reiterated the requirements already established, specifying the construction of free housing in all mining camps employing more than 200 workers and located more than six miles from the nearest village. It established, in a general way, an 8-hour day and a 48-hour week; exceptional cases aside, it limited the working day for women and for minors under 18 years of age to 7-hour days and a 40-hour week, and established a maximum of five hours for uninterrupted work'.

112   Lora 1994–2012, vol. 21, pp. 69 ff.

of Marxists to join the ranks of the unconditional supporters of Busch ... the bulk of the masses and not a few Marxists considered this body of laws to be synonymous with socialism ... Many authors of treatises and other exegetes wrote about the Busch Code and almost all of them are convinced that, especially in a backward country such as Bolivia, the exploited can be liberated by social legislation ... (the philo-Trotskyist university professor Alberto Cornejo) finds a presumed identity between the labour code and the Transitional Program of the Fourth International ... Cornejo fancies that the struggle for serious social legislation is nothing less than the Gordian knot of revolutionary activity.

As Lora said: 'State socialism, far from abolishing the principle of private property, would limit itself to modernising it, giving it the content of a social function'.[113]

Along with all this labour ferment and legislation, Busch imposed a great increase in the taxation of mines. When the tin mine owners from *Comite Permanente de Mineros* forced the government to abolish special taxes and foreign currency requirements, Busch responded in June 1939 with a Schacht-type system of currency controls. The decree required the mandatory handover of all foreign currency from mineral exports to the central bank, citing Germany, Russia, Spain, as well as Argentina, Brazil and Chile as antecedents. This measure increased state revenues by 25 percent.

The Bolivian representative in Berlin announced Bolivia's intention to withdraw from the International Tin Pool and put the *Banco Minero* in charge of tin exports, creating a state monopoly. The Germans saw this as an opening through which the Reich could acquire all Bolivian mineral production in exchange for mining equipment.[114] In July 1939, the Reich representatives in Bolivia, Walter Becker and Horst Koppelmann, were asked to reorganise German-Bolivian trade through the centralisation of the ASKI marks in the Central Bank, thereby obtaining all Bolivian mineral products (above all tin) in exchange for ASKI marks, and to sign a treaty, a *Convenio Comerical de Pagos* on all credit transactions between the two states.[115] Bolivia, like other countries which entered into these barter agreements with Nazi Germany, was flooded with cameras, Bayer aspirin and ASKI marks.[116]

113   Lora 1994–2012, vol. 20, p. 101.

114   Bieber 2004, pp. 70–1.

115   Bieber 2004, p. 71.

116   The standard joke in the late 1930s, in countries having a trade surplus with Germany

Busch then nationalised the Central Bank, and Alberto Ostria Gutierrez, a pro-Anglo-American diplomat, resigned from the government in protest at the drift of economic policy. On the same day German emissaries signed a preliminary protocol with the Ministry of Foreign Relations; in it, Germany and Bolivia agreed to give the Reich-Credit-Gesellschaft and the German Bank of South America the regulation of trade in ASKI-marks. The protocol also anticipated a five-year treaty under which Bolivia would sell all products to Germany for ASKI marks (with some exceptions for tin). The last part of the agreement proposed oversight of Bolivia's Central Bank by a mixed commission of Bolivians and the 'German Minister in Bolivia'. It also established the role of the *Reichsmark* and it reserved for Germany the right to use 50 percent of its *creencias de compensacion* (i.e., ASKI marks) in the purchase of Bolivian tin. The U.S., Britain and Japan attempted to exert counter-pressures, but six days later the two German banks signed an agreement with the YPFB, the state oil company, agreeing to help Bolivia in oil industry development. Walter Mehring, 'the special plenipotentiary of the YPFB' and a German citizen, was ordered to sign an agreement with the two German banks. Four million marks were slated for equipment in exchange for oil and raw materials.

This flurry of activity marked the high point of German-Bolivian commercial relations in the 1936–46 period,[117] but the anticipated exchanges never materialised and served more to focus U.S. attention on these developments; up to this point, the U.S. had been much more interested in the Bolivian-Paraguayan negotiations in the wake of the Chaco War, which dragged on until 1938, and which had taken precedence over concerns about Bolivian 'military socialism'. The German envoys ultimately left Bolivia empty-handed.

15   The Tin Barons Return to Direct Control of the State, 1940–3

'Military socialism' in Bolivia came to an abrupt end on 23 August 1939, with the (apparent) suicide of German Busch. There were widespread popular doubts that his death was indeed a suicide and many suspected that Busch had been assassinated by the tin barons and their 'superstate'.[118] Indeed, Busch was not

---

and finding themselves holding large stocks of aspirin and these special classes of non-convertible marks, was that Germany created the headache and then provided the remedy.

117   The German delegation to Bolivia at this point had 70 personnel, of whom only thirteen were declared.

118   Lora 1994–2012, vol. 21, p. 97.

replaced by Baldivian, his vice president, but instead a special commission convened to install General Carlos Quintanella as provisional president until April 1940. Quintanella promptly overturned the Busch decree on foreign currency and in late 1939 issued a modified decree suited to the wartime situation.[119]

Bolivian politics following the death of Busch entered a new period of the restoration of the oligarchy's power, albeit in suitably modified form, with an open orientation toward the emerging Allied side in the Second World War and a simultaneous right-wing shift on the domestic front. As early as September 1939, a rapid falloff in Bolivian-German trade took place as Bolivian trade with the U.S. eclipsed it. The German presence in Lloyd Aereo Boliviano was eliminated.[120]

The new period represented by the 1940–3 presidency of Enrique Peñaranda, following the Toro-Busch period of 'military socialism', marks a shift of the pendulum away from previous pro-fascist foreign policy and left-corporatist appeals to the working class, and toward a pro-Allied international stance combined with a hardening of the regime's relationship with workers and peasants. The pendulum would swing again after Peñaranda's ouster by the coup of December 1943, ushering in the 1943–6 return to the previous Toro-Busch dynamic, naturally modified for wartime conditions, under Villaroel. Following Villaroel's overthrow and lynching in July 1946, the pendulum swung back again, and hard, in the repressive *sexenio rosquero*,[121] the six-year period leading up to the MNR revolution, in which the tin baron 'superstate' returned to power with a vengeance, before being definitively overthrown in 1952. Hence it is necessary, as heretofore, to follow this crossover between international pressures and domestic developments in detail.[122] From 1940 onward, when the U.S.

---

119 Ibid. p. 89. 'The provisional government of Gen. Carlos Quintanella, following the mysterious death of President Busch, had the task of dismantling the Decree of June 7 and the suspension of its effects, pending another decree at the end of 1939 ... The considerations of the Decree of Pres. Quintanilla, which dissolved the bold measure of Busch with right-wing reaction, were that the European war required the dictation of "emergency dispositions" which would permit the country to receive "the maximum benefit as a producer of raw materials"'. In addition to changing the amount of foreign exchange that the mining companies were required to hand over to the central bank, the law watered down other aspects of the Busch decree to their advantage.

120 Germany had invested in airlines throughout Latin America. In April 1941, the U.S. helped Peru to expropriate the Lufthansa line operating there, and in the course of the war the US took over most Latin American air routes.

121 The 'Rosca', once again, was the popular term for the tin baron superstate.

122 Author's note: I feel that the detailed exposition of the developments of 1936–46 is imperative because the Anglo-American propaganda machine during these years repeatedly

turned its attention to Bolivia as the sole tin producer in the world not under Axis control, the u.s. and Britain engaged in a propaganda barrage depicting the emerging MNR as 'Nazi-fascist', and increasingly intervened in domestic Bolivian politics. After the war, during the *sexenio rosquero*, it was pointed out with some irony that under Bolivian 'fascism', workers were urged to unionise and peasant questions were at least theoretically addressed, whereas in 'democratic' (read: pro-Allied) phases, workers and peasants were repressed and massacred. In the decade before the outbreak of the Cold War in 1948, 'Nazi-fascist' was the epithet of choice reserved for anyone who opposed American interests, thereafter being replaced by 'communist'.

Beginning with its founding in 1940, the PIR (Partido de la Izquierda Revolucionaria – Party of the Revolutionary Left) emerged as the most influential self-designated Marxist party in Bolivia, with a pro-Soviet and an indigenous faction. The main personality of the PIR, Jose Antonio Arze,[123] was not, however (at least in Lora's view), a 'sectarian Stalinist'. In the absence of any established Communist Party in Bolivia, the PIR functioned effectively as the local pro-Stalinist party, and followed the Soviet line as faithfully as any CP elsewhere. From the time of Nazi Germany's attack on the Soviet Union in June 1941 to the outbreak of the Cold War, the PIR so aggressively depicted critics of the Allies, whether from the MNR or the Trotskyists, as 'Nazis', that it wound up in a close alliance with the tin baron superstate, ultimately even involving itself (in 1947) in bloody repression of workers. This abject pro-Allied, pro-'democratic' stance of the PIR so totally discredited it in the eyes of the Bolivian masses, especially the working class, that the party's mass support of 1940 simply evaporated by 1950, when it shrank to a miserable sect. This self-destruction of the PIR (hardly unique among pro-Soviet political parties in the 1940s) was an important factor in the emergence of Trotskyism as the dominant current in the Bolivian working class in the late 1940s and beyond.[124] During the war,

---

issued a flood of material portraying the MNR as 'Nazi', and were joined in this by the (Stalinist) PIR and the tin baron press in Bolivia itself. In this period, prior to Cold War anti-communism, any Latin American opposition to Anglo-American interests was 'Nazi', confirming George Orwell's remark that 'a fascist is someone I don't like'. Since, at the same time, I do feel that the RADEPA and La Calle groups were in fact deeply marked by European fascism, while recognizing the 'left corporatist' character of some social measures of the Toro-Busch, Villaroel and early MNR years, I feel it essential to sort out the differing strands which were crudely lumped together by the MNR's imperialist and domestic enemies.

123   A full portrait of Arze is in Lora 1994–2012, vol. 21, pp. 125–33.

124   Indeed, along with Vietnam and Ceylon in the 1930s and 1940s, Bolivia was the sole country

the MNR was pro-Axis, at least until U.S. pressures (and the imminence of German defeat) forced it to moderate its tone; the marginal *Falange* was pro-Axis throughout.[125]

Thus on 12 April 1940, Enrique Peñaranda was elected president, ending the provisional rule of Quintanilla and re-establishing the tin baron superstate's direct influence in the government. The 10,000 votes (out of 56,000 total) for Jose Antonio Arze, the PIR leader, were the real shock of the elections, particularly given the elite character of the enfranchised 2 percent. Peñaranda's priority of reorienting Bolivian foreign policy to the U.S. ran into the obstacle of Standard Oil's ongoing clamour for compensation for the 1937 nationalisation of its assets.

Alberto Ostria Gutierrez, who had resigned under protest from the Busch regime, was back in charge of diplomacy. He claimed to have forced Washington to back down on the oil issue in exchange for full cooperation in the war effort.[126]

In this new period, moderate left, middle-class intellectuals were anti-U.S. and influenced by fascist ideology.[127] The pro-German and pro-Italian 'national socialists' were in favour of the nationalisation of basic industries, above all the tin mines. In Klein's view, it was in their interest to foster a 'radical mine labour movement',[128] and the time was indeed propitious; in October 1940 there were wildcats in the mines and a major railroad strike.

---

in the world where the Trotskyists and not the Stalinists dominated the working class in that period.

125 Lora 1994–2012, vol. 20, pp. 300–1, has this to say about these configurations: 'There are no real reasons to doubt that the caudillos of "nationalism" had had contacts with the German embassy ... but their campaign against the government of Peñaranda expressed a popular sentiment and channelled the radicalisation of the masses. The errors of the presumed Marxists (both of the PIR and of Marof) directly contributed to the strengthening of the MNR and they were the ones who practically paved its way to power'.

126 Ostria Gutíerrez went into exile in Chile after the ouster of Peñaranda in 1943, and wrote a polemical (and somewhat tendentious) book, *Una revolucion tras los Andes* (Ostria Gutiérrez 1944), giving his version of events. He pointed to, in his view, striking parallels between the founding programme of the MNR and the programme of the German Nazis (see Ostria Gutírrez 1944, pp. 120–1; and below).

127 Klein 2003, p. 197.

128 Again, in parallel to the kind of organisation from above associated with Cardenas, as described previously.

16   The 'Nazi Putsch'; Peñaranda Fights to Retain Social Control; the
        U.S. Begins to Eclipse Germany in Bolivian Domestic Politics

The new dispensation under Peñaranda was accelerated by the so-called 'Nazi putsch'. A letter was published in Bolivian newspapers on 20 July 1941, ostensibly naming Bolivian attaché Elias Belmonte in Berlin and the German ambassador in La Paz in a plot for a Nazi takeover in Bolivia. Though the letter was actually a caper of British intelligence services,[129] it gave the Peñaranda government all the pretext it needed for harsh repression of those associated with the Toro-Busch years. The German ambassador was expelled from the country, German and Bolivian Nazis as well as MNR activists were jailed, the Italian contractors in Cochabamba were expelled, *La Calle* was shut down, and Carlos Montenegro was also jailed for four months. Up to that time, the MNR had been the loudest critic of compensation to Standard Oil. The 'Nazi putsch' also solidified the working alliance between the PIR, now (after the German invasion of the Soviet Union the previous month) in its anti-fascist 'Democratic Front' with the *Rosca* oligarchy. The military, however, never completely eliminated the nationalist younger officers who oriented to Toro-Busch military socialism, which would be important in the subsequent (1943–6) Villaroel period.

Not all went smoothly for the new right-wing course; in September and October 1941, Siglo XX miners and railway workers struck and won a 20 percent pay increase, and Ostria Gutierrez was forced out in controversies over the sales of minerals and the compensation questions. Nonetheless, by late 1941 the U.S., seriously in need of tin, enrolled Bolivia in its Lend-Lease programme. After Pearl Harbor (December 1941) the Peñaranda government issued a pro-U.S. statement, froze German and Japanese assets, and agreed to $1.5 million in compensation for Standard Oil.[130] In late January 1942, Bolivia broke diplomatic relations with Germany and expelled more German citizens.

The left parties did make big gains in the spring 1942 elections, in which the MNR also participated for the first time. But the Peñaranda government issued its infamous State Security Decree (*Decreto de Seguridad de Estado*), banning organisations with 'international ties', no doubt aimed at sympathisers of Germany and Italy. In June, Bolivia joined the Allied forces in the world war, and under this pressure the MNR began to take its distances from Germany. One early spur to this realignment was the Economic Cooperation

---

129   In 1972, the American political scientist Cole Blasier proved the letter was a British forgery;
        see Bieber 2004, p. 126.
130   In January 1942, Peñaranda admitted that secret compensation payments to Standard Oil
        had begun in 1937.

Agreement with the United States, which had resulted from the Inter-American Conference in Rio de Janeiro[131] and the report of the U.S. government's Bohan mission. The agreement provided $15 million for oil prospecting, highway construction and funding for the Bolivian Development Corporation (Corporacion de Fomento Boliviano – CFB), which would play a major role after the 1952 revolution. (Critics pointed out that the sum provided hardly made up for Bolivia's sales of tin and wolfram to the U.S. at below world market prices.)[132]

17   Fascist Overtones in the Founding of the MNR

The MNR was founded on 25 January 1941 (and more formally on 2 June 1942), with the *La Calle* intellectuals such as Montenegro, Cespedes, Paz Estenssoro and Cuadros Quiroga providing the main inspiration. One historian called it a 'uniquely Bolivian blend of nationalism and socialism, but never outright fascism'.[133] Augusto Cespedes, much later, agreed with Ostria Gutierrez that there was more than a whiff of Nazi influence in the founding programme, but went on to say that it was the 'fashion' (sic) of the time.[134] Another author[135] later asked Cuadros Quiroga, who drafted the programme, about the anti-Semitism in the original document of the MNR; the latter replied that it was due to (the Jewish tin baron) Hochschild. Cuadros Quiroga referred to the 'sinister figure of the Jew Mauricio Hochschild ... the pontiff of palace machinations'. In Cuadros Quiroga's view, anti-Semitic sentiment was widespread in Bolivia at

---

131   At the Rio conference, after Bolivia had reached a formal settlement with the U.S. for the Standard Oil expropriation, loans from the U.S. Export-Import (ExIm) Bank quickly followed. Lehman 1999, p. 78.

132   Bedregal 1999, p. 134.

133   Morales 2003, p. 117.

134   Abecia López 1997, pp. 195–6. Abecia Lopez refers to the 'fascism' of Cuadros Quiroga (p. 197).

135   Baptista Gumucio 1978, p. 8. His book provides further details on the author of the founding document of the MNR. 'Hochschild claimed to be to the "socialist" government what (tin baron) Patiño had been to the traditional parties: the master' (p. 180). 'We all saw how the Jewish parvenus contributed to the affirmation of the democratic faith' (p. 191). Ours was the 'struggle against socialism, the instrument of international finance' (p. 193). Liberal ideas penetrated Bolivia through the Masonic international, a dissolving internationalism 'with a dose of the Judaism which was cropping up everywhere' (p. 195). 'We can't construct our identity as a Nation while tied to the universalist ideology which is just being born in our country' (p. 196).

the time, but he claims that after the Holocaust he himself gave it up. For him, Hitler was seen in Bolivia as an 'alternative formula to bourgeois and oligarchic democracy'.

In Cuadros Quiroga's 'Principles and Action of the National Revolutionary Movement', the 1942 founding document of the MNR, the following points are enumerated:[136] 1) against false *entreguista*, or sell-out (to foreigners), democracy; 2) against the pseudo-socialism of a new exploitation. On the latter point, the document continues: 'we denounce as anti-national any possible relationship of the international political parties and the manoeuvres of Judaism'. It concludes with a call for the 'absolute prohibition of Jewish immigration, as well as any other immigration not having productive efficacy'. And finally, 3) a call for 'solidarity of Bolivians to defend the collective interest and the common good before the individual interest', possibly a direct translation of the Nazis' *Gemeinnutz vor Eigennutz*.[137]

It is enlightening to read some attempts to contextualise the collective views of the early MNR leaders, written decades later by MNR sympathisers. Walter Guevara Arze, in his 1988 book calling for a renewal of the movement, and commenting on the torrent of pro-Allied propaganda calling the MNR 'Nazi', wrote: '... unfortunately some texts of the party which confused the struggle against imperialism with support for Nazi-fascism appeared to justify, at a certain moment, this absurd accusation ... to this we have to add the declarations of some officers who believed, more or less sincerely, that this was the position most beneficial for the country ...'[138]

Guillermo Bedregal, in a massive study of Victor Paz Estenssoro, the most visible political face of the MNR over decades, writes that in 1939, World War Two

> ... gave rise to great expectations and obvious sympathy for the impressive military victories of Germany. Some people therefore believed that the matter was summed up in a twofold idea: the history of humanity, after capitalism and communism, was entering into a national-proletarian, national-peasant phase, whose paradoxical emergent form was then represented by European 'fascisms' (sic), and some were convinced that the advent of the new era had as its precondition the triumph of the Axis

---

136   Printed in full in Bedregal 1999, p. 99.

137   In 1983, Walter Guevara Arze, an MNR intellectual and later author of a book *Bases para replantear la revolucion nacional* (Guevara Arze 1988), on Bolivian national television called the 1942 document a 'creole version of Hitler's *Mein Kampf*'.

138   Guevara Arze 1988, p. 105.

in the world war ... Many young Bolivians believed in the European victory of the Axis and in a peace that might be favourable for the Indo-
American peoples ... Latin America had never had any problems with
German hegemonism or attempts at domination ... To this we have to
add the important influence of political developments in Brazil and in
Argentina ... (such as) an anti-u.s. politics enriched by the emergence of
the syndicalised workers' movement of the 'descamisados' of Eva and Juan
Peron ... the founding opposition of the MNR was driven by great passions
and also great disinformation. No one, until the final defeat of Nazi Germany, knew about the existence of the famous concentration camps ...
Sympathy, there was; disinformation, I repeat, there was in spades.[139]

(Presumably the crushing of all organisations – parties, unions – of the German
workers' movement as well as all other parties of the centre and the right,
concentration camps for enemies of the regime, 200,000 political refugees
before the outbreak of the war, the Nuremberg Laws on racial purity, the
expulsion of Jews from public life and the *Kristallnacht* had been insufficient
reasons for scepticism.)

Guevara Arze and Bedregal are at least willing to face up – to some extent – to
these currents for what they were. Consider, then, the attempt of Eduardo Arze
Cuadros, in his 2002 book (dedicated to ... Jose Cuadros Quiroga) to finesse the
same questions in a far more laudatory view of the early MNR.[140] For Arze, the
critics (presumably Marxists) who see the key struggle as 'class against class',
in opposition to the MNR's insistence on the 'nation against imperialism', are
'Eurocentric'. He makes virtually no mention of the existence of RADEPA. In
his chapter on *La Calle*, he invokes only its support for the Spanish Republic,
and makes no mention of its pervasive anti-Semitism. After this whitewash of
La Calle, Arze goes on to say that Bolivian anti-Semitism in this period has
been 'decontextualised'. Sinking further into quicksand, he continues with a
priceless passage:

> ... other objective elements of analysis of the period, such as the observ-
> able fact of the demographic and political gravitation of 'semitism' [sic]
> to the city of New York, the neuralgic point of the grave world crisis of
> 1929 and the principal headquarters of capitalist finance ... can under-
> score the objectivity of an association of big international finance capital

---

139   Bedregal 1999, p. 72.
140   Arze Cuadros 2002.

with semitism [sic] in a nation which had just emerged from a serious
defeat in a regional war and which was then involved, almost without
wanting it, in a new conflict ...[141]

With apologists such as these, the early MNR hardly needs critics.

18   The Catavi Mine Massacre Opens the Door to U.S. Domestic
        Intervention

While the MNR was making its entry into Bolivian politics, the labour situation
under Peñaranda was spinning out of control. In late September 1942, the
unions issued demands at the Catavi mine owned by Patiño; two weeks later
railroad strikes erupted.

    The strike wave intensified through November and December, until on 21–
2 December hundreds of assembled workers and their families were machine-
gunned by the Bolivian military at the Catavi mine.[142] The massacre became an
international issue; the U.S. ambassador had called the strikers 'Nazi saboteurs',
and Peñaranda later visited the U.S., where he was warmly received in the
Roosevelt White House. The two major U.S. union federations, the AF of L and
the CIO,[143] as well as the U.S. State Department, sent the Macgruder Commission to investigate, including Robert J. Watt of the AF of L and Martin
Kyne of the CIO, culminating in a devastating portrait of labour conditions
in Bolivia, published by the ILO. In Guillermo Lora's view,[144] the commission was mainly a probe to set the stage for U.S. aid. Such a bloodbath, in
the most important source of tin for the U.S. war effort, had to be a major
concern, and with forthcoming aid the U.S. began its serious intervention
into Bolivian domestic politics. Indeed, in April 1943, then-U.S. Vice President Henry Wallace visited Bolivia, and in August 1943, the U.S. Congress held
hearings on the massacre. (Wallace was quickly marginalised in dealings with
Bolivia by the more conservative Secretary of Commerce Jesse Jones, who

---

141   Ibid. p. 78.
142   On the Catavi massacre, see Lora 1994–2012, vol. 21, Ch. V; also Sándor John 2009, pp. 80–3.
143   They would not merge into the AFL-CIO until 1955. According to Grindle and Domingo
      2003, p. 101, the U.S. labor movement in the years leading up to the 1952 MNR revolution
      played a major role in explaining Bolivian politics in the U.S. (The AFL and CIO ultimately
      sent $5000 to the families of those killed.)
144   Lora 1994–2012, vol. 21, p. 284. Not only aid was mooted; Watt called for a 'mandate of 25
      years' to revamp the Bolivian economy. See Lehman 1999, p. 79.

had directed ties to the *Rosca*. The Patiño mines also established their corporate headquarters in Delaware to acquire the status of an American company.) In addition to tin, the U.S. wanted Bolivian quinine, tungsten, zinc, lead and rubber. From 1942 to 1945, Bolivia's tin production and the tin price did rise, but Mariano Baptista Gomucio argued that the fixed price during the war cost Bolivia $670 million, more than all U.S. aid to Bolivia into the 1960s.[145]

19 The Villaroel Regime, 1943–6: Second Dress Rehearsal for the MNR Revolution

The Catavi massacre also made possible something of a national political debut for MNR leader Victor Paz Estenssoro, who denounced it and strongly supported the strike, even though the MNR at that point was an urban middle-class party with no particular link to workers. Six months later, in July 1943, Paz went to Buenos Aires, where a pro-Axis group of military officers, including Colonel Juan Peron, had just come to power in a coup; Paz announced that he wanted a similar revolution in Bolivia.

The regime, though rapidly losing its grip on power, declared war on the Axis on 4 December 1943. It was of little avail for Peñaranda, who was overthrown in a coup led by RADEPA and the MNR on 20 December, marking another swing of the pendulum back in the direction of the pro-Axis, corporatist 'military socialism' of three years earlier.[146] The new head of state was Major Gualberto Villaroel, a member of RADEPA. His was the first Bolivian government to rule without at least one faction of the tin barons. Villaroel's Minister of Public Works and Communication was Colonel Antonio Ponce Montan, who had undergone German military training and was a great admirer of the Third Reich.[147] The new government was immediately recognised by Argen-

---

145 Lehman 1999, p. 79.

146 Bratzel and Rout 1986, p. 380, claim that 'the U.S. was able to ... verify that SD agents and Argentine army officers had conspired with Bolivian nationalists in the overthrow of Peñaranda'. Lora 1994–2012, vol. 21, pp. 349–54, also argues that the coup leaders were pro-Axis. Lora's portrait of Villaroel is in vol. 21, pp. 355–7. For his part, U.S. Secretary of State Cordell Hull in January 1944 described the MNR as 'Nazi' and attempted to link the MNR to Peron.

147 After the MNR Revolution in 1952, he joined the Bolivian Falange. The Falange had participated in the coup, at least in Cochabamba. Elias Belmonte, a founder of RADEPA and a tenacious opponent of the MNR, was a Falange deputy in Parliament.

tina, which itself would only declare war on Germany in March 1945.[148] One adviser of the chancellery was Dr. German Quiroga Galdo, a former professor of International Law at the heavily fascist-influenced Escuela de Guerra in Cochabamba, who in January 1944 made a speech calling for Bolivian support to the Axis. The cabinet included four officers from RADEPA and three leaders of the MNR, Augusto Cespedes, Carlos Montenegro and Victor Paz Estenssoro. According to Klein, the 'MNR backed Paz Estensssoro rather than the extreme fascist wing represented by Carlos Montenegro[149] and Augusto Cespedes'.[150] Cespedes, however, did become the general secretary of the Junta del Gobierno, while Paz Estenssoro became minister of economics. Paz Estenssoro had apparently met with Peron the night before the coup in Buenos Aires,[151] where he had spent the previous months.[152] Paz placed 'all the most rabidly anti-Semitic and fascist MNR members in the government'.[153] The MNR broadsheet *La Calle* became the official newspaper of the regime. German residents of Bolivia worked with the new government, Bolivian students went to study in Germany, and Germans were incorporated into the Bolivian police force.[154]

The international situation, however, was quite different from the Toro-Busch years, and within weeks of taking power, the Villaroel government had been forced to recognise the inevitability of an Allied victory in the war and to seek a new relationship with the United States. The U.S. and 18 other western hemisphere countries refused to recognise the Bolivian regime. In May 1944, Bolivia, then, formally declared war on the Axis, and expelled Germans and

---

148   The populist APRA of Haya de la Torre in Peru split on the question of Nazis in the Bolivian government.

149   Montenegro, who became Minister of Agriculture, was deeply involved in the coup. According to Abecia López 1997, p. 215, he had told the U.S. embassy that he was being paid by Germany, but would change sides if paid enough.

150   Klein 1969, p. 201.

151   Page 1983, p. 58.

152   On Paz Estenssoro's relations with the Argentine regime in this period, see Figallo 1996–7. Paz was honoured in Buenos Aires in July 1943. Figallo claims that prior to 1943, Paz Estenssoro was distinguished by his cult of Nazism and his frequent visits to the German legation in La Paz. According to Lora 1994–2012, vol. 21, p. 251, the Confedacion de Trabajo de America (CTLA), under the influence of the Stalinists and Lombardo Toledano, saw a conspiratorial link between Argentine coup of June 1943 and the Villaroel coup of December.

153   Klein 1969, p. 372.

154   Other fascist organisations, in addition to the Falange, that were active in Bolivia in these years were the Accion Nacionalista Boliviana, Estrella de Hierro and the CEHGA (Centro de Estudios Historicos Geograficos Andinos).

Japanese citizens from the country. The United States sent its ambassador, Avra Warren, to La Paz, where the Bolivian government handed over to him 81 Germans and Japanese considered to be 'dangerous'. The u.s. also agreed to buy tin at above the world price to assure price stability.[155]

The Stalinist PIR demanded an explanation for the presence of Nazi elements in the Villaroel government; the u.s. refusal to recognise the junta forced it to drop the more extreme MNR leaders and by July 1944 to remove MNR members altogether. Montenegro and Cespedes had left under this US pressure, with Montenegro becoming Bolivian ambassador to Mexico. Despite this departure of the main pro-Axis figures from the government, the RADEPA-MNR alliance lasted throughout the Villaroel period. In part in frustration at its ouster, the MNR intensified its turn to the labour movement.

Power was also taking its toll on RADEPA. Although Villaroel, increasingly in need of u.s. aid, had made efforts to purge his government of the ostentatiously pro-Axis members of the MNR, RADEPA (of which Villaroel was, it will be recalled, a member) was in the course of increasingly acting (apparently) on its own. It kidnapped Jewish tin baron Mauricio Hochschild and held him for several weeks; once released, Hochschild left the country, never to return. In July 1944, RADEPA was involved in the failed attempt on the life of PIR leader and vocal Villaroel opponent Jose Antonio Arze. Most serious, however, were the executions of ten anti-Villaroel politicians and military officers in Chuspipata in November 1944.[156] These executions, attributed to RADEPA, set off a political crisis that brought the MNR back into the government.

Argentina, for its part, had maintained relations with Germany until January 1944, and many Argentina nationalists remained strongly opposed to the break when it came. The United States sent a warship to Montevideo as a warning against any Argentine attempt to aid Bolivia; Argentina at this time was trying

---

155   A series of negotiations between the Villaroel government and the u.s. ensued over the prices of raw materials, and especially of tin. According to Villaroel's ambassador to the u.s., Victor Andrade, Bolivia asked for an increase in the tin price specifically for workers' wages, following the scandalous conditions in the mines revealed to international opinion after the Catavi massacre. See Andrade 1976, p. 31. The u.s. did agree to raise the tin price from $ 0.62 per pound to $ 0.635. Throughout the war, Bolivia sold rubber to the u.s. for $ 2 per pound, when Argentina was offering $ 5.

156   Andrade 1976, p. 49, wrote: 'For the Welles, the Bradens and other u.s. officials of their ilk, the shooting of ten civilians shook the foundations of civilization' (in contrast to their tolerance of the Catavi massacre of late 1942). Andrade was, for his part, a member of the far-right group Estrella de Hierro. Abecia López 1997, p. 241, argues that the totalitarian cell of RADEPA extended to national and departmental police chiefs.

to form a pro-Axis bloc in the Pan-American Union. To counter this trend, the U.S. in December 1944 sent Nelson Rockefeller, newly-appointed assistant secretary of state for Latin American affairs, to negotiate with Juan Peron. In these negotiations, Peron agreed to crack down on Axis spies, property, and propaganda in Argentina; for its part, the U.S. agreed to drop all economic sanctions and to sell Argentina military equipment.

20   Further Left-Corporatist Measures Under Villaroel

All these international realignments and reshufflings of the Bolivian govern-ment, however, hardly prevented ongoing ferment on the domestic social front. Strikes were rocking the countryside. Villaroel, to the extent possible, tried to relink with the 'military socialism' of the Toro-Busch years. In keeping with those corporatist precedents, the Villaroel government accepted the organisa-tion of a national miners' union, the Federacion Sindical de Trabajadores Min-eros (FSTMB), and decreed the abolition of the *ponguage*, the unpaid domestic labour for landowners that peasants were forced to perform. (This decree however remained a dead letter.) It announced plans for rural schools and began work on a rural labour code. In May 1945, it organised a national confer-ence of indigenous peoples, attended by 1,500 delegates. The conference drew up 27 demands, most of which were ignored. The landlords paid no attention to Villaroel's decrees, unleashing severe repression in the countryside, including attacks on schools and teachers.

The FSTMB became the biggest union in the country, under its leader Juan Lechin, who would be in the MNR government after 1952 and who was the key link, as shall be seen, between the MNR and the Bolivian Trotskyists.[157] The founding congress took place in June 1944 and was backed by the MNR and Villaroel to counter the influence of the PIR in the labour movement.[158]

In April 1945, Villaroel and his Economics Minister Paz Estenssoro ostensibly restored the Busch decree of 1939 on foreign exchange controls,[159] but its requirements on submitting income from foreign trade were not as extensive as the earlier decree. A month earlier, at the Chapultapec Conference in Mexico City, Paz had confronted the U.S. about its unfairly low payments for Bolivian tin.

---

157   See Sándor John 2009, pp. 87–90.
158   Lora 1994–2012, vol. 21, p. 363, considered the congress to be 'one of the most transcendent events in Bolivian social history'.
159   Ibid. p. 92.

The end of World War Two did not ease the pressure on the Villaroel government.[160] On 24 February 1946, Juan Peron was elected president of Argentina and took office in June. Peron's honeymoon with the Argentine working class from 1945 to 1950 undoubtedly had an influence on the evolution of the MNR, whose top leaders (along with many refugees from RADEPA) would spend the 1946–52 *sexenio rosquero* in exile in Buenos Aires. An MNR delegation did attend Peron's inauguration. The significance of these links, such as they were,[161] was Peron's attempt, well after the war, to organise a Latin American 'third way' against both the U.S. and Soviet blocs, beginning with the major countries of southern South America. Nonetheless, along with the clear impact of the Mexican Revolution and its institutions on the MNR, Peronist corporatism was definitely another influence.

Some solution to the ferment of the working class was clearly needed; the March 1946 Third Congress of the FSTMB marked a 'fundamental turn of the miners to the left'.[162] The press of the Stalinist PIR spoke darkly of the 'fascistization' of the miners, and other critics talked of a possible 'anarcho-syndicalist' deviation.

On 14 July 1946, however, Villaroel was overthrown in a popular revolt and lynched along with some of his aides in the Plaza Murillo in front of the parliament building in La Paz. The PIR had played a major role in the mobilisation that preceded it, as well as the forces of the tin baron (*Rosca*) 'superstate'. In subsequent revolutionary mythology, the murder of Villaroel would be converted into a major reactionary act and he would join the Bolivian revolutionary pantheon. Carlos Montenegro (in Mexico City at the time), in a posthumous work, blamed the coup on 'occult maneuvers' by the *Rosca* and lawyers for Standard Oil. The top leaders of the MNR and RAPEDA fled to Buenos Aires, and hundreds more members of both organisations were imprisoned. Thus the 1936–46 period of alternating pro-Axis populist and pro-Anglo-American anti-worker regimes ended in six years of harsh repression and the swan song of the tin

---

160 From 1945 to 1949, U.S. policy, backed by large reserves of tin accumulated during the war, kept the lid on the tin price. With the onset of the Korean War in 1950, as well as insurgencies in British Malaya and Indonesia, the price rose to $2 per pound, or almost 300 percent. The U.S. posture strengthened the appeal of the MNR. The mines employed only 3.2 percent of the Bolivian workforce, produced 25 percent of GNP, and 95 percent of Bolivia's foreign exchange (Lehman 1999, p. 97).

161 According to Knudson 1986, p. 128, Augusto Cespedes in a 1973 interview had denied any special link to Peron. But see the articles of Zanata and Aguas 2005; and Figallo 1996–7.

162 Lora 1994–2012, vol. 21, pp. 368 ff.

baron superstate, in which the MNR, from exile, would evolve into its mature form for the revolution of 1952.

21   Carlos Montenegro

Before entering into a discussion of the dark repression of the *sexenio rosquero*, the MNR in exile and finally of the 1952 revolution, it is important to analyse 'the' book which defined MNR nationalism, by one of the key founders we have followed through this narrative, Carlos Montenegro (1903–53). The book, published in 1953 as Montenegro was dying in exile, too sick with cancer to participate in the revolution, was *Nacionalismo y coloniaje* (Nationalism and the Colonial Period). In it, we can see the continuities and discontinuities of the MNR generation, relative to such earlier figures as Franz Tamayo.

We recall Montenegro's key role in the post-Chaco nationalism of his generation, his collaboration on the important MNR broadsheet *La Calle*, his conspiratorial role in the coups of Toro (1936) and Villaroel (1943), his close relationship with German Busch, his imprisonment after the 'Nazi coup', his ministerial portfolio (Agriculture) in the first Villaroel cabinet, his reassignment as ambassador to Mexico under U.S. pressure, and finally his Argentine exile during the *sexenio rosquero*.

Nacionalismo y Coloniaje is one long polemic against the 'anti-Bolivianist element of our historical culture', a counterposition of the 'foreign' elite and the 'true' Bolivian masses, above all the *mestizos*. Quoting Oswald Spengler, Montenegro refers to the elite as 'literate people who learned to read but not comprehend'.[163] Montenegro argues that Bolivian history has been written by those imbued with a 'complete lack of intelligence about the past ... condemning it with the ideas, prejudices and customs of the present ... [in this optic] the historical panoramic of Bolivia appears as nothing but a vision of horror'.[164] Bolivian journalism as well, from its nineteenth-century origins, showed a 'sudden and absorbing fever for foreign culture ... an impassioned surrender to modern spiritual foreign colonization'.[165] After 1879 and the loss of Bolivia's entire Pacific coastline to Chile, 'Bolivia was dispossessed of the very sense of itself'. Hilarion Daza, a military figure associated with the debacle, represented 'blood foreign to the nation'; he fled to Parisian exile and became a symbol of

---

163   Montenegro 1953, p. 28.
164   Ibid. p. 53.
165   Ibid. p. 77.

'the spiritually foreign', the personification of 'the anti-Bolivian ... the child of the colonialist spirit from which the domination of the learned and the rich draws its inspiration'.[166] By contrast, 'the most powerful personalities of our history ... Jose Ballivian and de Linares, belong by their origins to the lower classes'.[167]

In his last writings in exile, Montenegro made an extended attempt to delineate the MNR from any taint of Marxism. He argued that Bolivia had had neither feudalism nor capitalism, but rather a comprador class in the service of world empire. Bolivia was therefore colonialism and the servitude of the *indio*. The Bolivian Revolution was thus 'anti-colonial', in the interests of all classes. The MNR was a mass party, expressing the alliance between classes. For the left parties, the contradiction was between bourgeoisie and proletariat, whereas for Montenegro it was between colony and nation.

Montenegro, like Tamayo before him, attracted comment and hostility from many quarters. The Trotskyist Guillermo Lora pointed to the xenophobic rhetoric of *La Calle* and its 'indisputable Nazi derivation';[168] for Lora, Montenegro denounced 'all internationalism' with his 'messianic nationalism' and 'adulation of the lower classes'.[169] Montenegro 'tells us that "Bolivianidad", as the force which modelled the independent state, resided and resides in the vast social stratum of mestizos ...' In 1952, for Lora, 'the masses destroyed the feudal-bourgeois state apparatus which the MNR, proclaiming the general interests of the non-existent national bourgeoisie, hurried to reconstitute, as a state totally submissive to the imperialist metropole ... It is this which exposes the conservative and not merely Spenglerian[170] subjective and reactionary criticisms of Montenegro's perspective ... [for Montenegro] "Bolivianidad", "nationality" and the anti-foreign are synonymous with nativism'.[171]

Juan Albarracin Millan, in his book *Geopolitica Populismo* (1982), argues that 'Montenegro transposes this Spenglerism to the field of Bolivian history, through the dualism of nation-coloniaje, orienting that history in the direc-

---

166   Ibid. p. 158.

167   Ibid. p. 161. Jose Ballivian (1805–52) was a military figure in the war of independence and later president of Bolivia; Jose Maria Linares (1808–61) was another military figure and caudillo; president of Bolivia 1857–61.

168   Lora 1965, p. 49.

169   Ibid. pp. 53–4, 56.

170   Oswald Spengler's 1918 work *Decline of the West* was based on a biological metaphor of cultures rising and falling from youth to maturity to senescence; the biological interpretation of race seems to have been Spengler's legacy to Montenegro.

171   Ibid. pp. 64, 68.

tion of Indoamericanist populism, posing as the axis the Bolivian *mestizo* ... Montenegro, a populist ideologue, underscores the untameable masses as the historical root of the nation, counterposed to the "*chola*" oligarchy'. In Albarracin's view, 'going from the racial to the social analysis was not easy; it was the hardest task of Bolivian sociology. The actions of people were seen by racism in accordance with colour, bone structure, language, etc. Social analysis demanded an explanation of the place occupied by people within the social structure'. For Albarracin, the main characteristic of *Nacionalismo y Coloniaje* is 'its undifferentiated use of race and class in the concept of the people. The *mestizo* and the Indian class move hand in hand into populism'.[172] 'Montenegro calls his theory "Indoamericanism", following Haya de la Torre and, moreover, Spengler. In the concept of the "people" Montenegro telescopes his national thesis on race with the populist theory of the alliance of workers, peasants and the middle classes. This particularity of coupling race and people is the weak thread that Montenegro follows, at times toward racism and at other times toward populism ... Montenegro is ... the key figure of Bolivian sociological irrationalism ... Montenegro's key concepts are "*Bolivianidad*", counterposed to all other types of nationality; the "*antipatria*", or everything opposed to the untameable vision of the National Revolution; "genetic history", or history as a concept of biological maturation through which a new culture emerges against the decadent West ...'[173]

Coming from another angle, a later critic says of *Nacionalismo y coloniaje*: 'In this rewriting of history, the actual anti-colonial content of Indian struggles was erased and replaced by a nationalist narrative ... By the early 1940s, indigenous struggle was treated as one more current leading to national independence ... In the early twentieth century there was an uncanny silence about ... the great insurrection and civil war that consumed the Andean highland in the late colonial period'.[174]

The ultimate political message of Montenegro's work, then, is this alliance of all 'national' classes against the 'foreign' elite, ultimately the *Rosca* of the tin barons. In an essay published posthumously in 1954, he reiterates: 'Thirty years of the diffusion of communist theories and fifteen years of similar activ-

---

172   Quoted in Abecia López 1997, p. 280.

173   Ibid.

174   In Grindle and Domingo 2003, pp. 125–6, 129. Montenegro and Paz Estenssoro, as fellow exiles in Buenos Aires, daily discussed Montenegro's book as he was writing it: '... the essential was the discovery and the lived reality of the social contradictions of the parties based on the separation between the people (the nation) and the aristocrats of blood ... and money (the anti-nation)'. See Bedregal 1999, p. 251.

ity by fascism-Falangism never aroused the slightest interest by the national majorities, whose pronouncement in favour of the MNR ... underscores their conscious difference from the sham revolutionary ideals of European origin ... Let us proclaim the struggle against oppression and foreign conquest and against its favorite instruments, the international finance companies, the secret groups, the venal middlemen and the armed mercenaries ...'[175]

In short, the 'advance' of Montenegro over Tamayo is the half-step out of the latter's early twentieth-century German romantic race theory to a conflation of race and nation in a populist-nationalist multi-class ideology more suited to the modernisation of the Bolivian state, which the MNR would undertake after 1952. The rhetorical excesses of *La Calle* or the frankly fascist echoes of Cuadros Quiroga's 1942 MNR programme are trimmed away, but the core, irreducible, anti-universalist 'Bolivianess', counterposed to everything 'foreign' (a counterposition which could have been borrowed wholesale from Fichte), remained to drown the Bolivian masses in the corporatist-statist project of the MNR in power.

22   The 'Sexenio Rosquero'

In the immediate aftermath of the overthrow of Villaroel, the new right-wing government hunted down members of RADEPA and the MNR. Hundreds of members of both organisations were jailed and sometimes killed; thousands more were forced underground. The United States granted recognition to the new regime within weeks, and U.S. allies in the Americas followed suit. The MNR leaders – Paz Estenssoro, Cespedes, Montenegro – fled, as indicated, to exile in Peronist Argentina. (During those years of exile, Cespedes and Montenegro managed to work as journalists for *La Prensa*, a pro-Peronist newspaper.) They arrived in the midst of the 'Blue Book' campaign of the U.S. embassy, led by the notorious (aforementioned) Spruille Braden, depicting Peron, Villaroel and the MNR as 'Nazi'. Peron was in the midst of his honeymoon with the Argentine working class, and also conducting a vigorous foreign policy aimed at creating an anti-American bloc in southern South America. Events forced the MNR, both in exile and underground in Bolivia, more and more into an orientation toward labour.

It was a propitious time for such a turn since, despite intense repression, the 1946–52 period saw no falloff of worker and peasant ferment in Bolivia, starting

---

175   Ibid. p. 382.

with a number of general strikes. Villaroel's end had turned him into a martyr of the left, and workers went into the streets chanting his name,[176] which they associated with the gains they had made under his government.

More important still was the Extraordinary Congress of the FSTMB in Pulacayo in November 1946, called in response to this rising ferment. The congress adopted the famous 'Theses of Pulacayo', henceforth (in Lora's words) 'the Bible' of the Bolivian workers' movement. The Pulacayo Congress marked the clear ascendancy of Trotskyist influence in the movement, given the abject capitulation of the (Stalinist) PIR to the *Rosca* during the war and after. The FSTMB and the Trotskyist POR formed the 'Proletarian United Front', which subsequently managed to score electoral successes in the repressive atmosphere.

Because the Theses of Pulacayo became so influential in subsequent Bolivian working-class history, it is imperative to present them in some detail.[177] They were partly drawn from the Trotskyist Transitional Programme, calling for a sliding scale of wages and hours, workers' control of the mines, armed pickets and armed worker cadres. 'We must not', the Theses continued, 'make any bloc or compromise with the bourgeoisie', and then called for 'a proletarian united front' in contrast to 'the fronts which petty-bourgeois reformists are constantly proposing'. After calling for a 'Miners' Parliamentary Bloc' to transform the bourgeois parliament into a 'revolutionary tribune', to 'unmask the manoeuvres of the bourgeoisie from within the chambers themselves', the Theses spelled out their perspective:

> 'Worker' ministers do not change the structure of bourgeois governments. So long as the state defends capitalist society, 'worker' ministers become pimps for the bourgeoisie. The worker who exchanges his post of struggle in the revolutionary ranks for a bourgeois cabinet portfolio goes over to the ranks of traitors. The bourgeoisie invents 'worker' ministers the better to deceive the workers ...

> The FSTMB will never join bourgeois governments, because that would mean the most open betrayal of the exploited masses, forgetting that our line is the revolutionary line of the class struggle.

---

176   Lora 1994–2012, vol. 21, p. 415.
177   The following overview of the Theses of Pulacayo is drawn from Sándor John 1999, pp. 92–
         4.

S. Sándor John writes: 'Then, however, the Theses veer away from orthodox Trotskyism, pointing to the time, six years later, when the FSTMB would in fact support "worker ministers" in the first MNR government in 1952'. While calling the working class 'the revolutionary class par excellence', it went on to say that the coming revolution was 'bourgeois-democratic', though led by the working class rather than 'progressive' sectors of the bourgeoisie:

> ... those who claim we propose an immediate socialist revolution in Bolivia are liars ... since we know quite well that objective conditions for this do not exist.

For an international perspective, 'the Theses declared solidarity with North American workers ... the U.S. is a powder keg which a single spark can set off'.[178]

As Sándor John put it, concerning the confusion spread about a bourgeois revolution made by the working class, the Theses pointed to the 'fateful contradiction, played out in the ensuing years' of 'the role its authors played in entangling this combativity with illusions in the nationalist party'.[179]

The *sexenio rosquero* was, in spite of ongoing repression, hardly a time of social peace. It was, on the contrary, a period in which the now-clandestine MNR steadily gained ground as the voice of workers and peasants. Rural uprisings persisted throughout the year. In late January 1947, steel workers were massacred in Potosi by troops under the orders of a PIR Minister of Labour.[180] Still embedded in their 'anti-Nazi' alliance with the *Rosca* tin barons, PIR militants participated in the killing; although the PIR claimed it was merely fighting against the MNR and the Trotskyist POR, the party's reputation never recovered. By 1950, younger PIR cadre were leaving to found an actual Bolivian Communist Party, of negligible importance in the ensuing years.[181] This PIR-*Rosca* alliance, dating back to the beginning of World War Two, was one major factor in Bolivian Trotskyism's ability to win hegemony in the working class. During the same period, Juan Lechin, leader of the FSTMB (although himself having never been a worker) and like Tristan Marof a centrist capable of using Trotskyist language when necessary, emerged as a broker between the MNR and the POR, a

---

178   Ibid. 94–5.
179   Ibid. p. 95.
180   Lora 1994–2012, vol. 21, p. 373. Sándor John 1999, p. 98.
181   With the abject capitulation of the PIR to Rosca dominance, the influence of the international CTAL of Lombardo Toledano disappeared along with it. By June 1950 and the Sixth Congress of FSTMB, the rival Stalinist union federation, the CSTB, had virtually disappeared.

reality which would take on great significance in enlisting workers and other militants behind the MNR after 1952.

Despite its determination to use repression and outright terror to maintain control, the *Rosca* government of Enrique Hertzog was nominally committed to democratic forms and had to stage regular elections. The POR-backed *Frente Unico Proletario* had some success in the 1947 elections, a harbinger of things to come. Repression followed in May 1948 at the XX Siglo Mine, and in June, at the Fifth Congress of FSTMB in Telamayu, Lechin, who had made a secret deal with the government, showed truer colors and led the charge against the POR. In the radicalising climate, even the *Falange* (FSB) had to adopt workerist language. In the May 1949 elections, the MNR elected eleven deputies. Mass demonstrations and mass repression followed. Large numbers of MNR supporters were again in prison. But under the pressure of increasing instability, Hertzog resigned the presidency, and was replaced by the aristocrat Mamerto Urriolagoitia. He had hardly assumed power when in August–September 1949 a mini-civil war of 20 days erupted between MNR supporters attempting a coup and the forces of the government, with the government gaining the upper hand by the aerial bombardment of some cities[182] and afterward putting hundreds of MNR militants in a concentration camp on the Isla Conti in Lake Titicaca. Again in May 1950, the government responded to a general strike with the bombing and shelling of the La Paz working-class neighbourhood of Villa Victoria.

The last act of the *Rosca*, however, was at hand. As a snapshot of the social reality underlying this chronic instability, it should be kept in mind that as of 1950, 0.7 percent of property owners in Bolivia had 49.6 percent of the land, while people owning less than 1000 hectares were 93.7 percent of the population, with 8.1 percent of the land.[183] 0.1 percent of the population

---

182   Through all this, nonetheless, such august American newspapers as the *Washington Post* were still referring to the MNR as 'Nazi'.

183   Klein 1969, p. 395. Also by 1950 a study by the U.S. embassy had concluded that the MNR and the army were the main bulwark against communism, and the MNR's fascist past and nationalism were no longer liabilities. See Lehman 1999, p. 95. 1950 also saw the visit of the United Nations' Keenleyside Commission, which attempted to draw a profile of the Bolivian economy in view of future aid, again reflecting U.S. concerns about access to Bolivian raw materials (ibid.). Released in 1951, the commission's report was critical of the Urriolagoitia government, as informed opinion in the West increasingly realised the non-viability of the status quo, and the potential of the MNR as the only solution, once the U.S. government had concluded that there was no communist or Peronist influence. Grasping for analogies, the Keenleyside report likened the MNR to Kerensky and saw the centrist Lechin as Lenin (ibid.).

controlled 68 percent of mining, 100 percent of the railroads, and 26 percent of finance capital.

The February 1951 elections opened the end game for the *Rosca* with a landslide victory for Paz Estenssoro (still in exile after five years)[184] and the MNR. There was of course no question of accepting these results, and three months later, in May, a military junta took over. A deadlock ensued that would only end with the April 1952 revolution. 'Abandoning traditional fascism and economic orthodoxy', wrote Klein, 'the MNR moved to a totally revolutionary position',[185] meaning a no-holds barred commitment to the overthrow of the *Rosca* regime (though hardly revolutionary in the socialist sense).[186]

23   The 1952 Revolution and After

> ... in the same way but at a different stage of development, Cromwell and the English people had borrowed for their bourgeois revolution the language, passions and illusions of the Old Testament. When the actual goal had been reached, when the bourgeois transformation of English society had been accomplished, Locke drove out Habbakuk.
>
> MARX, *The Eighteenth Brumaire*

∴

Thus did Marx describe the way in which fulsome ideological excess serves to midwife an ultimately banal result. One could say of the Bolivian MNR that by the time it succeeded in overthrowing the *Rosca* and pushing through its corporatist nationalisations and half-baked agrarian reform, massive U.S. aid

---

184   According to Paz's main biographer, the MNR leaders in exile were studying the Mexican Revolution and even the Russian Revolution (Bedregal 1999, p. 249). They were also hardly immune to the influence of Peron's 'justicialismo' in the surrounding ambience. According to Labor Action, the weekly paper of the U.S.-based Independent Socialist League led by Max Schactman (4 July 1952), the POR backed the Peronist Congress of Workers' Unions, organised by Peron's agents in Asuncion.

185   Bedregal 1999, p. 401.

186   To keep the regional perspective in mind, it should be noted that in November 1951, Juan Peron was re-elected president of Argentina with 62.4 percent of the vote. Peron, however, had not backed the MNR in the February 1951 elections.

drove out its earlier infatuations with Mussolini, Hitler and, on a different register, Peron.

The Bolivian Revolution of April 1952 began initially as another coup attempt by the MNR, similar to the failure of 1949. The coup had the tentative support of General Seleme of the Carabineros and of the Falange, but the latter backed out at the last moment. Even the much-reduced Bolivian Communist Party (attempting to demarcate itself from the debacle of the PIR) supported the MNR by 1951. Fighting lasted three days in La Paz; at first the government seemed to have the upper hand but the intervention of armed workers turned things around. The Bolivian army simply collapsed, and suddenly the MNR found itself in power on the basis of the armed Bolivian working class, which had hardly been its intention. Fortunately for the MNR, the ideology of the 'national revolution' whose emergence we have followed throughout, as best articulated by Carlos Montenegro, dominated worker consciousness long enough to permit the re-establishment of a state apparatus and the requisite 'special body of armed men'.[187] In this endeavour, the MNR had no small help from both the FSTMB and especially from the COB (*Central Obrera Boliviana*) and its leader Juan Lechin. Lechin had created this broader confederation in the heady first week of the revolution, and in its first years the COB was not merely a union grouping but in fact the organisation of a broad swath of social groups, of which the miners of the FSTMB were the backbone.[188] Coming up behind these mass organisations, but weighing significantly in the overall balance of forces despite its smaller numbers, was the Trotskyist POR of Guillermo Lora and Edwin Moller, which ended up providing a far-left cover for the establishment of the new state.

Paz Estenssoro and other top MNR leaders returned in triumph from their Buenos Aires exile, met by rejoicing throngs. These throngs had not caught up

---

187   Only seven weeks after the revolution, Paz Estenssoro authorised the opening of a new air force college in Santa Cruz to rebuild the shattered military. The Colegio Militar reopened in 1953 to form a new generation of 'nationalist officers'. Showing the continuity of the pre-World War Two German influence, Dómich Ruiz 1993, p. 50, writes: 'The high commands of the Allied armies absorbed from fascist sources a whole series of justifications, theory and models of conduct and ... acquired the "values" of the dead'. Dómich Ruiz sees the origins of the post-1945 doctrine of 'national security' in the work of German theoreticians such as Ritter, Raetzel, Haushofer, Kjellen and Mackinder, i.e., the notorious Anglo-German geopolitical school (p. 55).

188   Other groups 'relied on the COB to resolve problems that would, elsewhere, have been the province of government functionaries'. Sándor John 1999, p. 120. Lechin was also named Minister of Mines and Petroleum.

with the MNR's refurbished rhetoric, however, and were chanting 'Down with the Jews' at Paz's first public appearance.[189] Before leaving Argentina, Paz had also affirmed that the MNR was 'completely anti-Communist'.

The four main reforms introduced on the momentum of the MNR's early mass support were 1) nationalisation of the mines of the three tin barons, but with full compensation amounting to $22 million; 2) universal suffrage, decreed in July 1952; 3) land reform; and 4) abolition of the hated *ponguaje* and other quasi-feudal practices in the countryside. All this occurred within the framework of the revamping of the Bolivian state, with important corporatist overtones. It should be kept in mind that Peronism had just achieved its second electoral triumph in Argentina in November 1951, and that a Peronist-style government under Ibañez would be elected in Chile in November 1952.[190] In this regional context, Peron's ongoing attempt to create a South American 'third way' would exert its pull on Bolivia under the MNR during the latter's brief glory days.[191] The MNR Revolutionary Committee in fact included Colonel Sergio Sanchez, who became Minister of Labour and who was known as 'Peroncito' or the 'Bolivian Peron'. According to Beatriz Figoll,[192] Argentina provided arms for the MNR uprising, though Paz Estenssoro was alienated by Peron's tendency to use him to advance Argentina's interests. (Peron also backed Ibañez, who had been a dictatorial president of Chile from 1927 to 1931, who had been close

---

189 Dunkerley 2006, p. 42. This was not a unique outburst. According to Labor Action (18 August 1952): 'The "Trotskyist" POR also speaks in empty revolutionary phrases about the "workers' revolution" of April 9th, about the fight between the "left" and "right" wings of the Nationalist party, and about the "revolutionary maturity of the Bolivian proletariat" – while trade union elements protest against the "Jewish oppressors' class" and demand "freedom of pogroms". And this is against a few Jewish small industrialists, owners of little factories – this is the "maturity" of the Bolivian proletariat, which entirely backs the Nationalist party while the Trotskyist POR backs not only the "left wing" of the MNR led by Lechin, but also the government of Paz Estenssoro.'

190 'A political phenomenon which could not be alien to Paz Estenssoro was that of Gen. Juan Domingo Peron. Argentine 'justicialism' was a peculiar military-worker symbiosis that expressed a new reality for Paz and his party. Peron was the vanguard of a front-line struggle against ... the agrarian oligarchy ... and the manipulative presence of U.S. interests ... justicialism combined political categories from Marxism and other aspects of British trade unionism and the social reformism of the Mexican PRI' (Bedregal 1999, p. 251).

191 On the overall Peronist strategy of an anti-communist 'third position' independent of Washington and Moscow in the Southern Cone, see Zanatta and Aguas 2005; and Figallo 1996–7.

192 See Figallo 1996–7.

to Chile's Nazi movement in the 1930s, and who was supported by the small vestige of the Chilean Nazi party in the 1951 election).

To this end of rebuilding the state, the regime's first move toward nationalisation required tin exports to be processed by the state-controlled *Banco Minero*, with all foreign exchange earnings having to be converted by the *Banco Central*;[193] this was effectively the reinstatement of German Busch's attempts at controls in 1939. The U.S., for its part, had controlled tin prices from 1945 to 1949, and stymied the International Tin Committee. The outbreak of the Korean War and insurgencies in then-British Malaysia and in Indonesia had run the tin price up to $2 per pound, strengthening the posture of the MNR. At the time of the revolution, tin miners were 3.2 percent of the work force, producing 25 percent of GNP, which in turn accounted for 95 percent of Bolivia's foreign exchange income.

A larger context conditioning the new Bolivian regime's relations with the hemispheric hegemon, the U.S., was the international atmosphere of crisis in the early years of the Cold War. In 1952, the U.S. was bogged down in the Korean War, the regime of Mossadegh in Iran was preparing to nationalise British oil assets there, and the Arbenz government in Guatemala was moving on U.S.-owned United Fruit. (The Arbenz regime was the first country to grant recognition to the MNR government.) With many fires to put out, the U.S. could ill afford another open counter-insurgency in the developing world. Instead, building on the ties established with Bolivia going back to 1942[194] and the orchestrated outcry over the Catavi massacre, followed by commissions of enquiry, aid, and agreements on the tin price, the U.S. opted for entrapping Bolivia and its immense natural resources[195] with aid aimed, not surprisingly, at strengthening the most pliable elements in the MNR. The MNR, for its part, jumped into this trap with both feet and by the late 1950s Bolivia was receiving more U.S. aid per capita than any other country in the world. After Dwight Eisenhower's 1952 election as president, his brother Milton Eisenhower visited Bolivia on a fact-finding mission, and in Washington, the Bolivian ambassador Victor Andrade (who had served earlier under Villaroel) convinced the Eisen-

---

193   Ibid. p. 54.

194   As already noted above, after visiting Bolivia on the commission investigating Catavi, which had disclosed the abysmal situation of the wage-labour workforce there, the AF of L's Worth had called for a 'mandate of 25 years' to recoup the Bolivian economy (Lehman 1999, p. 81). Bolivians resented the 'scores of North American experts and diplomatic attachés who descended on their country during the war' (ibid. p. 89).

195   In addition to tin, oil and natural gas, these included lead, zinc, copper, wolfram and bismuth.

howers that the Bolivian nationalisations had nothing to do with communism (as was in fact the case).

There was of course great pressure in the working class for nationalisation (without compensation) and after five months of deliberations by a commission devoted to the issue, this took place in October 1952, with compensation of $22 million. It affected only the large mines, and left small and medium-size mines in private hands. The nationalisation also involved a corporatist type of 'workers' control', but (in contrast to, e.g., the workers' councils and soviets of the German and Russian revolutions after 1917) in collaboration with the managers of the COMIBOL (Corporacion Minera de Bolivia). As Dunkerley puts it, 'a key component of the revolution was in the process of being managerialized'.[196] The COMIBOL was effectively a holding company; it had 30,000 employees with ownership of most mineral production, as well as medical centres and railroads. Decrees in April and June 1952 required the COMIBOL to rehire workers laid off during the *sexenio rosquero*.

As *Labor Action* commented at the time:

> The nationalization of the mines has been decreed, but not according to the program and wishes of the majority of the workers. The nationalization bill provides for indemnity to the proprietors if they pay all taxes and back debts to the government. Of course, the question is purely theoretical, since the government has no money, and hence will not pay. The *Central Obrera* had demanded workers' administration, administration of the mines by workers' committees elected by general meetings of all workers, and a national committee to be elected by all mine committees. But the government, while accepting the principle of workers' control formally, has passed a bill which creates a *Corporation Minera Boliviana* as a great state mining trust in the place of the three private capitalist corporations. In the new trust the representatives of the workers are in a minority, and are to be nominated by the government.

> In this bureaucratic form, workers' control has been transformed into control over the workers.[197]

---

196   Dunkerley 2006, p. 57.
197   Labor Action, 8 December 1952. Most subsequent quotes from Labor Action are from the pamphlet of the League for the Revolutionary Party (LRP), 'Bolivia: The Revolution the Fourth International Betrayed', available online at: http://www.lrp-cofi.org/pamphlets/boliviailetter.html.

The tin barons of the *Rosca* were down but not out, and from exile they conducted a massive propaganda campaign designed to present the MNR and its nationalisations as 'communist'. Patiño, Hochschild and Aramayo, who had long been shifting assets abroad, hired the New York public relations firm Nathanson Brothers to convince the U.S. government, Congress and the 'public' of this, ultimately in vain. The *Rosca's* propaganda machine put out disinformation on the danger to foreign technicians and their families, and quoted such technicians to the effect that nationalisation would ruin the mines.[198] The *Rosca* hired U.S. Senator Millard Tydings of Maryland to trumpet their cause in Congress; Tydings threatened to stop the U.S. purchase of Bolivian tin, but he died shortly thereafter. The U.S. State Department issued calls for full compensation. The *Rosca* campaign was countered by the services of Gardner Jackson, a politically moderate worker-intellectual whose activities in the U.S. labour movement dated from the Sacco-Vanzetti campaign of 1927. (In fact, most sympathy in the U.S. for the MNR came initially from the labour movement.)

Further complicating matters for the MNR was the fall of world tin prices from $1.21 to $0.70 per pound as the Korean War wound down in 1953, costing Bolivia $20 million in income in that year, and bringing the Bolivian state to the verge of bankruptcy; nationalisation had in effect saved the mines from such a fate. In the same year direct U.S. aid to the regime began, and the Chinese Revolution was causing the world price of tungsten and wolfram to rise.

The nationalised mines faced multiple problems quite apart from the international campaign of the *Rosca* and the fall of tin prices. Friction arose between engineers and workers in the management of the mines, and labour leaders and military officers filled the vacuum. The COMIBOL in fact became a refuge for retired military officers and retired second-rate politicians. In addition to these managerial and pork barrel complications, the long-term trends in production worked against tin; in 1927, just before total tin exports had peaked in 1929, tin made up 74.2 percent of Bolivia's exports, whereas by 1956 that percentage had fallen to 56.5 percent. The slack was taken up to some extent by increases in exports of lead, tungsten, zinc and oil.[199] But the tin barons had responded to the depression and to the threats of the 'military socialism' of Toro and Busch, and later to Villaroel, with a general policy of disinvestment, so that the mining equipment nationalised in 1952 was quite out of date. (During the Busch years, the tin barons had lowered production to 19,000 tons annually on the

---

198   The propaganda battle between the well-funded public relations campaign of the Rosca and the Bolivian government is recounted in Andrade 1976, pp. 135–46.

199   Bedregal 1999, p. 350.

pretext that reserves were being exhausted.) In light of this, the MNR's national-isation parallels, e.g., Britain's nationalisation in the same period of mines, steel, and railroads that were no longer profitable. Decrees in April and June 1952 required the COMIBOL to rehire workers laid off during the *sexenio rosquero*. The industries controlled by the COMIBOL had had 24,000 employees in 1951, and by 1956 had 36,000. Further ties to Western imperialism, in addition to U.S. aid, U.S. trade unions, and the various reports and commissions of inquiry were developed when in 1953 the COMIBOL signed a contract with the British tin smelter William Harvey Company. The working population as a whole paid for the losing proposition of the COMIBOL through taxation, and U.S. aid pressured the COMIBOL to return to orthodox management.

The agrarian reform undertaken by the MNR had some of the same ambigu-ities as the nationalisation of the large mines. It was undertaken 16 months after the revolution in response to land takeovers by armed peasants. It included, as indicated, the abolition of the quasi-feudal *pongueaje*. The leadership of the popular umbrella organisation, the COB, for its part vacillated between protest-ing the repression of the peasants and denouncing 'provocation' by peasants influenced by the POR.[200] According to Sándor John, the POR was actually lukewarm toward peasant mobilisations, arguing that peasants only wanted individual plots of lands for themselves. As Sándor John put it, the POR policy 'resembled what Stalin told Chinese Communists in 1925–27: curb peasants' land seizures because they threaten the party's bloc with the nationalist Guom-ingtang'. The reference to China is apt, since the Chinese Communist Party's 'bloc of four classes' in the 1949–53 period (workers, peasants, industrial cap-italists and the progressive middle class) was a frequent reference of the MNR leaders. Shortly after the revolution, Paz Estenssoro had appointed MNR leader Hernan Siles Zuazo to head a commission on agrarian reform. The commission reflected a general lack of expertise on such matters. Further, it was domin-ated by members of the reduced (Stalinist) PIR wedded to their stagist idea of a bourgeois-democratic revolution (above all PIR agrarian expert Arturo Urquidi Morales), even further to the right and more cautious than the MNR's own per-spective of a 'national revolution'. In keeping with the corporatist reality already manifest in nationalised industry, in agriculture as well the revolution had cre-ated a 'new national and organic image of the State as a basic structure for transformation, representation, integration and development'.[201] Paz Estens-soro had carefully studied the Mexican agrarian reform under Cardenas, but

---

200   Sándor John 2009, pp. 143, 146.
201   Begregal 1999, p. 448.

the PIR influence on the commission was oriented to maintaining 'an important nuclei of traditional latifundist power' through the euphemism 'small and
medium-size properties',[202] which were to be preserved. Peasants themselves
mobilised in western Bolivia from January to August 1953, placing increasing
pressure on the commission, but the latter continued to support the 'micro-
fundia', tying peasants to those plots. The decree on agrarian reform came at the
beginning of August 1953. In the view of Bedregal, the commission supported
a 'semi-democratic agrarian reform of the landowners' and of the 'progressive
hacendados', leaving the latifundias with some power. The agrarian reform had
to accept a modus vivendi 'leaving an ample sector of growers and cattle owners
to define what the law meant: "land to those who work it"'.[203] Urquidi, for his
part, saw the reform transforming the latifundists into 'progressive agricultur-
ists', better equipped than the indigenous population to advance the rural economy. The reform 'did not resolve the key question of the historical survival of
latifundist and microfundist factors which, over the long term, would become
the most serious problem of Bolivian backwardness, by which the agrarian
counter-reform could put down roots and derail the capitalist development
which was the immediate objective of the national revolution'.[204] Protected by
this thrust of the reform were the latifundias of the Beni and Pando provinces
(in the latter there were 3000 properties of 2000 hectares or more).

24   The Role of the Trotskyist POR

Following these brief sketches of the MNR nationalisations and agrarian reform,
it is imperative to analyse, in conclusion, the dynamic of class forces in which
these changes acquired their concrete meaning. In contrast to the other cases
of Latin American corporatism in more developed economies, as discussed
earlier, the 'national revolution' of the MNR could not base itself, at least initially, on a modernising military and state already in place, since the army, the
'special body of armed men', quite simply disintegrated in April 1952, leaving the
MNR precariously atop the armed militias of the Bolivian working class which
it had to contain and, initially, to appease. Coming right behind the working
class were the indigenous rural masses, largely trapped in pre-capitalist immis-
eration with quasi-feudal overtones, who went into motion at the beginning of

---

202   Ibid. p. 451.
203   Ibid. p. 455.
204   Ibid. p. 458.

1953. Confronting these forces and trying to ride them, the MNR was drawn from 'intellectual sectors of the Bolivian elite and upwardly mobile members of the middle class'.[205] Out of this array of forces, the MNR leadership had set itself the task of revamping the Bolivian state it had taken away from the *Rosca* to 'complete the bourgeois revolution', using Bolivia's rich endowment of resources and a reformed agriculture to build a viable capitalist nation-state that could hopefully at last escape from the 'colonial' status which MNR nationalist theoreticians such as Carlos Montenegro ascribed to it.

The MNR that seized power in 1952 had evolved from its origins around the anti-Semitic broadsheet *La Calle*, via the Toro-Busch 'military socialism' mixing clear German and Italian fascist influences with corporatist elements drawn from the Mexican Revolution, by way of the Nazi imprint on its founding programme of 1942, to the force recognised by the U.S. State Department in 1950 as the sole real alternative to 'communism' in Bolivia.

The MNR did not have to deal with 'communism' in the form of a mass pro-Soviet party, because that party, the PIR, had totally discredited itself by its services rendered since 1940 to the *Rosca*'s 'democracy'. Thus the sole ideological and practical force of any consequence to its left was the Trotskyist POR. Bolivia was, along with Vietnam and Ceylon (now Sri Lanka) one of the few countries in the world in which Trotskyism, and not Stalinism or Social Democracy, became for a time the mass current in the working class.

Undoubtedly the key figure in all but wedding the POR to the 'left wing' of the MNR was Juan Lechin, the presumed 'Lenin' to Paz Estenssoro's 'Kerensky'. As Dunkerley put it, 'a disparity between words and deeds ... was to be a consistent feature of the COB leader's erratic career'.[206] Lechin, a member of the MNR, had been politically educated by Guillermo Lora. Lechin was the restraining link to the Bolivian working class that the MNR desperately needed in 1952. Sándor John is succinct:

> While presenting their own viewpoint in articles and manifestos, Bolivian Trotskyists[207] were becoming a radical appendage to *lechinismo* in the labor movement, while Lechin guarded the MNR's left flank ... [quoting Lora]: 'Everything [the POR did in this period] led objectively to the numerical, but not political [sic] strengthening of the MNR'.[208] Paz Estens-

---

205   Sándor John 2009, p. 123.
206   Dunkerley 2006, p. 57.
207   I have left a theoretical discussion of Trotsky and the vicissitudes of post-Trotsky Trotskyism to the Appendix, in order not to excessively burden the main text.
208   Sándor John 2009, p. 89.

soro made constant attacks on Trotskyism, while he set about co-opting leaders and bureaucratizing structures. Ultimately more a pressure group than an independent party, the POR, in flat contradiction to the Theses of Pulacayo, supported not only Lechin but also other 'worker ministers'. In May 1952, Guillermo Lora declared these 'worker ministers' a conquest of the labor movement as textile workers decided to impose their conditions on the right wing of the MNR.[209]

Here is how the Latin American correspondent of U.S.-based Labor Action analysed the role of the POR at the end of 1952:

> On the other hand, the government ushered the Trotskyist 'leaders' into very profitable positions in the official machinery, such as the Agrarian Commission, the Stabilization Office, the Workers' Security Administration, etc. The *PORista* theoretician, Alaya Mercada, is a member of the Agrarian Commission with a salary of 70,000 pesos, which is 100 per cent higher than a minister's salary. Another 'theoretician' of the POR, Lora, a collaborator of Lechin's, is now a member of the President's Stabilization Office. The Secretary of the POR, Moller, is director of the Workers' Savings Bank [*Caja de Seguro y Ahorro Obrera*].

> Many other POR militants have also gotten good posts in the official government machine. In this way the Nationalist government has liquidated the 'Communist' and 'Trotskyist' danger in Bolivia, and now the whole Bolivian 'left' is collaborating with the regime, with the claim that it is thus 'saving the revolution' from capitalist restoration.

> Parallel to all this, the government party is absorbing leading elements from the left, especially from the POR. Two former general secretaries of the POR, Edwin Moller and Jorge Salazar, and the POR theoretician Ernesto Ayala Mercada, as well as Lechin's ex-secretary Josa Zogada, have entered the MNR officially. Thus a part of the POR staff has capitulated to the MNR, as we predicted long ago. Ideological capitulation preceded the personal and organizational capitulation. The right turn of the MNR is complemented by the capitulation and disintegration of the 'Left'.[210]

---

209   Ibid. p. 135.
210   Labor Action, 22 December 1952.

Along the same lines, Sándor John writes: 'Complete control of the state by the left wing of the MNR became a leitmotiv of the (POR's) propaganda'.[211] The Ninth Congress of the POR in September 1952 supported the MNR's 'progressive measures' and the left-wing of the MNR. In early 1953, the party sent a message to the MNR's national convention saying that 'to fulfil its historic mission' the convention 'should be the scene of reaction's defeat'. If the left-wing wins and the MNR acquires a 'proletarian physiognomy', the Congress declared the POR would even consider fusion. At times of crisis, such as the attempted (and failed) coups by the Falange and the *Rosca* in June 1953, the POR called on left-wing ministers to take control. When Paz Estenssoro responded to the coup attempts with anti-business rhetoric, the POR newspaper *Lucha Obrera* headlined 'Radicalization of Paz Estenssoro'. 'THE PRESIDENT, REVISING ALL OF HIS PAST POLITICAL STANCES, POINTED OUT ANTI-CAPITALIST OBJECTIVES FOR THE REVOLUTION, NOT JUST ANTI-IMPERIALIST AND ANTI-FEUDAL ONES'. 'All this struggle must center on the slogan, "Total control of the state by the left wing of the MNR"'. 'The people who join ministries as workers' representatives will not be doing so simply as personal collaboration by particular leaders ... [but on the basis of the] program especially approved by the COB'.[212] In early 1954, the POR supported a member of the MNR Left during the MNR's internal elections to its La Paz Departmental Command.

For all the POR's efforts on its behalf, the Paz government in 1954 increased repression against the Trotskyists, including large-scale arrests of POR workers and peasants, blacklists, and a crackdown on *Lucha Obrera*.[213]

In sum, the Bolivian POR was by rough analogy rather like the Spanish POUM (Partido Obrero de Unificacion Marxista) during the Spanish Revolution and Civil War, which was widely denounced as 'Trotskyist', but which was in fact a centrist political formation supporting (and participating in) the bourgeois Republican government. In Spain, the real Trotskyists were expelled from the POUM and with a handful of others formed the 'Bolshevik Leninist' group.[214]

---

211   Ibid. p. 136. Most of the material on the POR's role beginning in 1952 is from this source.

212   Ibid. p. 137.

213   The POR, following these developments, entered an internal crisis in 1954–5. The crisis was related to the 1951–3 split in the (Trotskyist) Fourth International, pitting Michel Pablo and Ernest Mandel against the American Trotksyist James Cannon. Guillermo Lora attempted to avoid aligning with either faction. The pro-Pablo faction did not enter the MNR. The great majority of Lora's faction opted for 'entrism' into the MNR, though Lora broke over the question of entrism at the last moment.

214   A rough analogy, indeed. The POR never formally entered the MNR government, though its members occupied posts therein; the POUM vehemently denied it was Trotksyist, whereas

During these first years after the revolution, the u.s. was more and more successfully pulling Bolivia into the fold. Aside from the crucial question of access to Bolivia's natural resources, u.s. aid was also prompted by the propaganda value of appearing to support a non-Communist version of reform. Paz Estenssoro on May 1953 had proclaimed his intention to open diplomatic relations with newly-Communist Czechoslovakia, but under the impact of u.s. aid in the following months, the initiative was dropped. By fall 1953 the u.s. was providing millions of dollars worth of surplus food, as well as funds for technical assistance and road construction. Because they were no longer profitable, the nationalisation of the mines had ultimately revealed Bolivia's dependency on outside help. By 1954, the Bolivian government was backing the u.s.'s anticommunist measures at the Inter-American Conference in Caracas. Accelerating inflation, which reached 179 percent in 1956, and other economic disruptions brought a stabilisation team headed by u.s. corporate executive George Eder, which proposed more opening to market forces and a dismantling of the public sector. The Eder stabilisation plan was adopted in December 1956, with the scrapping of the multiple exchange rates left over from the earlier currency controls; the Bolivian currency was allowed to fluctuate with international supply and demand just as tin prices were contracting in the 1957 world recession.[215] The momentum of the revolution of 1952 was long since broken, and the Bolivian working class and peasantry were left to endure ensuing decades of coups, counter-coups, hyperinflation, and a quasi narco-state, much of it under a refurbished military and the u.s. 'national security' doctrine worked up, once again, from interwar fascist sources.

Conclusion: The Inability of the Left to Distinguish Between Corporatism and Socialism

The MNR revolution in Bolivia and the little-remembered ideological sources from which it developed provide an unusually clear example of the myopia of much of the self-styled left, both on the scene and internationally. Taking the

---

the POR claimed that it was. See Bolloten 1979, pp. 381–3. 'In its polemic with the Trotskyists the POUM argued that its presence in the Catalan government was a transitional step toward complete working-class power ... [for the Trotskyists this] ... was inconsistent with the POUM's participation in a government that ... decreed the dissolution of the workers' committees ...'

215   The information in this paragraph is based on Lehman 1999, pp. 109–24.

example of the currents of Trotskyism, particularly the Mandel-Pablo variety dominant in the Fourth International at the time, we see evolving a methodology repeated again and again whereby different variants of the far-left set themselves up as the cheering section and often minor adjuncts to 'progressive' movements and governments in fact quite alien to their ostensible goal of socialist revolution, movements and governments strictly committed to a restructuring (or creation) of a nation-state adequate to the present realities of world capitalism. This methodology involves imagining (as has been shown in the relationship of the POR with the MNR) a healthy 'left' wing of a bourgeois or nationalist or 'progressive' or Third World 'anti-imperialist' movement that can be 'pushed to the left' by 'critical support', opening the way for socialist revolution (there is nothing specifically 'Trotskyist' about this; see appendix below). This methodology has been employed again and again, from Bolivia under the MNR to Algeria under the FLN to Mitterand's France to the Iranian mullahs after 1979. The far-left groups in question see themselves in the role of Lenin's Bolsheviks to Kerensky's Provisional Government, when in fact their role is to enlist some of the more radical elements in supporting or tolerating an alien project which sooner or later co-opts or, even worse, represses and sometimes annihilates them.

In the case of Bolivia, the multi-class nationalism epitomised by MNR intellectual Carlos Montenegro, with its problematic of the 'nation' versus the 'foreign', combined in practice the corporatist models attempted by 1936–40 'military socialism' and the 1943–6 Villaroel regime, and was influenced to different degrees by Mussolini's Italy, the Primo de Rivera dictatorship in Spain, Nazi Germany, Vargas's Brazil, Peron's Argentina and the Mexico of Cardenas. Though the standing bourgeois army in Bolivia (in contrast to these other experiences) simply dissolved and had to be rebuilt (as it quickly was), theoretical disarmament set the stage for the practical disarmament of the worker militias. The statist backing of the FSTMB and later of the COB, the creation of the COMIBOL to administer the nationalised mines, and state-sponsored agrarian reform gave Bolivia its variant of the twentieth-century adaptation to the post-1929 world conjuncture, in which the old liberal ideologies and party organisations no longer sufficed.

Appendix: Trotskyism, Permanent Revolution and the Case of Bolivia

I felt the preceding text was complex and tortuous enough that I did not wish to burden it with excessive theoretical baggage. I have used the term 'Trotskyist' throughout in a neutral way to refer to those who designated themselves as such. The blur of unfamiliar names and events is difficult enough for the unapprised reader, and indeed for some more apprised, without adding on what might seem like a detour into the labyrinth of mutually hostile self-proclaimed Trotskyist currents that existed even before the assassination of Trotsky in 1940, not to mention after. Yet in this case, the question of Trotskyism cannot be avoided because, as indicated, Bolivia was one of the few countries in the world where Trotskyism became the mass movement, as opposed to a small group (or sect) on the fringes of the mass movement. Hence its actions, particularly as they involved the POR and prominent POR leaders such as Guillermo Lora, are highly relevant to our story. In fact, as the comments of Sándor John and of the correspondent of Labor Action have already indicated, the Bolivian POR, at the high point of its influence from 1946 into the early 1950s, had a rather tenuous relationship (at best) to 'orthodox Trotskyism'.

My own distance from Trotskyism, orthodox or otherwise, is not the issue here.[216] So many people have been exposed to Trotskyism as a blur of warring sects of no apparent historical weight that the attempt to distil a 'true Trotskyism' might seem as futile as an attempt to distil a 'true Christianity'.

In the case of Bolivia, however, the self-styled Trotskyists of the POR were not a 'warring sect' but a significant party with a mass working-class base. What is most relevant for the purposes of the Bolivian Revolution and the relationship of the POR to the MNR is Trotsky's theory of permanent revolution, and the related theory of combined and uneven development.

That theory, stated most bluntly, held that any bourgeois revolution in a semi-developed or underdeveloped country must necessarily unleash forces beyond itself (most notably the working class) and 'cross over' into a proletarian revolution, which can be successful in the medium-to-long term only if it successfully links up with a proletarian revolution in the capitalist heartland. Such was the strategy of the Bolshevik Revolution in its early (1917–21) phase, predicated as it was on the urgent necessity of revolution in Germany at the very least.

---

216   See my articles on the Break Their Haughty Power website http://home.earthlink.net/
      ~lrgoldner: 'Introduction to the Johnson-Forest Tendency and the Background to "Facing
      Reality"' (Goldner 2004); 'Facing Reality 45 Years Later: Critical Dialogue With C.L.R. James
      /Grace Lee/Pierre Chaulieu' (Goldner 2002); 'Max Eastman: One American Radical's View
      of the "Bolshevization" of the American Revolutionary Movement and a Forgotten, and
      Unforgettable, Portrait of Trotsky' (Goldner 2006); and 'The Situation of Left Communism
      Today: An Interview with the Korean SaNoShin Group' (Goldner 2008).

The Trotsky-Parvus recovery of the mootings of permanent revolution in the pre- and post-1848 writings of Marx and Engels, and their use of that theory to understand, through the explosion of 1904–5, that the coming revolution in Russia would be a working-class and not a bourgeois revolution, was a fundamental contribution to revolutionary theory in the twentieth century. One does not have to be a 'Trotskyist' to recognise this. (At the time of this formulation, it should be recalled, Trotsky was highly sceptical of Lenin's Bolshevik conception of the vanguard party).[217]

The theory of permanent revolution is adumbrated by Marx and Engels in some of their writings of the 1840s and on the revolution of 1848. From their earliest period, by way of their assessments of the failed revolutions of 1848, Marx and Engels portrayed the German bourgeoisie, in contrast to the English or the French, as having come historically 'too late':

> If one were to proceed from the *status quo* itself in Germany, even in the only appropriate way, that is, negatively, the result would still be an anachronism. Even the negation of our political present is already a dusty fact in the historical lumber room of modern nations. If I negate powdered wigs, I am still left with unpowdered wigs. If I negate German conditions of 1843, I am hardly, according to French chronology, in the year 1789 and still less in the focus of the present ... We have in fact shared in the restoration of modern nations without sharing in their revolutions. We have been restored, first because other nations dared to make revolutions, and secondly because other nations suffered counter-revolutions ... Led by our shepherds, we found ourselves in the company of freedom only once, on the *day of its burial*.[218]

Engels, in his 1851 book *Revolution and Counter-Revolution in Germany*, diagnosing the timidity and impotence of the German liberal bourgeoisie in 1848, made this more concrete:

---

217 'In the internal politics of the Party these methods lead, as we shall see below, to the Party organisation "substituting" itself for the Party, the Central Committee substituting itself for the Party organisation, and finally the dictator substituting himself for the Central Committee ...' This quote is from Trotsky's *Our Political Tasks* (Trotsky 1904), a text rarely referred to by Trotskyists. See: http://www.marxists.org/archive/trotsky/1904/tasks/ch03 .htm.

218 'Toward the Critique of Hegel's Philosophy of Law: Introduction', in Marx 1967 [1843–4], p. 251.

The Revolution of February upset, in France, the very same sort of Government which the Prussian bourgeoisie were going to set up in their own country. The Revolution of February announced itself as a revolution of the working classes against the middle classes; it proclaimed the downfall of middle-class government and the emancipation of the workingman. Now the Prussian bourgeoisie had, of late, had quite enough of working-class agitation in their own country. After the first terror of the Silesian riots had passed away, they had even tried to give this agitation a turn in their own favor; but they always had retained a salutary horror of revolutionary Socialism and Communism; and, therefore, when they saw men at the head of the Government in Paris whom they considered as the most dangerous enemies of property, order, religion, family, and of the other Penates of the modern bourgeois, they at once experienced a considerable cooling down of their own revolutionary ardor. They knew that the moment must be seized, and that, without the aid of the working masses, they would be defeated; and yet their courage failed them. Thus they sided with the Government in the first partial and provincial outbreaks, tried to keep the people quiet in Berlin, who, during five days, met in crowds before the royal palace to discuss the news and ask for changes in the Government; and when at last, after the news of the downfall of Metternich, the King made some slight concessions, the bourgeoisie considered the Revolution as completed, and went to thank His Majesty for having fulfilled all the wishes of his people. But then followed the attack of the military on the crowd, the barricades, the struggle, and the defeat of royalty. Then everything was changed: the very working classes, which it had been the tendency of the bourgeoisie to keep in the background, had been pushed forward, had fought and conquered, and all at once were conscious of their strength. Restrictions of suffrage, of the liberty of the press, of the right to sit on juries, of the right of meeting-restrictions that would have been very agreeable to the bourgeoisie because they would have touched upon such classes only as were beneath them – now were no longer possible. The danger of a repetition of the Parisian scenes of 'anarchy' was imminent. Before this danger all former differences disappeared. Against the victorious workingman, although he had not yet uttered any specific demands for himself, the friends and the foes of many years united, and the alliance between the bourgeoisie and the supporters of the over-turned system was concluded upon the very barricades of Berlin. The necessary concessions, but no more than was unavoidable, were to be made, a ministry of the opposition leaders of the United Diet was to be formed, and in return for its services in saving the Crown, it was to have the support of all the props of the old Government, the feudal aristocracy, the bureaucracy, the army.[219]

Thus Marx and Engels, before, during and after the 'springtime of peoples' of 1848, already saw the dynamic by which the struggle for the bourgeois revolution necessarily opened the way for the independent emergence of the working class, 'even before (the working man) had uttered any specific demands for himself'. This 'crossover' process between the bourgeois and proletarian revolutions was the kernel of what was later elaborated by Trotsky and his collaborator Parvus in 1904–5 in the mature theory of 'permanent revolution'.

Permanent revolution was intimately linked, for Trotsky, with the theory of combined and uneven development. This theory was a direct rejection of the linear- 'stageist' view of history widely held in the parties of the Second International, in which every country had to pass through the bourgeois revolution before arriving at the socialist revolution. It was based on the perfectly reasonable insight, strengthened by the history of capitalism, that each individual country does not (indeed cannot) recapitulate all the 'stages' undergone by other countries. Trotsky saw his theory confirmed already in 1905 with the vacillations of the timid liberal bourgeoisie in its feeble battles with Tsarism, all too aware of the workers, in contrast to Germany, already articulating demands of their own. Even at the beginning of 1917, Lenin still shared this stageist view. Trotsky and Parvus, on the other hand, linked up with the Marx-Engels germ of the theory of the 'crossover' between the two revolutions, based on seeing individual capitalist countries as part of one single international system, in which developing countries tapping into the cutting edge of world technological innovation not only could but were compelled to 'leap' over stages passed through by others. Thus on the eve of its 1905 and 1917 revolutions, Russia had some of the largest and most modern factories in the world, surrounded by a much larger sea of backward agriculture.

> The law of combined development reveals itself most indubitably, however, in the history and character of Russian industry. Arising late, Russian industry did not repeat the development of advanced countries, but inserted itself into this development, adapting their latest achievements to their own backwardness. Just as the economic evolution of Russia as a whole skipped over the epoch of craft guilds and manufacture, so also

---

219   Engels 1851, available online at: http://www.marxists.org/archive/marx/works/1852/germany/cho6.htm.

the separate branches of industry made a series of special leaps over technical productive stages that had been measured in the West by decades ... The social character of the Russian bourgeoisie and its political physiognomy were determined by the condition of origin and structure of Russian industry. The extreme concentration of this industry alone meant that between the capitalist leaders and the popular masses there was no hierarchy of transitional layers ... Such are the elementary and irremovable causes of the political isolation of the Russian bourgeoisie. Whereas in the dawn of its history it was too unripe to accomplish a Reformation, when the time came for leading a revolution it was overripe.[220]

The triumph of Stalinism by 1924 was, among other things, a full restoration of the linear, Second International stage theory, having among its first fruits the catastrophic Comintern policy of allying with Chiang kai-shek's Nationalist movement in China in the years 1925–7.

Whatever the problems of Trotsky himself, Trotskyism after his assassination was mainly an affair of mediocrities, of the Barneses and Cannons and Pablos and Mandels. Trotsky had predicted that the coming Second World War would be followed by world revolution similar to the aftermath of World War One; he also believed that the Stalinist regime in Russia would be swept away in the process. Instead, his followers in 1945 and thereafter found themselves confronted with a giant step forward in Stalinist power in Eastern Europe, China, Korea and Indochina, a giant step in which the working class had played no role. Western Trotskyists such as Mandel were egging on the 'reformist' Stalinists in such places as Czechoslovakia and Yugoslavia, while the NKVD and their local counterparts were tracking down and assassinating their own Trotskyist comrades.

Probably the worst case was that of Michel Pablo, who by 1950 had concluded that the world was entering centuries of Stalinist hegemony, and called on Trotskyists to engage in 'deep entry' into the Stalinist parties, like Christians in the catacombs. Pablo's adaptation to current events was blown sky high only a few years later with the 1953 uprising of workers in East Berlin and in 1956 with workers' movements that shook Stalinism to its foundations in the Polish Autumn and the Hungarian Revolution. But the damage maturing since 1940 had been done, and a methodology of adaptation to Stalinist expansionism as well as various Third World 'national liberation fronts' and progressive regimes had been set down for decades. The list is long, from the adaptation

---

220   Trotsky 1967 [1930], vol. 1, pp. 26–8.

of most[221] Trotskyists (with their 'revolutionary opposition' buried in fine print in footnotes) to such sundry movements and regimes as the Algerian FLN, the Vietnamese NLF,[222] Castro's Cuba, Allende's Chile, the Iranian mullahs, the Nicaraguan Sandinistas, and Polish Solidarnosc.

And to the Bolivian MNR.

At the time of the April 1952 revolution, the most significant Bolivian Trotskyist, Guillermo Lora, was in Paris conferring with the leaders of the Fourth International, who were by then firmly in the camp of Pablo and who apparently did not impress him. Lora did not join the Pablo faction, and those in Bolivia who did so did not join the MNR government. Nevertheless the relationship between the POR and the MNR we have documented in the main text speaks for itself.

The theory of permanent revolution dictated for Bolivia, as for all other underdeveloped countries, the impossibility of a stable bourgeois democratic regime and the necessary 'crossover' of the bourgeois into the proletarian revolution. Bolivia was of course not Russia in 1917, and, in contrast to Russia, did not possess some of the largest and most modern factories in the world. It certainly shared with Russia a vast majority of the population working in backward, mainly pre-capitalist agriculture. Fundamental agrarian reform was and is the sine qua non for any true bourgeois revolution. Instead, as we have seen, the Bolivian land reform of 1953 was compromised by preservation of the holdings of the 'progressive *hacendados*' and sizeable micro- and latifundia lands which later became the base of a conservative peasantry.

Similarly, the 'nationalisation of decline' by the COMIBOL, with full compensation to the three tin barons, burdened the revolution from the beginning with the dead weight of the past.

Between these two halfway measures, and the accommodation with the United States, the runaway inflation of 1955–6 was hardly a surprise.

Let us then pose the question point-blank: would a different, 'truly Trotskyist' policy of the POR in 1951–3 have resulted in a proletarian revolution in Bolivia? When one considers that in April 1952 the 'nationalist revolution' of the MNR had the overwhelming support of the armed working class, the peasantry and the urban middle class; that 85 percent of the members of the POR

---

221 The varieties proliferated with the passing decades.

222 See the remarkable books of Ngo Van (in French, e.g., Ngo Van 1995; a review on the Break Their Haughty Power web site summarises the book in English: http://home.earthlink.net/ ~lrgoldner/vietnam.html). See also the English translation of his autobiography (Ngo Van 2010), in which he details the massacres of the Trotskyists by Ho Chi Minh's Stalinists in 1945 and thereafter.

ultimately entered the MNR in those years; and when a figure of the stature
of Guillermo Lora decided not to enter only at the last moment, the question
seems moot. The real question is why the national revolutionary ideology and
organisation was so popular, to the point that it was even attractive to the great
majority of POR members. The Trotskyist view, with its belief that the 'crisis of
leadership' is paramount in such situations, makes the question of the presence
or absence of the revolutionary party the deux ex machina of such crises, when
the real historical question is what conditions make possible or militate against
the existence of such a party in the first place.

In 1952, the Cold War was at its peak and a resulting World War Three
seemed a real possibility. Developments in Guatemala, Iran, China, Korea and
the struggle of the two blocs to influence de-colonisation in Asia and Africa
were so many flashpoints. In such a conjuncture, surely a proletarian revolution in Bolivia could have had ripples far beyond a poor, remote, landlocked
country of three million people. (We bracket for a moment the question of the
possibility of a working-class revolution in the capitalist heartland, a necessary
counterpart to the theory of permanent revolution, when in fact the working
class everywhere in Europe and the U.S. had been contained or defeated by
1952; recall, to the credit of the POR, the declaration of solidarity – cited earlier –
with North American workers.)[223] Bolivia's ability to command the attention of
the United States, for reasons we have described in detail, when there were so
many other, seemingly larger fires to put out, already attests to its explosive
potential. Nevertheless, such calculations surely weighed on the thoughts of
Bolivia's workers as well, and they made their decisions accordingly. To 'blame'
the POR for 'betraying' the Bolivian Revolution is to fall into the idealist trap of
saying 'they had the wrong ideas' instead of explaining why they had the ideas
they did.

---

223   Sándor John 2009, pp. 94–5.

References

Abecia López, Valentín 1997, *Montenegro*, La Paz: Honorable Senado Nacional.

Alexander, Robert J. 1999, *The Anarchists in the Spanish Civil War*, 2 Volumes, London: Janus.

Anderson, Kevin 2010, *Marx at the Margins: On Nationalism, Ethnicity, and non-Western Societies*, Chicago: University of Chicago Press.

Anderson, Perry 1974, *Lineages of the Absolutist State*, London: New Left Books.

Andrade, Victor 1976, *My Missions for Revolutionary Bolivia, 1944–1962*, Pittsburgh: University of Pittsburgh Press.

Arnade, Charles W. 2008, *Histografía colonial y moderna de Bolivia*, Bolivia: Amigos del Libro.

Arze Cuadros, Eduardo 2002, *Bolivia, el Programa del MNR y la revolución nacional: del movimiento de reforma universtaria al ocaso del modelo neoliberal (1928–2002)*, La Paz: Plural Editores.

Atkinson, Dorothy 1983, *The End of the Russian Land Commune, 1905–1930*, Stanford, CA: Stanford University Press.

Balabanoff, Angelica 1968 [1938], *My Life as a Rebel*, 3rd ed., New York: Greenwood Press.

Baptista Gumucio, Mariano 1978, *Yo fuí el orgullo: vida y pensamiento de Fran Tamayo*, La Paz: Editorial los Amigos del Libro.

Barcelli, Augustín 1957, *Medio siglo de luchas sindicales revolucionarias en Bolivia: 1905–1955*, La Paz: n. p.

Baynac, Jacques 1979, *Les socialistes-révolutionnaires, de mars 1881 à mars 1917*, Volume 1, Paris: R. Laffont.

Bedregal, Guillermo 1999, *Víctor Paz Estenssoro, el político: una semblanza crítica*, Mexico: Fondo de Cultura Económica.

Belmonte Pabón, Elías 1994, *RADEPA: sombras y refulgencias del pasado*, La Paz: n. p.

Bennigsen, Alexandre 1986, *Sultan Galiev, le père de la révolution tiers-mondiste*, Paris: Fayard.

Bernecker, Walther L. 1982, *Colectividades y revolución social: el anarquismo en la guerra civil española, 1936–1939*, Barcelona: Editorial Crítica.

Bernstein, Irving 1960, *The Lean Years: A History of the American Worker, 1920–1933*, Boston: Houghton Mifflin.

Bettelheim, Charles 1974, *Les luttes de classes en URSS*, Volume 1, *Première Période*, Paris: Maspero.

Bieber, León Enrique 1984, *Las relaciones económicas de Bolivia con Alemania, 1880–1920*, Berlin: Colloquium.

———— 2004, *Pugna por influencia y hegemonía: la rivalidad germano-estadounidense en Bolivia, 1936–1946*, Frankfurt: Lang.

————— 2010, *Presencia judía en Bolivia: la ola inmigratoria de 1938–1940*, Santa Cruz de la Sierra: Editorial El País.

Bolloten, Burnett 1979, *The Spanish Revolution: The Left and the Struggle for Power during the Civil War*, Chapel Hill, NC: University of North Carolina Press.

Bookchin, Murray 1998, *The Spanish Anarchists: The Heroic Years, 1868–1936*, San Francisco: AK Press.

Bordiga, Amadeo 1975, *Russie et revolution dans la theorie marxiste*, Paris: Spartacus.

Borkenau, Franz 1937, *Spanish Cockpit: An Eye-Witness Account of the Political Conflicts of the Spanish Civil War*, S.I.: s.n.

Braden, Spruille 1971, *Diplomats and Demagogues: The Memoirs of Spruille Bragden*, New Rochelle, NY: Arlington House.

Brady, Robert Alexander 1933, *The Rationalization Movement in German Industry: A Study in the Evolution of Economic Planning*, Berkeley: University of California Press.

Bratzel, John F., and Leslie B. Rout 1986, *The Shadow War: German espionage and United States counterespionage in Latin America during World War II*, Frederick, MD: University Publications of America.

Brenan, Gerald 1950 [1943], *The Spanish Labyrinth: An Account of the Social and Political Background of the Civil War*, Cambridge: Cambridge University Press.

————— 1974, *Personal Record, 1920–1972*, London: Jonathan Cape.

Cano Ruiz, B. 1985, *Que es el anarchismo?*, Mexico: Editorial Nuevo Tiempo.

Carr, Edward Hallett 1953, *The Bolshevik Revolution*, Volume 3, London: Macmillan.

Carrère d'Encausse, Hélène 1981, *Réforme et révolution chez les musulmans de l'Empire russe, Bukhara, 1867–1924*, Paris: Presses de la Fondation nationale des sciences politiques.

Çağatay, Ergun, Doğan Kuban et al. 2006, *The Turkic Speaking Peoples: 2,000 Years of Art and Culture from Inner Asia to the Balkans*, Munich: Prestel.

Casanova, Julián 1985, *Anarquismo y revolución en la sociedad rural aragonesa, 1936–1938*, Madrid: Siglo Veintiuno.

Chaquèri, Cosroe 1995, *The Soviet Socialist Republic of Iran, 1920–1921: Birth of the Trauma*, Pittsburgh: University of Pittsburgh Press.

Chiaradia, John 2013, 'Amadeo Bordiga and the Myth of Antonio Gramsci', available at http://bthp23.com/Chiaradia.pdf; and https://libcom.org/library/amadeo-bordiga -myth-antonio-gramsci-john-chiaradia.

Cohen, Stephen F. 1973, *Bukharin and the Bolshevik Revolution: A Political Biography, 1888–1938*, New York: Alfred A. Knopf.

Cooper Busch, Briton 1971, *Britain, India, and the Arabs, 1914–1921*, California, University of California Press.

Córdova, Arnaldo 1974, *La política de masas del cardenismo*, Mexico: Ediciones Era.

Crisenoy, Chantal de 1978, *Lenine face aux moujiks*, Paris: Seuil.

Cruz, Rafael 1987, *El Partido Comunista de España en la Segunda República*, Madris, Alianza Editorial.

Daum, Walter 1990, *The Life and Death of Stalinism: A Resurrection of Marxist Theory*, New York: Socialist Voice Publishing Co.

Davis, Mike 2006, *Planet of Slums*, London: Verso.

Deutscher, Isaac 1980, *The Prophet Armed: Trotsky, 1879–1921*, Oxford: Oxford University Press.

Dómich Ruiz, Marcos 1993, *Militares en la revolución y en la contrarevolución*, La Paz: Institutio de Investigaciones Sociológicas.

Dosman, Edgar J. 2008, *The Life and Times of Raúl Prebisch, 1901–1986*, Montreal: McGill-Queen's University Press.

Dumont, Paul 1997, *Du socialisme ottoman à l'internationalisme anatolien*, Istanbul: Les Editions Isis.

Dunkerley, James 2006, *Orígenes del poder militar: Bolivia, 1879–1935*, 3rd ed., La Paz, Bolivia.

Engels, Frederick 1851, *Revolution and Counter-Revolution in Germany*, available online at: https://www.marxists.org/archive/marx/works/1852/germany/.

Erlich, Alexander 1960, *The Soviet Industrialization Debate, 1924–1928*, Cambridge, MA: Harvard University Press.

Elbe, Ingo 2008, *Marx im Westen: die neue Marx-Lektüre in der Bundesrepublik seit 1965*, Berlin: Akademie Verlag.

Etchebehere, Mika 1976, *Ma guerre d'Espagne à moi*, Paris: Denoël.

Figallo, Beatriz 1996–7, 'Bolivia y la Argentina: los conflictos regionales durante la Segunda Guerra Mundial', *Estudios Interdisciplinarios de América Latina y el Caribe*, 7, 1.

Gallego, Ferran 1991, *Los origenes del reformismo militar en America Latina: La Gestion de David Toro in Bolivia*, Barcelona: PPU.

Gerschenkron, Alexander 1943, *Bread and Democracy in Germany*, Berkeley: University of California Press.

Glenny, Misha 2000, *The Balkans: Nationalism, War, and the Great Powers, 1804–1999*, New York: Viking.

Gomes, Gustavo Maia 1986, *The Roots of State Intervention in the Brazilian Economy*, New York: Praeger.

Grindle, Merilee Serrill, and Pilar Domingo 2003, *Proclaiming Revolution: Bolivia in Comparative Perspective*, London: Institute of Latin American Studies.

Glyn Williams, Brian 2001, *The Crimean Tartars: The Diaspora Experience and the Forging of a Nation*, Leiden: Brill.

Goldner, Loren 1981, 'Remaking of the American Working Class: Restructuring of Global Capital, Recomposition of Class Terrain', available at http://breaktheirhaughtypower.org/the-remaking-of-the-american-working-class-the-restructuring-of-global-capital-and-the-recomposition-of-class-terrain/.

——— 1983, 'On the Non-Formation of a Working-Class Political Party in the United

States, 1900–1945', available at: http://breaktheirhaughtypower.org/on-the-non
-formation-of-a-working-class-political-party-in-the-united-states-1900-1945/.

———— 1991, 'Communism is the Material Human Community: Amadeo Bordiga Today', available at http://breaktheirhaughtypower.org/communism-is-the-material
-human-community-amadeo-bordiga-today/.

———— 2000, *Ubu Saved From Drowning: Worker Insurgency and Statist Containment
in Portugal and Spain, 1974–1977*, Cambridge, MA: Queenqueg Publications; full text
available online at: http://bthp23.com/Portugal-Spain.pdf.

———— 2001, *Vanguard of Retrogression: 'Postmodern' Fictions as Ideology in the Era of
Fictitious Capital*, New York: Queequeg.

———— 2002, 'Facing Reality 45 Years Later: Critical Dialogue With C.L.R. James/Grace
Lee/Pierre Chaulieu', available online at: http://breaktheirhaughtypower.org/facing
-reality-45-years-later-critical-dialogue-with-jamesleechaulieu/.

———— 2004, 'Introduction to the Johnson-Forest Tendency and the Background to
"Facing Reality"', available online at: http://breaktheirhaughtypower.org/
introduction-to-the-johnson-forest-tendency-and-the-background-to-facing
-reality/.

———— 2006, 'Max Eastman: One American Radical's View of the "Bolshevization" of
the American Revolutionary Movement and a Forgotten, and Unforgettable, Portrait
of Trotsky', available online at: http://breaktheirhaughtypower.org/max-eastman
-one-american-radicals-view-of-the-bolshevization-of-the-american-revolutionary
-movement-and-a-forgotten-and-unforgettable-portrait-of-trotsky/.

———— 2008, 'The Situation of Left Communism Today: An Interview with the Korean
SaNoShin Group', available at: http://breaktheirhaughtypower.org/the-situation-of
-left-communism-today/.

Grigor Suny, Ronald 1972, *The Baku Commune, 1917–1918: Class and Nationality in the
Russian Revolution*, Princeton, NJ: Princeton University Press.

Grog, Dieter 1973, *Negative Intergration und revolutionärer Attentismus: die deutsche
Sozialdemokratie am Varaben des Ersten Weltkrieges*, Frankfurt: Ullstein Buch.

Guevara Arze, Walter 1988, *Bases para replantear la revolución nacional: con el Manifi-
esto de Ayopaya*, La Paz: Librería Editorial 'Juventud'.

Guillén, Abraham 1980, *El error militar de las "izquierdas": estrategia de la guerra revolucionaria*, Barcelona: Hacer.

———— 2002, *José Cuadros Quiroga: inventor del Movimiento Nacionalista Revolucionario*, La Paz: n. p.

Ingerflom, Claudio Segio 1988, *Le citoyen impossible: les racines russes du léninisme*,
Paris: Editions Payot.

Harris, George S. 1967, *The Origins of Communism in Turkey*, Stanford, CA: Hoover
Institute on War, Revolution, and Peace.

———— 2002, *The Communists and the Kadro Movement: Shaping Ideology in Atatürk's
Turkey*, Istanbul: Isis Press.

Heyd, Ulrich 1950, *Foundations of Turkish Nationalism: The Life and Teachings of Ziya Gokalp*, London: Luzac and Co.

Hopkirk, Peter 1985, *Setting the East Ablaze: Lenin's Dream of an Empire in Asia*, New York: Norton.

———— 1992, *The Great Game: The Struggle for Empire in Central Asia*, New York: Kodansha International.

Hostler, Charles Warren 1957, *Turkism and the Soviets: The Turks of the World and their Political Objectives*, London: G. Allen & Unwin.

Hovannisian, Richard G. 1971–1996, *The Republic of Armenia*, 4 Volumes, Berkeley: University of California Press.

Iglesias, Ignacio 1977, *León Trotski y España (1930–1939)*, Madrid: Júcar.

Insurgent Notes 2010, 'The Historical Moment that Produced Us: Global Revolution or Recomposition of Capital', available at: http://insurgentnotes.com/2010/06/historical_moment/.

International Communist Current n.d, 'Left Wing of the Turkish Communist Party, 1920–1927', n.p.: International Communist Current.

James, C.L.R., and Grace Lee Boggs and Cornelius Castoriadis 1974, *Facing Reality*, Detroit: Bewick.

Junco, José Alvarez 1976, *La ideología política del anarquismo español (1868–1910)*, Madrid: Siglo Veintiuno de España Editores.

Italian Communist Left 1960, 'Bilan d'une revolution', *Programme Communiste*, 40–2.

Kautsky, Karl 1988 [1899], *The Agrarian Question*, translated by Pete Burgess, 2 Volumes, London: Zwan Publications.

Kingston-Mann, Esther 1983, *Lenin and the Problem of Marxist Peasant Revolution*, Oxford: Oxford University Press.

Klein, Herbert S. 1969, *Parties and Political Change in Bolivia, 1880–1952*, London: Cambridge University Press.

———— 2003, *A Concise History of Bolivia*, Cambridge: Cambridge University Press.

Klein, Naomi 2007, *The Shock Doctrine: The Rise of Disaster Capitalism*, New York: Metropolitan Books.

Kohn, Hans 1960, *Pan-Slavism: Its History and Ideology*, New York: Vintage Books.

Köprülü, Mehmet Fuat 1929, *Influence du chamanisme turco-mongol sur les ordres mystiques musulmans*, Istanbul: Zellitch frères.

Knudson, Jerry W. 1986, *Bolivia, Press and Revolution, 1932–1964*, Lanham, MD: University Press of America.

Krader, Lawrence 1975, *The Asiatic Mode of Production: Sources, Development, and Critique in the Writings of Karl Marx*, Assen: Von Gorcum.

von Laue, Theodore H. 1963, *Sergei Witte and the Industrialization of Russia*, New York: Columbia University Press.

League for the Revolutionary Party (LRP) 1952, 'Bolivia: The Revolution the Fourth International Betrayed', available online at: http://www.lrp-cofi.org/pamphlets/bolivia1letter.html.

Lehman, Kenneth D. 1999, *Bolivia and the United States: A Limited Partnership*, Athens: University of Georgia Press.

Lenin, V.I. 1960–70, *Complete Works*, 45 Volumes, Moscow: Foreign Languages Publishing House.

———— *One Step Forwards, Two Steps Back (The Crisis in Our Party)*, in Lenin 1960–1970, Volume 7.

LeRoy Love, Joseph 1996, *Crafting the Third World: Theorizing Underdevelopment in Rumania and Brazil*, Stanford, CA: Stanford University Press.

Lewin, Moshe 1968a, *Lenin's Last Struggle*, New York: Pantheon.

Lewis, Bernard 2002, *The Emergence of Modern Turkey*, Oxford: Oxford University Press.

———— 1968b, *Russian Peasants and Soviet Power: A Study of Collectivization*, translated by Irene Nove, Evanston, IL: Northwestern University Press.

Lih, Lars T. 2006, *Lenin Rediscovered*: What is to be Done? *in Context*, Leiden: Brill.

van der Linden, Marcel 2007, *Western Marxism and the Soviet Union: A Survey of Critical Theories and Debates since 1917*, Leiden: Brill.

Lora, Guillermo 1965, *Fue revolucionario Carlos Montenegro?*, n. p.: n. p.

———— 1994–2012, *Obras completas*, 69 Volumes, La Paz: Ediciones Masas.

Lorenzo, Anselmo 1974, *El proletariado miltante*, Madrid: Alianza Editorial.

Lorini, Irma 2006, *El nacionalismo en Bolivia de la pre y posguerra del Chaco, 1910–1945*, La Paz: Plural Editores.

Luxemburg, Rosa 2004 [1912], *Introduction to Political Economy*, in *The Rosa Luxemburg Reader*, edited by Peter Hudis and Kevin Anderson, New York: Monthly Review Press.

———— 2008 [1906], *The Mass Strike*, in *The Essential Rosa Luxemburg: Reform or Revolution and the Mass Strike*, Chicago: Haymarket.

Maitron, Jean 1975, *Le mouvement anarchiste en France*, 2 Volumes, Paris: F. Maspero.

Malefakis, Edward E. 1970, *Agrarian Reform and Peasant Revolution in Spain: Origins of the Civil War*, New Haven: Yale University Press.

Marof, Tristán 1934, *La tragedia del altiplano*, Buenos Aires: Editorial Claridad.

Marot, John Eric 2012, *The October Revolution in Prospect and Retrospect: Interventions in Russian and Soviet History*, Leiden: Brill.

Marx, Karl 1967 [1843–4], *A Contribution to the Critique of Hegel's Philosophy of Right*, in *Writings of the Young Marx on Philosophy and Society*, edited by Lloyd David Easton and Kurt H. Guddat, New York: Doubleday.

———— 1972, *The Ethnological Notebooks of Karl Marx*, edited by Lawrence Krader, Assen: Van Gorcum.

———— 1973 [1857], *Grundrisse: Foundations of the Critique of Political Economy*, translated by Martin Nicolaus, New York: Vintage.

———— 1975b [1844], *Economic and Philosophic Manuscripts of 1844*, in Karl Marx and Frederick Engels 1975–2004.

———— 1978 [1857] *Die Geschichte der Geheimdiplomatie des 18. Jahrhunderts: über den asiatischen Ursprung de russischen Despotie*, edited by Bernd Rabehl, Berlin: Olle & Wolter.

Marx, Karl, and Frederick Engels 1975–2004, *Collected Works*, 50 Volumes, New York: International Publishers.

Mazower, Mark 2004, *Salonica, City of Ghosts: Christians, Muslims, and Jews, 1430–1950*, New York: Alfred A. Knopf.

Meyer, Karl E., and Shareen Blair Brysac 1999, *Tournament of Shadows: The Great Game and Race for Empire in Central Asia*, Washington, DC: Counterpoint.

Millán, Juan Albarracín 1981, *El pensamiento filosófico de Tamayo y el irracionalismo alemán*, La Paz: Akapana.

Millward, James 2007, *Eurasian Crossroads. A History of Xinjiang*, New York: Columbia University Press.

Montenegro, Carlos 1953, *Nacionalismo y coloniaje*, La Paz: Alcaldía Municipal.

del Moral, Juan Díaz 1969 [1929], *Historia de las agitaciones campesinas andaluzas-Córdoba: antecedentes para una reforma agraria*, Madrid: Alianza.

Morales, Waltraud Q. 2003, *A Brief History of Bolivia*, New York: Facts on File.

Morat, Daniel 2007, *Von der Tat zur Gelassenheit: konservatives Denken bei Martin Heidegger, Ernst Jünger, und Friedrich Georg Jünger, 1920–1960*, Göttingen: Wallstein.

Morrow, Felix 1938, *Revolution and Counter-Revolution in Spain*, New York: Pioneer.

Munck, Ronaldo, Ricardo Falcón, and Bernado Galitelli 1987, *Argentina: From Anarchism to Peronism: Workers, Unions, and Politics, 1855–1985*, London: Zed Books.

Munis, Grandizo 1948, *Jalones de Derrota, promesa de victoria: Critica y teoria de la revolución española (1930–1939)*, Mexico: Editorial Lucha Obrera.

O'Connor, Timothy Edward 1988, *Diplomacy and Revolution: G.V. Chicherin and Soviet Foreign Affairs, 1918–1930*, Ames: Iowa State University Press.

Oliver, Juan García 1978, *El eco de los pasos*, Barcelona: Ruedo Ibérico.

Olivera, Oscar 2004, *Cochabamba!: Water War in Bolivia*, Cambridge, MA: South End Press.

Orwell, George 1952 [1938], *Homage to Catalonia*, New York: Harcourt, Brace.

Ostria Gutiérrez, Alberto 1944, *Una revolucion tras los Andes*, La Paz: Editorial Nascimento.

Page, Joseph 1983, *Peron: a Biography*, New York: Random House.

Paz, Abel 2000, *La cuestión de Marruecos y la République española*, Madrid: Fundación de Estudios Libertarios Anselmo Lorenzo.

Peñaloza Cordero, Luis 1987, *Nueva historia ecónomica de Bolivia*, Volume 7, La Paz: Editorial Los Amigos del Libro.

Pereira, Blithz Lozardo 2007, *Cosmovisión, historia y política en los Andes*, La Paz: n. p.

Petras, James F., and Henry Veltmeyer 2005, *Social Movements and State Power: Argentina, Brazil, Bolivia, Ecuador*, London: Pluto.

Poullada, Leon B. 1973, *Reform and Rebellion in Afghanistan, 1919–1929: King Amanullah's Failure to Modernize a Tribal Society*, Ithaca, NY: Cornell University Press.

Pirani, Simon 2008, *The Russian Revolution in Retreat, 1920–24: Soviet Workers and the New Communist Elite*, London: Routledge; available online at: https://libcom.org/history/russian-revolution-retreat-1920-24-soviet-workers-new-communist-elite-simon-pirani.

Preobraženskij, E.A. 1965 [1926], *The New Economics*, translated by Brian Pearce, Oxford: Clarendon Press.

Reinaga, Fausto 1970, *Franz Tamayo y la revolución boliviana*, La Paz: Editorial Casegural.

Rexroth, Kenneth 1966, *An Autobiographical Novel*, Garden City, NY: Doubleday.

Roberts, David D. 1979, *The Syndicalist Tradition and Italian Fascism*, Chapel Hill: University of North Carolina.

Rozdolski, Roman, and John-Paul Himka 1986, *Engels and the 'Non-Historic' Peoples: The National Question in the Revolution of 1848*, Glasgow: Critique Books.

Rubel, Maximilian 1972, *Die russische Kommune: Kritik eines Mythos*, München: Carl Hanser.

Ruiz, Marco Dómich 1978, *Ideología y mito: los orígenes del fascismo boliviano*, La Paz: Editorial Los Amigo del Libro.

Sabatier, Guy n.d., *The 1918 Treat of Brest-Litovsk: Curbing the Revolution*, available at: http://libcom.org/book/export/html/45641.

Salvattecci, Hugo García 1979, *Sorel y Mariátegui*, Lima: E. Delgado Valenzuela.

Salvemini, Gaetano 1936, *Under the Axe of Fascism*, New York: Viking.

Sándor John, S. 2009, *Bolivia's Radical Tradition: Permanent Revolution in the Andes*, Tucson: University of Arizona Press.

Santillán, Diego Abad de 1940, *Porque perdimos la guerra*, Buenos Aires.

Schorske, Carl 1955, *German Social Democracy, 1905–1917: The Development of the Great Schism*, Cambridge: Cambridge University Press.

Serge, Victor 1936, 'The Death of Ivan Nikitich Smirnov', available at: http://www.marxists.org/archive/serge/1936/08/smirnov.htm.

Seton-Watson, R.W. 1972 [1935], *Disraeli, Gladstone, and the Eastern Question: A Study in Diplomacy and Party Politics*, New York.

Shanin, Teodor 1983, *Late Marx and the Russian Road: Marx and the 'Peripheries of Capitalism'*, London: Routledge.

———— 1986, *The Roots of Otherness*, Volume 2, *Russia 1905–07: Revolution as a Moment of Truth*, New Haven: Yale University Press.

Shaw, Stanford J., and Ezel Kural Shaw 1976–77, *History of the Ottoman Empire and Modern Turkey*, 2 Volumes, Cambridge: Cambridge University Press.

Schmidt, Michael, and Lucien van der Walt 2009, *Black Flame: The Revolutionary Class Politics of Anarchism and Syndicalism*, Oakland: AK Press.

Sternberg, Fritz 1932, *Der Niedergang des deutschen Kapitalismus*, Berlin: Rowohlt.

Stinas, A. 1990, *Mémoires: un révolutionnaire ans la Grèce du XXe siècle*, Montreuil: La Brèche-PEC; excerpts in English available at: http://www.geocities.com/antagonism1/stinas/index.html.

Taboada Terán, Néstor 2007, *Franz Tamayo: Profeta de la Rebelión*, Cochabamba: Editora HP.

Tamaya, Franz 1979, *Obra escogida*, Caracas: Biblioteca Ayacucho.

Tibi, Bassam 1981, *Arab Nationalism: A Critical Enquiry*, New York: St. Martin's Press.

Ticktin, Hillel 1973, 'Towards a Political Economy of the USSR', *Critique: Journal of Socialist Theory*, 1, 1: 20–41.

Thomas, Hugh 1965, *The Spanish Civil War*, Harmondsworth: Penguin.

Trotsky, Leon 1904, 'Our Political Tasks', available online at: https://www.marxists.org/archive/trotsky/1904/tasks/

——— 1931, *The Permanent Revolution*, available online at: https://www.marxists.org/archive/trotsky/1931/tpr/pr-index.htm.

——— 1964–71, *The Trotsky Papers, 1917–1922*, edited by Jan M. Meijer, 2 Volumes, The Hague: Mouton.

——— 1967 [1930], *History of the Russian Revolution*, translated by Max Eastman, 3 Volumes, London: Sphere.

Valdez, Abraham 1996, *La nación boliviana y Franz Tamayo*, La Paz: Ediciones Casa de la Cultura.

Valentinov, Nikolay 1968, *Encounters with Lenin*, translated by Paul Rosta and Brian Pearce, London: Oxford University Press.

Van Ngo 1995, *Viêt-Nam, 1920–1945: révolution et contre-révolution sous la domination coloniale*, Paris: L'Insomniaque.

——— 2010, *In the Crossfire: Adventures of a Vietnamese Revolutionary*, translated by Ken Knabb, Oakland: AK Press.

Venturi, Franco 1960, *Roots of Revolution: a History of the Populist and Socialist Movements in Nineteenth Century Russia*, translated by Frances Haskell, New York: Knopf.

Vourkoutiotis, Vasilis 2007, *Making Common Cause: German-Soviet Secret Relations, 1919–22*, Basingstoke, Palgrave Macmillan.

Weber, Eugen 1976, *Peasants into Frenchmen: The Modernization of Rural France, 1870–1914*, Stanford, CA: Stanford University Press.

Webber, Jeffrey 2008a, 'Rebellion to Reform in Bolivia, Part I', *Historical Materialism*, 16, 23–58.

——— 2008b, 'Rebellion to Reform in Bolivia, Part II', *Historical Materialism*, 16, 55–76.

——— 2008c, 'Rebellion to Reform in Bolivia, Part III', *Historical Materialism*, 16, 67–109.

White, James D. 1996, *Karl Marx and the Origins of Dialectical Materialism*, New York: St. Martin's Press.

Zanatta, Loris, and Mariano Aguas 2005, 'Auge y declinación de la tercera posición: Bolivia, Perón y la guerra fría, 1943–1954', *Desarrollo Económico*, 45, 177: 25–53.

Index